ΑΩ

The Almega Project

Tom Galligan

Tom Galligan

Copyright © 2013 Tom Galligan
All rights reserved.
ISBN:1477522093
ISBN-13:978-1477522097

DO NOT GO GENTLE INTO THAT GOOD NIGHT

Do not go gentle into that good night,
Old age should burn and rage at close of day;
Rage, rage against the dying of the light.

Though wise men at their end know dark is right,
Because their words had forked no lightning they
Do not go gentle into that good night.

Good men, the last wave by, crying how bright
Their frail deeds might have danced in a green bay,
Rage, rage against the dying of the light.

Wild men who caught and sang the sun in flight,
And learn, too late, they grieved it on its way,
Do not go gentle into that good night.

Grave men, near death, who see with blinding sight
Blind eyes could blaze like meteors and be gay,
Rage, rage against the dying of the light.

Dylan Thomas Page

Tom Galligan

Prologue

Just a few men have dramatically changed the course of human history in each century. Jesus Christ was one such man, but so was Adolph Hitler. On this first day of June, 2000, Sean Patrick Gallagher, a wealthy venture capitalist, thought about the decision he had made, many months ago, to start a revolutionary secret project. He had agonized over the decision because the outcome would determine whether the history books would put his name in the Jesus column or in the Hitler column.

"May God have mercy on my soul for what I am about to do", he said, softly, to himself.

He was standing on the patio of his La Jolla home on La Jolla Farms Road. It was perched on the edge of a three hundred foot bluff overlooking the Pacific Ocean. He looked much younger than his approaching seventieth birthday. Whatever silver strands he had were hidden by his blond hair. He was quite tall, six foot four, and weighed a trim two hundred pounds, thanks to regularly playing tennis, surfing, or jogging on the beach below.

He glanced to the other side of the patio and looked at his wife, the former Sarah Goldman. He still marveled at how she had aged so gracefully. When she walked by, most men turned their heads to admire this tall, raven haired beauty.

Sarah was talking to two husky men who were Israeli Mossad agents. Their navy blazers concealed shoulder holsters that contained Uzi semi-automatic pistols. Their primary function was to ensure Sarah's safety. She was in charge of the secret project that caused Sean's concern for his immortal soul.

Sarah finished talking to the men and went back into the house. She emerged a few minutes later, carrying two Margaritas. She offered one to Sean. He took a long sip and smacked his lips. "Thanks, I needed that. What were you talking about to the men?

"Oh, I was asking them if they had any concerns about the security of our home and they said they didn't. They have double-checked all systems and everything seems fine. They were glad to get away from our laboratory in Tijuana for a few days. They really like it here in La Jolla."

Sean replied, "I hope they are right. We have been lucky so far that no one has discovered your project, but I have the uneasy feeling that something bad is going to happen. We're so near to our dream coming to fruition."

Sarah smiled. "Don't be such a worry wart."

Sean shrugged and took another long sip of his drink. In doing so, his eyes looked up. He saw a large number of hang gliders and paragliders flying lazily in the afternoon sky. They launched themselves from the Torrey Pines Glider Port just a few hundred yards to the north. It was the same spot where, years ago, Lucky Lindberg practiced his aviation skills in fixed- wing gliders.

Nowadays, the site primarily hosted these two modern birds of flight. The winds coming off the Pacific hit the bluff and created the strong updrafts that were so necessary for gliding. The brightly colored fabric panels of these crafts created an interesting mosaic in the azure blue sky.

Sean noted something odd. One hang glider stood out. It was all black, and its rider was clothed completely in black. It reminded him of the ominous raven in the poem by Edgar Allen Poe. He felt a slight shiver run down his spine.

He remembered the one time that he felt brave enough to try hang gliding at the glider port. He was strapped piggyback fashion to an instructor. When they leaped off the bluff, the adrenalin surged through his veins. He felt equal sensations of fear and elation. It was so quiet and peaceful as they soared over the Pacific. Looking to the south, he could see the brown hills of Tijuana, Mexico. To the north, he saw the world famous Torrey Pines Golf Course. Directly below the launch area was Black's Beach, one of the best surfing spots in San Diego. It also happened to be a clothing optional beach.

The flight reminded him of the Greek myth of Daedalus and Icarus, who had attached bird feathers to their arms with wax, in order to fly away and escape from the Labyrinth prison on the island of Crete. Daedalus told his son that when he took to flight, neither to fly too high, lest the wax should melt in the sun and the wings drop off, nor to fly too near the sea, lest the pinions should be detached by the dampness. However, Icarus, thrilled by his newfound ability to fly, disregarded his father's instructions, and soared ever higher and higher in an attempt to join the gods in their heavenly home. Alas, the wax melted, and he fell into the sea and perished. Thus, thought Sean, did the gods deal with the hubris of man.

He now wondered if his own hubris would cause a similar fate. He dismissed that thought for the time being and turned his attention to the majestic buildings standing between his home and the glider port. They contained the facilities of the Salk Institute for Biological Studies. Dr. Jonas Salk, of Polio vaccine fame, had founded this world-renowned medical research center in 1960 with a gift of land from the City of San Diego and the financial support of the March of Dimes. The Institute's two current major areas of focus were molecular biology and genetics. Sarah had a PhD in Biology and worked at Salk, heading a genetics research team.

Her old friend and mentor, Francis Crick, had joined the Institute in 1976. He and James Watson were attending Cambridge University when they discovered the secret of the double helix structure of DNA in 1953. They eventually were awarded a Nobel Prize. Sarah had met them while she was a student at Cambridge. She helped out in their lab and they became lifelong friends.

Sarah believed she had found the ideal situation in her profession. Since the Institute was only a few hundred yards away, she could choose to walk to her office, where some of the foremost scientific minds in the world surrounded her.

The world famous architect, Louis I. Kahn, designed the physical facility. It was universally regarded as an architectural masterpiece of concrete buildings that had magnificent views of the ocean and the coastline. Sean privately referred to it as "Stonehenge West", not only because of its unique slab-like monolithic structures, but also because he thought that what they produced there was akin to a kind of magic.

That is where his dilemma started. A few years ago, Sarah was approached at the Salk Institute by a consortium of officials of the Israeli government. She was asked to head up a secret project that they said would be vital to the survival of the state of

Israel. Israel was surrounded by enemies out to destroy it, and this project would help to minimize or eliminate that threat. The Israeli government would fully fund it and give it any other support she would need.

Sarah was stunned when they told her of the details. The project was fraught with legal, moral, and ethical implications. She felt compelled to discuss it at great length with Sean, before giving her assent.

After much soul searching, Sean told her to go ahead with it. He promised to give her any additional help she needed.

They named it the Lazarus Project. They based the operation in nearby Tijuana, away from the prying eyes of U.S. governmental agencies.

The Lazarus project was very close to success.

Sean had an agreement with Sarah that, if the Lazarus project were successful, he would personally finance another, more audacious undertaking that he called the Almega Project. He promised to give her the details at a later date.

Almega was an acronym he had coined from a combination of the Greek letters Alpha and Omega, meaning the first and the last, or, the beginning and the end. Only he and Sarah would be involved in this new project. If it were successful, it would be the most startling event the world had seen in the last two thousand years. The project was intended to benefit all of mankind, but there were serious risks involved. As he well knew, the strongest law in the land was the law of unintended consequences.

To the east of Salk, across North Torrey Pines Road, was the University of California San Diego, where Sarah also lectured on a part time basis. Five Nobel Laureates were currently on staff there. Over the years, the Salk Institute and UCSD had provided La Jolla with twenty-three Nobel Laureate residents, more than any other community in the world.

The presence of these two giant institutions, with their illustrious scientists, caused a host of large and small biomedical and technical corporations to spring up around them, an area that Sean called "Biotech Beach."

Qualcomm, founded by a former UCSD professor, was located just a few miles away, in an area that also hosted a number of other telecommunication companies. Sean referred to this area as "Wireless Valley."

These two areas had provided Sean's venture capital company with a number of successful investments that had made him a very wealthy man.

Sean took another long sip of his Margarita. He now turned his attention to the sun, which was in the process of sinking into the ocean.

"I wonder if I'll see it this evening", he mused. The "it" was the Green Flash, a somewhat rare phenomenon that, under the right climatic conditions, caused the sun to emit a brilliant emerald green flash of light just as it sank completely into the Pacific Ocean. Green had always been his favorite color. Most people thought that it was because green was the color of money, but that was not so. Green reminded him of Ireland, the Emerald Isle, his parents' birthplace. He never knew his father. He had been a New York City police officer who died a hero's death and was buried on the same day that Sean was born.

More importantly, however, green reminded him of his dearly beloved mother, Kathleen. She was a beautiful woman. With her flashing green eyes, flaming red hair and creamy white complexion, she was the "spitting image", as the Irish would say, of Maureen O'Hara. His mother had long since departed this world and his heart still ached for her. She had sacrificed so much in raising him by herself. He liked to think that the Green Flashes were messages from her. It was as if she were saying from heaven, "Sean, I'm here. I still love you. I'm praying for you. I'm so proud of you."

Sean's mother would have much to be proud of. His was truly a rags to riches story. He felt sad that she did not live long enough to share in his enormous financial success. Sad, too, that she had not lived to see her only child marry and produce the grandchildren that she had so dearly wanted. His identical twin sons, Brian and Liam, had her green eyes and fair complexion, but they inherited his blond hair.

Perhaps it was best, after all, that his deeply religious mother was not alive to witness the momentous project in which he planned to engage. He knew, for certain, that his mother would not approve. "Sean", she would say, "What you are planning to do is wrong! It is evil! It is the greatest of mortal sins! Don't do it!"

She would weep and beg him not to proceed. When that failed, she would go to her parish church, light candles, and make a special novena to the Virgin Mary. He could hear her pray, "Dear Mother of God, do you know what my son is trying to do to your Son? I beg you, don't let it happen. I couldn't bear the thought that it was I who gave birth to the person that would inflict such a sacrilege on the world, a person who may even be responsible for the coming of the anti-Christ. Please stop him, please, please, please."

Then, all of a sudden, there it was, the Green Flash! It was the brightest and longest lasting one he had ever seen. A new thought flashed through Sean's mind. Maybe this Flash was really an affirmative sign from God. After all, Sean, as a devout Catholic, believed that God knew what he was thinking, and maybe God wanted to show him a sign that He approved of the project and, as a matter of fact, it was part of His Divine Plan. Sean desperately wanted to believe that.

His reverie was interrupted when Sarah rejoined him. She pointed to the sky and said, "Look!"

Sean saw that the black hang glider was circling high over their house. That was against the glider association rules. As it dropped nearer, he saw that the rider was wearing an extremely bulky vest emblazoned with a red crescent moon and star. Wires were hanging out of the vest and were attached to some sort of device in the man's hand.

That was odd.

The hang glider made a lazy turn directly overhead and started to dive at them. The rider repeatedly shouted, "Allahu Akbar. Die infidels, die!"

Sean immediately realized what was about to happen. He shouted, "Everybody get down! Suicide bomber!"

He pushed Sarah to the ground and rolled on top of her.

The two security guards immediately sprang into action. They drew their automatic weapons, which they emptied at the attacker. The impact of the bullets caused the rider's body to convulse. He lost control of the steering bar and overshot the patio. The hang glider dropped down a hundred feet, veered to the right, crashed into the side of the cliff, and exploded with a deafening roar.

Sean jumped up, looked down at the smoking hole, and groaned, "Oh, my god!"

The security guards rushed over to make sure that Sarah and Sean were unhurt. One of them said, "That was a close call. It looks like some Muslim group found out about your project. We have to leave this place at once. There may be others waiting with a plan B."

Sean agreed and all four of them hurried to their armored SUV The guards hopped into the front seat while Sean and Sarah collapsed into the back .They sped down Interstate 5 to their well-guarded facility in Tijuana, about a half hour away.

As the adrenaline rush wore off, Sean fell into a dreamlike state. His mind wandered over the series of events in his background that led up to his current status.

Tom Galligan

Part 1

The Past

Tar éis a chítear gach beart

(It is afterwards events are understood)
Old Irish Proverb

Tom Galligan

Chapter 1

Daniel Patrick Gallagher, Sean's father, stood in the stern of a steamship headed for America watching the Irish shoreline disappear in the early morning mist. The year was 1920. Dan was twenty years old and a wanted member of the Irish Republican Army.

Yesterday, he had barely escaped from British troops, who wanted him for the murder of one of their officers. He felt that he might never see his native land again.

He thought of the family farm in the seaside town of Howth, just a few miles north of Dublin. His father, Patrick Joseph, known to all as PJ, was a successful breeder and trainer of horses. Dan adored him and followed him everywhere.

Their farm attracted many visitors. One frequent caller was a tall, gaunt, college math professor, Eamon deValera, nicknamed the "Long Fellow." Dan would often sit by the fireside and listen to the two men talking politics into the wee hours of the night.

Their conversations often revolved around the centuries-old British occupation of Ireland and their vicious suppression of any attempt to establish Irish independence.

King Henry VIII, and his many successors, vainly tried to impose the Anglican religion, the English language, and English culture on the recalcitrant Irish natives. They murdered thousands of Irish citizens to enforce their rule. The English confiscated the land from the Irish owners, and placed it in the hands of a few loyal and wealthy Protestant families.

Many of them were absentee landlords who set foot on their properties once or twice a year, if at all. They often utilized local agents to manage their estates while living lavishly in London or in Europe, off the rents paid by Catholics for land their ancestors had once owned.

Since the Irish peasant population no longer owned any land, they had to trade their labor to become tenant farmers. They paid backbreaking rents for the use of a dwelling, which consisted of a one-room, windowless, mud cabin, with no chimney, plus a few acres of land for their own use.

They worked in their landlords' fields of oats, rye, or other grains. For their own families, they planted only potatoes, which cost little and yielded more food per acre than any other crop. The only tool needed was a simple spade, for digging on almost any kind of soil. Potatoes thrived on this rented land where the soil was usually unfit for the landowners' own grain or animals.

More than three million Irish peasants subsisted solely on this vegetable, which is rich in protein, carbohydrates, minerals, and vitamins. It was possible to stay reasonably healthy on a diet of potatoes, alone, as long as it was occasionally supplemented by a little buttermilk and the use of salt, cabbage, or fish, as seasoning.

When a blight ruined the potatoes, between 1845 and 1849, one and a half million men, women, and children died of starvation, or related diseases, such as cholera. Another million people were lucky enough to immigrate to America, Canada, or Australia. Meanwhile, during this entire period, the mostly absentee aristocratic English landowners continued to raise large amounts of wheat, barley, oats, and other grains that they shipped to England. They had to sell their products abroad because most of them were living well above their means and had contracted enormous debts. Their estates were encumbered and mortgaged to the hilt. They needed the cash.

There was more than enough food available to feed the population of Ireland, if the people could afford to pay for it. The impoverished tenant farmers could not, and, consequently, paid the ultimate price.

The British government could have solved the problem in a number of ways, but they did nothing, until it was too late.

Dan heard his father state, "What the British did to Ireland was an out and out act of genocide. They looked on us as sub-humans, and were glad to be rid of us. Between the famine and emigration, our population dropped in half, from eight million to four million by the year 1900. They ruined our country."

De Valera replied, "You're right. It's a sad legacy the Brits have left us, and we must change it. We have to get rid of these oppressors. We've tried peaceful means, for at least a hundred years, to become an independent nation, and we have failed at every turn. The Brits have broken every promise of land reform and independence. They cannot be trusted. We have no other recourse except violence, just like the Americans once did."

"But Dev, we're only a few miles from England while the Americans were three thousand miles away. Besides, weapons have changed. They now have tanks, machine guns, and long range artillery. We still have nothing but rifles and pitchforks."

"That's true, PJ, but things can change. We just have to wait for the right opportunity. In the meantime, I have joined a secret organization called the Irish Republican Brotherhood. We have guns and we are practicing military maneuvers so we will be ready to strike when the time is right. Other groups are doing the same. Will you join me?"

PJ hesitated for a moment and then said, "Yes."

By the spring of 1916, England was fully engaged in the middle of World War 1. They had pulled some of their troops out of Ireland and shipped them to the battlefront in France. The IRB and other militant groups thought the time was ripe to start their revolution. On Easter Monday, April 24, 1916, about fifteen hundred rebels captured the General Post Office in downtown Dublin, and made it their headquarters. They also captured a few other nearby government buildings.

The rebel leaders issued a proclamation claiming the right of the Irish people to have their own sovereign Irish Republic, and claimed themselves to be the Provisional Government of that nation.

The British army quickly retaliated. They cordoned off the downtown area and began firing on the Irish strongholds. They brought in artillery and gunships and began to shell the buildings. After five days of intense fighting, downtown Dublin lay in ruins. The Irish held on for a week but had to surrender on Sunday, April 30.

De Valera's unit was the furthest from the General Post Office. It was the last to receive the orders to surrender. He told his men to lay down their arms and follow him to the British lines. PJ accompanied him, holding a white flag on a pole.

When they neared the British lines, an officer told them to halt. The British officers had been given instructions that the rebels had put themselves outside the law and were not to be treated as prisoners of war. Hence, the slightest suspicion was sufficient to get them killed on the spot.

The British officer asked Dev, "Who are you?"

"I am Captain Eamon de Valera. My men and I have come to surrender." Dev reached for his sword to hand it over to the officer, as was the tradition of a defeated enemy. An enlisted man behind the officer saw this as a threatening gesture, and raised his rifle to fire. PJ, still holding the white flag, noticed this, and shouted, "No, no." He flung himself in front of Dev, just as the rifle exploded. The bullet hit him in the heart and he slouched to the ground, dead.

Chapter 2

DeValera and the remainder of his troops were arrested and put in jail.

About ninety rebel men were tried by court martial for treason and collaboration with the enemy. Fifteen of them were sentenced to death by firing squad, including De Valera. However, the British discovered that he was born in New York City, therefore, an American citizen. They didn't want to antagonize their American allies by executing one of its citizens, so they abolished his death sentence and sent him to jail in England.

The general public in Ireland was outraged over the executions. The people were further radicalized by the threatened imposition of conscription of young Irish men into the British army to fight in the First World War.

The British realized that they could ill afford a hostile Ireland that could foment a civil war while they were engaged in battle on the continent. In June, 1917, the British released DeValera and his comrades under amnesty.

In 1918, DeValera and his colleague, Michael Collins, formed the Sinn Fein political party and declared an independent Irish Republic. The Irish Republican Army was formed about the same time, with Michael Collins as its head.

At this point, Dan, who was still seething over his father's death, approached deValera to volunteer to join the IRA.

DeValera told him, "Dan, I know how you feel about your father's death. I, too, still grieve for him. Your mother needs you and I will not allow you to endanger your life by becoming an active fighting member. However, you can help our cause immeasurably by acting as an intelligence gatherer and courier. Your trading of horses requires you to travel all over the countryside without arousing suspicion. It's a perfect cover for a very important job and it exposes you to less danger."

"I'll do as you say, sir."

When the British attempted to suppress the IRA and its support of independence, Collins began a guerilla campaign known as the Irish War of Independence. They attacked the Royal Irish Constabulary, a police organization formed by England for the security of the country.

The native Irish members of the RIC were warned to quit or suffer the consequences. After a number of them were assassinated, mass resignations followed. The British faced a serious problem. They found themselves without enough constables to control the increasingly restive Irish rebels, so they formed a paramilitary force of almost ten thousand men to bolster the shrunken ranks of the RIC.

The English recruits to the RIC were mainly unemployed veterans of World War 1, as well as newly released convicts. They signed on for an indefinite period of service with no pension rights. Their pay was ten shillings a day.

When the first recruits arrived in Ireland on March 25, 1920, after three months of training, they looked like the irregulars they were. Since there were not enough RIC uniforms for the new men, they were equipped with some army khaki clothing items supplemented with pieces of constabulary uniforms, so that they appeared in a strange mixture of khaki and dark green, with the black leather belts of the RIC.

This mixture gave rise to their nickname, "The Black and Tans", not only based on the colors of their uniforms, but also as a reference to a famous pack of foxhounds from Limerick. These mercenaries behaved like a pack of undisciplined and brutal animals. They were an occupation army that had been given the mandate to make Ireland "hell for rebels to live in."

They ruthlessly attacked and killed many innocent civilians at the slightest provocation. They burned and sacked a number of small towns and villages. They alienated the people against the British government in Ireland. The same soil that nurtured the potato now harbored the bitter weed of hatred.

On November 22, 1920, Dan's mother was spreading hay near their horse corral when Dan rode in on a large black stallion.

"How did your horse do today?" she asked.

"He did very well, ma. We practiced jumping walls and fences today. He has the makings of a champion steeplechase racer."

At that moment, they heard the sound of many horses coming up the road. It was a squad of Black and Tan soldiers. The captain leading the entourage stopped at the gate to the farm and asked, "Is this the Gallagher farm?"

Dan's mother answered, "Yes. Who are you and what do you want?"

"I am Captain Gordon and I have an arrest warrant for your son, Daniel Patrick Gallagher."

"What has he done to deserve an arrest warrant?"

"He is accused of aiding members of the Irish Republican Army that murdered fourteen members of our intelligence service yesterday, in Dublin. I have orders to bring him back to the barracks for questioning."

The captain drew his sword and, leaning over his horse, used it to unlatch the gate. He guided his horse through the narrow opening toward Dan. Brigid, holding the pitchfork in her right hand, raised her left fist and shook it at the captain saying, "Haven't you people done enough to my family? You murdered my husband and now you want to take my only child? I won't let you."

Gordon looked with disdain at the woman, urged his horse forward, saying, "Get out of the way you old hag."

The horse's chest brushed against Brigid, and she started to stumble backwards. She raised both arms in the air in an effort to regain her balance. Out of the corner of his eye, the captain saw the pitchfork rising in the air toward him and took this movement as a threat. He raised his sword and slashed viciously at her. His sword sliced across her throat, almost decapitating her. She fell to the ground, mortally wounded, the blood gushing from the ugly cut.

Dan stared in disbelief at what he saw. He leapt forward to kneel at his mother's side, while shouting, "You killed my mother you cowardly bastard."

"I'll kill you too if you give me any trouble. I don't care if I take you back dead or alive," snarled Gordon, as he backed his horse away.

Dan's left hand grabbed the pitchfork from his mother's lifeless body and his right hand snatched the bloodstained shawl from her shoulders. He stood up and ran at the captain. A tight smile crossed Gordon's lips as he raised his sword once again to skewer another piece of Irish trash. As Dan neared the captain, he threw the shawl over the horse's eyes. The horse became so startled that he reared up on his hind legs, his front legs pawing at the air, trying to rid himself of the blinding shawl.

The captain kept the reins clutched in his left hand and stood straight up in the stirrups to maintain his balance to avoid being thrown from his saddle. Dan grabbed the pitchfork in both hands and thrust it with all his might under the armpit of the captain's upraised right arm. Then, as easily as he would toss a bale of hay, Dan lifted the captain completely out of the saddle and threw him over his shoulder. Captain Gordon landed on his head with a sickening sound as his neck snapped. He lay on the ground, his neck bent at a grotesque angle, his lifeless eyes staring at the sky. A stream of dark blood oozed from between the tines still imbedded in his side.

It all happened so quickly that the cavalrymen waiting in the road had no time to intervene. Now, they were startled into activity. They spurred their horses to try to reach their fallen leader. The first two horses collided and wedged themselves within the confines of the narrow gate. It took some moments before they could back up their steeds and enter single file. During the confusion, Dan ran back to his horse and vaulted into the saddle. He spurred the horse forward and easily cleared the stone fence. Half of the soldiers chased after him while others dismounted and fired their rifles in his direction. Dan had the advantage of being a superior horseman as well as being astride an outstanding jumper. He also had the knowledge of the countryside and chose an escape route that included all the highest fences that his mount took with ease. The soldiers following him were soon forced to give up the chase.

Dan raced to Dublin. There, he went to a secret hideout to report to Michael Collins, the "Big Fellow." Collins heard Dan's story and said, "You won't be safe in this country since the Brits know who you are. They will be looking for you everywhere.

"There's a ship leaving from Cobh, for America, tomorrow morning. The captain is one of our friends and he will smuggle you aboard. We have some blank passports that we stole from the Brits, and we'll forge the proper documents for you. Nobody will question them on the other end.

"I'm going to write a letter to our mutual friend, deValera. He's been in the States for the past year raising money for our cause. I want you to deliver it personally to him. He'll take care of you. I'm also giving you the name and address of a contact in New York City who will make arrangements for you.

"Good luck, lad. I'll personally look after your mother's burial. Always remember that your mother and father did not die in vain. They are heroes who gave their lives for a worthy cause. God be with you."

Chapter 3

Dan arrived safely in New York and met his contact. He stayed with the man for a few days, until de Valera arrived in New York. Dev welcomed him with open arms.

"I heard about your mother, Dan, and I am truly sorry. Your family made the ultimate sacrifice for our country. May God bless them. Now, we will have to get you situated here in the States. You obviously need some kind of job.

"You're a big strong lad who has proven you can handle yourself quite well. What I propose is that you accompany me on my fund raising trip through the States as a sort of personal bodyguard. By the time I have to return to Ireland I'll have figured out something for you. You realize you can't return to Ireland, at least until we drive the Brits out."

"I understand, Mr. de Valera."

Dan accompanied Dev on his trips throughout the country as he met a number of expatriates. Dev raised over five million dollars from various Irish organizations. The transplanted Irish were more than glad to donate to the cause of freeing their beloved homeland from the reviled English.

When Dev was scheduled to depart the United States, he introduced Dan to Michael O'Brien, a captain in the New York City Police Dept. He gave O'Brien a brief history of Dan and his family's patriotism. "Michael, could you use another Irishman in your department?"

O'Brien looked Dan over from top to toe of his six foot frame. "Dev, any friend of yours is a friend of mine. We can always use another stout lad who is obviously not afraid of danger. Danny boy, I would be proud to have you join our force. Are you interested?"

Dev nodded his head to Dan, who said, "Yes. Thank you sir. I'd like that."

After Dev sailed back to Ireland, Dan joined the police department and completed the training program. Captain O'Brien knew about Dan's expertise with horses, and assigned him to the mounted police force. He started in the horse training facility, tending the new mounts, shoeing, feeding, and training them. He worked hard and, after many months, was promoted to a full-fledged mounted officer.

He started his on-the-job training with an experienced officer, patrolling Central Park, an eight hundred acre oasis in the heart of midtown Manhattan. It was a convenient meeting place for young women who were acting as domestic servants and nannies for wealthy families. These privileged people lived in the nearby brownstone mansions on Fifth Avenue and Park Avenue.

The park offered a refuge of wide-open spaces, with lots of trees and pretty landscaping. There was a carousel with hand carved wooden horses, and a zoo, to keep the children amused while their nannies gossiped with each other.

Many of these nannies were young Irish girls. These young lassies were particularly sought after by wealthy Jewish families. It was not uncommon for a family to have a staff composed entirely of Irish servants. The girls worked for relatively low wages, but, most of the time, they were further compensated with free room and board. These newly arrived immigrants thus had built in companions who helped to assuage their initial fears and loneliness in their new country. As long as they were treated fairly, they were more than happy to stay with the same family for a number of years.

The Irish girls made excellent nannies since many of them had come from large families and were used to taking care of young children. Most were also raised on farms and were accustomed to long hours and hard work. Their major advantage over other European immigrants was, obviously, the fact they spoke English. Many a young Jewish child grew up in New York speaking English with a slight Irish brogue. This greatly amused the parents as well as the nannies.

It was in the park that Dan first met Kathleen McCarthy, who was taking care of two young children for a Jewish doctor's family. She came from a small farming town in County Mayo. She was an only child when, at age ten, her parents died during an influenza epidemic. An aunt raised her until, at age eighteen, she decided to immigrate to America.

They struck up a friendship and started to "keep company". After a year, Dan proposed marriage and she accepted.

Dan had been sharing an apartment with another officer, on 57th street near 8th Avenue, a rough section of Manhattan near Madison Square Garden known as Hell's Kitchen. He had chosen the area because it was predominantly Irish and the rent was cheap. However, he was not about to have Kathleen live in such a rowdy neighborhood. He heard of a nicer area in upper Manhattan, near the City College of New York. The residents called it Vinegar Hill. Although the area contained immigrants from all over Europe and Puerto Rico, the Irish formed the majority and, consequently, got the naming rights.

The area was named after a site in Ireland, outside the town of Enniscorthy, in County Wexford, where one of the bloodiest confrontations in Irish history took place. On June 21, 1798, Protestant English forces were flogging Catholics and burning their homes in a drive to enforce a disarmament decree. Fully believing that a massacre of Catholics was imminent, Father John Murphy led a small band of Catholic rebels to fight the Protestants at a place called Vinegar Hill. Since the rebels were armed with little more than pikes against government forces with muskets, they were massacred, as were most of the town's innocent women and children. Vinegar Hill became a constant reminder of the price the Irish had to pay if they hoped to obtain political and religious freedom.

The Vinegar Hill neighborhood consisted of a three block wide strip of land rising from 125th Street up a hill to 140th Street. The center of the strip was Amsterdam Avenue. It was sandwiched between Convent Avenue on the east and Broadway on the west. Amsterdam Avenue was lined with four and five story tenement houses, most of which featured street level shops. It was a vibrant and convenient commercial sector. There was little need to go outside this small community for the necessities of life.

The area was blessed with many transportation options. An electric trolley car line ran up Amsterdam Avenue. Bus lines could be found on Convent Avenue and Broadway. An IRT subway line had twos stop on Broadway, at 125th St., and 137th Street.

Dan found an affordable apartment in a tenement house situated on the southeast corner of Amsterdam Avenue and 136th Street. He rented a top floor unit of the five-story walk-up. There were four apartments on each floor. Kathleen was ecstatic over the fact that, for the first time in her life, she had a place of her own.

The house was directly across the street from Lewisohn Stadium, a multi-purpose facility situated on the southern boundary of the campus of CCNY. Diagonally across Amsterdam Avenue was the Hebrew Orphan Asylum, a huge building occupying two square city blocks.

Kathleen discovered an unusual array of eight schools within a six-block radius of her apartment. There were two colleges, two high schools, one junior high school, one public grammar school, and two Catholic grammar schools. Just a few blocks further south of the Vinegar Hill community was the prestigious campus of Columbia University.

The local Catholic Church, Annunciation, was located four blocks away, on Convent Avenue. It faced the campus of Manhattanville College, a Catholic college for women. The campus also contained the parish high school and grammar school for girls.

Knickerbocker Hospital was conveniently located across the street from the campus and church.

Kathleen made a point to meet the other tenants. She became quite friendly with an older Russian couple, Boris and Ivana Semenova, who lived in an adjacent apartment. They were Jews who had left Moscow to escape the pogroms that seemed to come more and more frequently. Both had been university professors. Boris was fortunate to have obtained a job at CCNY, teaching Russian Literature. Ivana busied herself at home where she taught piano lessons, as well as English language lessons for fellow Russian émigrés.

Rosa Morelli, who lived in the apartment just below her, became her closest friend. She was born in this country. Her husband, Vito, had arrived from Italy some years ago. They operated a small grocery store a few blocks away.

Part of the ground floor was home to the Vinegar Hill Bar and Grill, a popular watering hole for local Irish cops and firemen. Kathleen once said to Dan, "I can't believe that all of our neighbors are immigrants from so many different countries. It's so interesting. It's like our own little League of Nations. This is so different from Ireland."

"Yes, it is. They all left their homeland to escape from persecution or poverty, the same as we did. Here, no one cares who your parents were or what clan or tribe you came from. I think that this is the first country in history that doesn't have a class system. I love it here."

By this time, Dan had acquired enough seniority and influence on the force to get a transfer to the mounted patrol beat in his new neighborhood. The mounted police had a stable on 129th St. and Amsterdam Ave., a few blocks from home. It was adjacent to the huge trolley car garage that serviced all of Manhattan's trolleys.

He spent the first few weeks getting familiar with the area. He made a special point to meet with the heads of all the schools and other institutions to determine if they had any specific problems that could need his help.

Rabbi Bernie Kattler, head of the Hebrew Orphan Asylum, told him of having his children harassed on Amsterdam Avenue on their way from the HOA to classes at P. S 43, a junior high school, about seven blocks south.

"I hate to tell you this, officer Gallagher, but I believe most of those hooligans are Irish kids. They call my kids derogatory names and sometimes throw stones or snowballs at them. My boys are under strict orders not to get into fights with them. It makes them very angry not being able to fight back."

"I can understand that, Rabbi, I'd feel the same way myself. However, I guarantee you that I'll have the problem solved within a week or so. Believe me, I know firsthand what religious persecution is like."

For the following two mornings, Dan dressed in civilian clothes and followed the HOA children as they walked to school.

He was able to pinpoint five older boys who appeared to be the ringleaders of the rowdies. On the third morning, he donned his uniform and mounted up. When he was astride his horse, Dan towered more than ten feet above the ground. He posed an intimidating figure to the five troublemakers as he rounded them up. He took their names and addresses. The rabbi was right. They were all Irish.

Dan accompanied each boy to visit his parents. There, he explained what had happened. To each he said, "The Irish have been persecuted for centuries by the British because of their religion. You know how it felt. That's why you left the old country. I will not allow your child, or anyone else on my beat, to harass any other human being because of his or her religion. If I ever catch your son doing it again, I will arrest him and keep him in jail as long as the law allows. I will also report your son to his school principal and recommend that if he breaks the law again, he be severely punished or possibly expelled. Do I make myself clear?"

The fear of the law was thus instilled into the parents, who, in turn, instilled it into their sons, sometimes with the aid of a stout strap.

The next morning, Dan rode down Amsterdam Avenue. As he saw each of the five boys, he said, "Good morning, lad."

They replied, "Good morning, officer Gallagher, sir."

Dan smiled to himself and, over the next few weeks, he made a point to talk at length to each of them. He told them that he expected them to be his helpers in keeping the peace by riding herd on any other boys who tried to start trouble with the HOA students. As a reward for good service, he allowed each of the boys to ride on his horse with him for a few blocks. In a remarkably short time, there were no further incidents on the streets.

The junior high schoolyard was another matter. Fights would break out at recess, and after school, when Dan wasn't around.

Dan talked to Rabbi Kattler, saying, "I have an idea that I hope will meet with your approval. The police department has been teaching us self-defense lessons, known as Judo. I have become one of the instructors. I would like the opportunity to teach your kids some of these techniques."

Kattler thought for a minute and replied. "I don't want my children to become aggressive fighters, Dan. I think that would only create more antagonism against us."

"I didn't mean that I would teach them to be aggressive, only how to defend themselves if they are attacked. Bullies in the schoolyard usually begin by pushing around smaller kids. There are a few defensive moves that will allow smaller opponents to neutralize their superior strength and weight. They don't have to use their fists and hurt someone. Let me demonstrate a typical move. Push your hands against my chest, like you were trying to shove me backwards."

Kattler did as instructed. Dan clapped the palms of his hands over the back of Kattler's hands, pinning them to his chest. He then took a short step backwards while simultaneously bending slightly at his waist. This maneuver caused Kattler's hands to bend back against his wrists causing some pain.

Dan explained, "Now, see what happens if I bend forward a little more."

Dan applied a little more pressure and the Rabbi felt so much pain that he had to fall to his knees. "Wow that really hurts."

"Yes, it does. You can see that even small girls can use this technique. It doesn't really require any strength. This is the type of thing I'm talking about, it's simply self-defense, not aggressive offence. It will give your kids a good deal of confidence and, after a while, nobody will want to pick on the Jewish kids."

"Dan, I'm impressed. Let's talk about how to start a program at our gym."

Thereafter, Dan spent a few hours each month, on his own time, on a Sunday, teaching the children some rudimentary techniques. He used Kathleen as his training partner. She really enjoyed meeting and working with the children who started to call them Auntie Kate and Uncle Dan.

While Dan was attending to his police duties, Kathleen started to prepare herself for the eventual citizenship exam when she and Dan became eligible.

Rosa asked Kathleen if she would help Vito to study for the same exam. Kathleen readily agreed. Then, she realized that, perhaps, some of the other tenants might also be interested. They were, so she organized a study group that would meet on a rotating basis in each participant's apartment. Ivana Semenova became a member of the group. Her husband was able to get some books from the college and persuade some of the language teachers from CCNY to volunteer to help on occasion. After each session, the host family would prepare one of their favorite national desserts to feed everyone. It became a truly warm and bonding experience.

Chapter 4

Kathleen and Sean were very happy in their marriage. Their major disappointment was the fact that, after many years, Kathleen had not conceived a child. She made many a novena to the Blessed Virgin, but to no avail.

She was genuinely pleased when her best friend, Rosa Morelli, became pregnant. Rosa's doctor advised her to stop working at the store when she started her seventh month.

Rosa had a ten-year-old niece, named Lucy. She came to spend a few weeks of her summer vacation to help Rosa. One Saturday evening, Lucy decided to escape the summer heat in the apartment by sitting on the backyard fire escape. She heard the front door open and close as Vito came home from work. Shortly after, she heard a knock on the front door.

When she peered through the curtains, she saw Rosa answer the door. Three large men appeared in the entranceway, each carrying a gun. One of them immediately grabbed Rosa and clamped a hand over her mouth. The second man put his finger to his mouth, indicating to Rosa that she be quiet. The third man went back outside, and closed the door.

The two men quietly pushed Rosa into the dining room where Vito was sitting, listening to the radio.

"Who was at the door, Rosa?" he inquired.

One of the gunmen shoved his pistol into the back of Vito's head and said, "Be quiet and do what I say and no one will be hurt."

"What do you want?"

"We want the money."

"What money?"

"Don't be cute with us. You know what money. We've been casing your store and know what you're doing. Every Saturday night you take money home in a paper bag. We followed you home tonight, and know you have it here, somewhere. If you don't cooperate we'll beat it out of you."

Turning to his companion, he continued, "Hey, Gino, turn up the radio, close that window, and lock it. Pull down the window shade, too"

At this point, Lucy sucked in her breath and silently scrambled up the fire escape ladder to the next floor. As she reached the Gallagher's open window and slid through, she heard the downstairs window slam shut.

Kathleen and Dan were seated at the dining room table, having dinner. Kathleen was the first to notice her. "Why, hello Lucy, what brings you here at this time of night? Does Rosa need something?" Then she noticed that Lucy was as white as a sheet, and was trembling. "Lucy, what's wrong?"

Lucy stood there, terrified and unable to speak. Dan went over and took her in his arms. "Lucy, what's wrong? Speak up or we can't help you."

It took a few moments of quiet questioning for Dan to understand the fact that two thugs were threatening Vito and Rosa while an armed guard was standing outside their apartment.

Dan thought that, if he tried to overpower the guard, he might make enough noise to alert the two guys inside. He couldn't slip into the apartment from the fire escape because the window was locked, and the curtains were drawn. He would have to break the glass to get in, and this would give the hoods enough warning and time to shoot him before he could get at the two of them. He said to himself, "At times like this I wish we had a telephone."

After pondering the situation for a few more moments, Dan asked Lucy, "Is the door to your dumbwaiter locked?"

"No", Rosa always leaves it open during the day. She locks it at night before going to bed."

"Good", said Dan. "I have a plan. This is what I want you to do, Kathleen. Pretend you are going down to the Vinegar Hill Bar to get me to come home. There are always some off duty cops there. Tell them what the situation is.

"Meanwhile, after you leave, I'm going to get on top of the dumbwaiter and lower myself down to Morelli's apartment. I'll wait about five minutes to give you time to bring some of the boys back up with you. When they've taken care of the lookout, knock three times on the door, softly. The dumb waiter is close enough to the front door so that I can hear the knocking. When I hear your signal, I'll slip into the apartment. I'm hoping the thugs will be so busy intimidating Vito and Rosa that they won't hear me and I can get the drop on them. I know you have a key to their apartment. Give me a few minutes before you open the door."

Kathleen headed out the front door. As she passed the man standing outside the Morelli's door, she muttered out loud, "That husband of mine is such a lazy lout. He spends all his free time playing cards and drinking booze in the bar downstairs. Meanwhile, his dinner is getting cold. I'm going to give him a good piece of my mind."

The man smiled, and watched her proceed down the stairs, still talking to herself. When Kathleen hit the front stoop, she paused and looked up and down the street to see if any more thugs were around. Not seeing any, she walked quickly around the corner and entered the Vinegar Hill Bar and Grill. There, she was relieved to see Billy Donovan and Pat McDonald, two of Dan's fellow officers, sitting at the bar.

Kathleen's practiced eye saw the bulges under their jackets, proof that they were armed while off duty. She hurriedly told them the story. Pat grabbed a phone and called the precinct house. He told the desk sergeant that an officer was in trouble, gave him the address, and told him to roll whatever patrol cars they had, without using their sirens.

As they walked up the five flights of stairs with Kathleen, Pat and Billy started to sing "When Irish Eyes Are Smiling." When they arrived at the fourth floor, the gunman was still standing there with his right hand inside his jacket. The guard smiled. His hand dropped away from his jacket when he saw the two apparently intoxicated men behind Kathleen. As Pat stumbled by, he grabbed the thug's gun hand. Billy shoved a gun to the man's head, clamped a hand over his mouth and whispered, "Don't make a sound or else I'll blow your head off. Kathleen then proceeded to gently knock three times on the door. "Good Lord", she prayed, "I hope Dan can hear that."

In the interim, Dan had cautioned Lucy to remain in the apartment and to keep quiet. He warned her not to unlock the front

The Almega Project

door for anyone except Kathleen or himself. He then pulled the dumbwaiter up to his level, stood on top of it, and quietly lowered himself down to Vito's apartment. He put his ear to the door, opened it just a crack, and waited for the three knocks on the front door.

He heard faint voices coming from the dining room. Fortunately, its entrance was around the corner. When he heard the knocking signal, he pushed open the dumbwaiter door ever so slowly, and then slipped into the hallway. The loud radio music masked whatever sounds he made. Dan moved quickly toward the dining room entrance. The occupants were around the corner, out of sight.

There was a breakfront opposite Dan and, in its glass door, he could see a reflection of the interior of the room. There, he saw Vito and Rosa tied and gagged in two chairs. One of the hoods held a gun against Vito's head as he said, "Look, you've stalled us long enough, now we're going to get rough. Hey, Gino, get out your knife. If this guy doesn't nod his head to give us the information I want you to cut off the bitch's nose. Let's see how pretty she looks then."

Vito's eyes bulged out, and guttural noises came from his throat as he frantically strained against his bonds. He then nodded his head.

Dan decided he had to act fast. He stepped into the room; his revolver pointed at the gunman near Vito. He shouted, "Police. Drop your weapons." The gunman wheeled around and started firing wildly in Dan's direction. However, Dan had dropped to a crouching position and fired three shots squarely into the gunman's chest. He was dead before he hit the ground. The man with the knife lunged at Dan and stabbed him in the left arm. As the man tried to pull the knife back out, Dan emptied the rest of his revolver into the man's stomach. The man's mouth gaped open in surprise as he clutched Dan and slid slowly to the floor, his life forces oozing out of him.

At this point, the front door flew open, and Pat and Billy dashed into the apartment, followed by five more uniformed cops, all with their guns drawn. Billy rushed over to Dan, who was covered with blood. "For God's sake, man, are you all right?"

"Yeah. The bastard stuck me in my arm, and it hurts like hell. But it'll take more than a pig sticker to bring down a thick mick like me. I'll be all right if you can get a doctor to patch me up. I think those two guys on the floor are dead."

"Well done, boyo", Billy laughed. He yelled at one of the uniforms "Get on the car radio and send an ambulance over here right away, we have an officer wounded. And also tell them to send for the coroner."

At this moment, Kathleen muscled her way through the mob of uniformed officers and grabbed Dan. "Are you all right, Dan", she sobbed, "I heard all that shooting and commotion. I prayed to God that you weren't killed."

"Do I look like a ghost, woman? I'm fine, thank God. Your prayers were answered. I just got a little nick in my arm."

The precinct captain, Cormac O'Neill, soon arrived on the scene, along with the doctor and ambulance crew. "Well, Danny boy, I understand you're all right, and you got two of the bastards. Imagine them threatening to cut a pregnant woman. What kind of animals were they, trying to do something like that? What the hell were they doing up here?"

"I don't know, captain", shrugged Dan. "You'll have to ask the Morellis."

"They are so shook up that they can't even think straight right now" said O'Neill. "They worked Vito over pretty well. He has a black eye and a swollen jaw. I'll have them come to my office tomorrow for a statement. Meanwhile, let's have the doctor look at you."

The doctor examined Dan's arm and concluded that all he had to do was to clean the wound and put in some stitches. He told him to take a few days off. "Come in next week and I'll take out the stitches."

"Thanks, Doc."

When everyone left, Dan said to Vito, "You and I are going to have a private talk tomorrow morning. You better have some good answers to what was going on here this evening."

Vito nodded numbly and Rosa replied, "We'll tell you everything tomorrow. Meanwhile, I'm terribly grateful to you for saving our lives. I don't know how we can ever repay you."

"That's OK," said Dan. "That's what friends are for. I was just doing my job and I'm glad I was home when this happened. Kathleen and I are very fond of you folks. She'd skin me alive if I let something happen to you. So, get a good night's sleep and I'll see you in the morning."

Chapter 5

At nine o'clock the following morning, Dan knocked on the Morelli's door. Rosa answered it and ushered Dan into the dining room, where Vito was drinking coffee.

"Please have a seat, Dan. I'll pour you some fresh coffee."

"Thanks, Rosa. Now will someone please tell me what in God's name is going on?"

"Dan, Vito asked me to tell you the whole story since his jaw is swollen and he can't talk very well. Let me start at the very beginning. My maiden name is Castiglia. Does that name mean anything to you?"

Dan shook his head, "No, it doesn't."

"How about the name Frank Costello?"

"Of course, everybody knows about Frank Costello. He's one of the biggest racketeers in the city."

"Yes, but his real name was Francesco Castiglia. I'm his first cousin. Our families come from the same town in Calabria, Italy. My folks moved here shortly before I was born. Frank, together with his mother and sister, had moved here a few years earlier. We lived near them and were friends. Unfortunately, Frank got involved with a bad crowd."

"That's putting it mildly," said Dan, shaking his head.

"I know. I don't approve of what he does, but he's still family. My mother didn't want me to get involved with anyone in that crowd so she kept me as far away from them as she could. She was very happy when I met and married Vito. He had been working in a nice restaurant in Little Italy, where we were living. Vito had been sent to America, from Sicily, when he was sixteen, to live with an older brother. He started in the restaurant, washing dishes.

"He became a busboy, worked his way up to waiter, and then as assistant to the chef.

"One night, there was a big private party at the restaurant for a local mob family. At midnight, a group of rival gangsters burst into the restaurant and started shooting at everybody. They killed a number of people, including the owner of the place. The restaurant closed down and Vito was out of work. Times were tough then and Vito couldn't find another job.

"My mother asked Frank to help Vito get a job that wouldn't involve the rackets. Frank had always liked me and my mom and he agreed to help. He said that he would lend us the money to open a store, or restaurant, so we could be our own boss. I wanted to get away from Little Italy and all its problems. I didn't want to live in another Italian neighborhood.

"Someone told me about the Vinegar Hill area. I liked this apartment house. It's a safe neighborhood, with some Italians, but most of the people are from other countries. The Catholic Church and school are only a few blocks away, there are nice parks close by, and there's good public transportation. So, we moved here and opened our delicatessen. It was a struggle to make an honest living, but we were able to get by.

"As you know, when I became pregnant I eventually had to quit working there. That's when Frank approached Vito and said that he could earn some badly needed extra money by doing something on the side."

"And what was that something, Rosa?"

"Well, Frank wanted to run a numbers racket in this neighborhood. He needed a space for the operation. We had a small storeroom in our store, which we seldom used, and Vito allowed Frank to use it. One of Frank's men stayed in the room during the day and collected the bets from the runners. When he left at night, he took the money with him, except on Saturdays.

"On Saturdays, for some reason, he gave the money to Vito in a brown paper bag. Vito brought it home for safe keeping, overnight, and returned it to the store the following morning. One of Frank's bagmen then picked it up.

"Vito never told me about this deal. I just found out about it last night. Frank had convinced Vito that he had enough influence with the police department that Vito would never have a problem. He convinced Vito that he wouldn't actually be involved in anything really bad.

"With the baby coming, Vito knew we needed the money badly, and he figured that this was a pretty safe thing to do for the family.

"Apparently, the goons that came after us last night found out about the numbers racket and thought that Vito was an easy target."

"Are you telling me the whole truth?" asked Dan skeptically. "My captain is going to ask me a lot of questions about you and Vito. I don't want to be embarrassed about the relationship that Kathleen and I have with you two."

"Dan", I swear I'm telling you the whole truth. You and Kathleen have been such good friends that I wouldn't do anything to get you into trouble or put you in danger."

"All right, Rosa, I believe you. I have to go to the station house and meet with the captain. I'll tell him that you gave me your statements. I'll let you know what happens."

When Dan went to the station house, the captain informed him that the captured hood told the police that he and his two dead companions lived in Chicago and were visiting New York to see if they could make some easy scores.

"Tell me, Dan, why did they pick on Vito?"

"I'll tell you the whole story, captain, but then I'm going to ask you for a favor."

"I can't promise you anything in advance, Dan, but continue."

Dan told him everything he knew about the incident as well as the personal relationship he had with the Morellis.

"They are really fine people, captain, and I wouldn't want them to get into any further trouble over this. Can you see your way to not putting some of this in your report?"

"Well, Dan, I have a confession to make. I've been aware of Vito's situation for a little while but I was under orders not to interfere."

"Why?"

"Frank Costello has a number of politicians and police officials in this town on his payroll. It wouldn't really do any good for me to put Vito's problem in an official report. I would certainly lose some Brownie points with the higher ups. But the cat's out of the bag now. The press is already snooping around and they will eventually learn the truth.

"Tell Vito that I will have to close his store, otherwise the press will crucify me and the department.

"By the way, those crooks didn't know that they were trying to rob a Frank Costello operation, or that Rosa was his cousin. When I told the survivor, the guy turned white. He said he would confess to anything I wanted as long as I would send him out of town before Frank could reach him."

Dan said, "I don't blame him."

Captain O'Neill then smiled and said, "That was real smart thinking, Dan, the way you handled the situation. I could use a cool-headed guy like you in the Detective squad. Would you be interested? It would mean a promotion in rank and more pay."

Dan took the offer on the spot. A few weeks later, Rosa delivered a healthy boy whom they named Joseph.

Chapter 6

The police closed Vito's store. Frank Costello felt sorry for Rosa and Vito. He knew they needed money, but he also knew that Rosa would not accept any further help from him unless she was convinced that everything was on the up and up.

Frank came up with another idea. He owned a building in the Bronx, on Arthur Avenue, a predominantly Italian neighborhood. A large pizza parlor had formerly occupied the street level space. The owner recently died and the store was vacant.

Frank brought Vito to the store and said, "Vito, I know you have restaurant and food preparation experience. I want you to be my partner and reopen this place as a nice restaurant."

Vito shook his head, "Frank, you know Rosa. She won't let me get involved with you in anything illegal."

"There will be nothing illegal about this. It will be strictly legit. I'll straighten it out with Rosa. Let me tell you my plan. I've been talking to some of the other Italian gangs and we all agree that we want to have a neutral place to meet, occasionally, to discuss some mutual problems. They all pledged to make such a place safe. Think of it as a kind of sanctuary like one provided by a church. If anyone violates their pledge, the other members promise to take swift care of the problem.

"I think a restaurant here, that served really good Italian food, would be an ideal place. There are too many eyes and ears in Manhattan for our purpose. Furthermore, you're Sicilian and everybody trusts you.

Vito thought for a while and said, "If you can convince Rosa, I'll do it."

Frank told the police captain of the local precinct what the plan was and personally guaranteed that there would be no trouble there. The captain was informed by his superiors to go along and not to interfere. He was also instructed to keep the place under tight surveillance.

Rosa was leery of the plan when Frank explained it to her. She insisted on talking to the local police captain to verify what he said. When the captain told her that the police department had no objections, she relented and gave her approval to Vito.

When the remodeling was complete, the place was opened as "Vito's Ristorante". It was an immediate success.

Dan found his new detective work exciting. He got to travel in various parts of the city and meet many interesting people. The Irish throughout the city knew of his involvement with Eamon de Valera and the IRA. He was one of their own so they trusted him. They would tell him things they wouldn't tell anyone else. Some of this information enabled him to crack cases that had stumped the department for some time.

From the start of his career, Dan was active in the Emerald Society, the Irish police officers fraternal and protective organization. Every high and low ranking officer of Irish descent belonged to this group. Eventually, he became its president, a highly visible position. Everyone knew him. He was moving up the ladder.

Also helping his rapid climb was his friendship with Vito Morelli. If some ambitious outside mobster tried to horn in on a Mafioso's action, the mob found it much more effective to let the police handle the situation for them. Vito would be told to let Dan know about certain names, places, dates and criminal activity. The miscreants would soon find themselves in jail. Dan's arrest record became the talk of the police force.

To top it all off, Kathleen became pregnant. Life was looking good.

One evening, Dan was leaving the subway stop at 137th street and Broadway when he heard someone call his name. He turned and saw Rabbi Kattler walking toward him.

"Hello, Rabbi, it's good to see you again. I'm sorry that I don't get to see you and the kids too often since I got this new job."

"I'm sorry too, Dan. You don't know how happy you made the kids feel when you taught them your self-defense classes. It really helped their confidence. The neighborhood bullies aren't picking on them anymore, even though you're no longer pounding this beat. By the way, how is Kathleen feeling, now that she's nine months pregnant?"

Dan replied, "She's feeling just great, thank God. She's ready to give birth any day now. We finally got a telephone in our apartment and I check in with her a couple of times a days. Say, what are you carrying in that bank bag?"

"Oh, this is the payroll for the week. I just picked it up from the bank up the street. Payday is tomorrow. By the way, I'm glad I ran into you. I think I'm being followed. There's a young black man who was in line behind me at the bank. He saw all the money put in my bag and he followed me out. He's still walking behind me."

Dan stopped walking and pretended to let out a loud sneeze. He turned slightly to his right, reached into his pocket for a handkerchief and made a great show of blowing his nose. While performing this act, he was able to look behind him. He saw the black man, who had also stopped, and was making a great pretense of looking in a store window.

Dan said, "You might be right but we only have to walk up the hill to Amsterdam Avenue and we'll both be home. I'll make sure you get into your place safely. If he follows us up the hill and tries to pull anything, I'll be ready."

When Dan replaced his handkerchief, he unobtrusively slid his hip holster toward the front and unfastened its restraining strap for quicker access. As they started to walk up the steep incline of 136th street, Dan periodically looked behind him but saw no one. "I guess we were both wrong, the street is deserted. We can both relax."

When they were about half way up the hill, a car suddenly screeched to a halt beside them. Two black men were in the car. The passenger jumped out. He was the man that had been following them on foot. He raced over and pointed a gun at the Rabbi as he snarled, "O.K. you whiteys, this is a stickup. I want the moneybag and both your wallets. If you don't do as I say, I'll shoot you."

Dan instinctively reached up to grab the robber's right hand while trying to draw his own gun. He jumped in front of the Rabbi. The gunman, startled by this sudden move, fired his gun, hitting Dan squarely in the chest. Dan threw himself against the hoodlum and pumped four shots into his heart, killing him instantly. Dan's momentum caused him and his assailant to fall to the ground. Dan's gun fell from his grip. He found himself pinned underneath the other man, seriously wounded and unable to move. Meanwhile, the driver jumped out of his car and ran over to his companion. He bent over and tried to feel his pulse. There was none. He then looked at Dan who gazed up at him with semiconscious eyes. He snatched Dan's gun from the sidewalk and put it against Dan's head screaming, "You killed my younger brother. I'm gonna make you pay for that."

He pulled the trigger twice. Brain parts scattered all over the street. He reached into Dan's jacket and took the wallet containing Dan's money and gold Detective shield.

Then he turned his attention to the Rabbi, who was staring in disbelief at what was happening. He told the Rabbi to hand over the moneybag and his wallet. The shell-shocked Rabbi quickly complied. The gunman muttered, "I can't leave no witnesses." With that, he pressed the gun against the Rabbi's temple and pulled the trigger. There was no sound but a loud click. The gun was empty. The gunman stared at the gun in disbelief.

By this time, some of the neighbors in the tenements across the street were opening their windows and one of them was shouting, "What's all the noise down there? We've called the cops. What's going on?"

The yells startled the gunman who quickly turned around, raced back to his car, jumped in and sped away.

A stunned Rabbi Kattler shouted for someone to call the hospital. Within minutes, the street was crawling with cops and ambulances.

.

Chapter 8

Kathleen heard the sirens of the ambulances and squad cars as they raced past her apartment house and turned west on 136th street. She looked out her window but since all the vehicles were below the crest of the hill, she could only see evidence of flashing red lights in the evening dusk.

"Some poor soul must have had an accident", she thought to herself, "I hope it's not anyone I know."

About an hour later, Kathleen heard a knock on her door. When she opened it, she saw Captain Cormac O'Neill, Monsignor Quinn and Rabbi Kattler.

"Jesus, Mary and Joseph", she wailed, "Something's happened to Dan!"

The three men entered the apartment. Captain O'Neill was the first to speak. "Kathleen, I'm sorry to be the one to tell you, but Dan was shot dead not more than a hundred yards from here."

Kathleen felt the child in her womb give her stomach a violent kick. She started to double over in pain. All three men grabbed her before she could fall to the ground. They gently escorted her to the living room and sat her down on the couch. Over the next hour or so, Kathleen was informed of the entire incident. Rabbi Kattler was so grief stricken that Dan had to give his own life in order to save his friend that he was barely able to talk. Msgr. Quinn told her that he would personally take care of all the funeral arrangements.

Capt. O'Neill said, "We know who the killer is. The slain man is Luther Jones and his companion is his older brother, Lincoln. These two guys have long records. They usually operate in Harlem. I have no idea why they came into this neighborhood.

Rest assured that whole department won't rest until Dan's killer is caught. If you need any help, Kathleen, call me personally."

When Rosa heard all the commotion in the stairway, she asked a policeman what had happened. When she heard the story, she raced upstairs and pushed her way to Kathleen's side. Kathleen hugged her and sobbed on her shoulder.

Rosa told everyone that she was going to take charge of Kathleen and asked everyone to please leave. They willingly complied.

Kathleen spent the next few days in a daze. Msgr. Quinn and Rosa took care of everything. Cashman's Funeral Parlor, that was only two blocks from the church, was chosen for the wake. The neighborhood had never witnessed such an outpouring of people. The mayor, police commissioner, and every politician, Irish or not, came to pay their respects as well as every member of New York's Finest.

Rabbi Kattler led a large contingent of Jewish notables to the parlor. There were so many floral bouquets that they had to put most of them in the other viewing rooms.

The ladies in the Altar and Rosary Society did their best to put on a good old- fashioned Irish wake. There was a great deal of food available as well as Irish whisky, compliments of the Emerald Society. They even provided the traditional Irish clay pipes.

There was much storytelling and laughter at the wake because the Irish firmly believed that the dearly departed were entering a far better life with God. This passing was supposed to be a cause for rejoicing as much as it was for grieving.

A Solemn High Requiem Mass was scheduled and attendance inside the church was by invitation only. Every seat was taken. Hundreds more waited outside, filling the sidewalks of Convent Avenue for two blocks. Dan's former colleagues in the Mounted Police force were kept busy keeping things in order.

The Hebrew Orphan Asylum's award winning band marched from their building, past Dan's apartment house and made a right turn onto Convent Avenue, all the while playing Irish tunes. They were led by a boy carrying a pole, on which hung a blue banner with the initials HOA. When they reached the church they stopped.

At this point, a gust of wind twisted the banner around. An Irish mounted policeman, whose back had been turned to the parade, turned his head and noticed the banner, which to him, now appeared to read AOH. He looked at the young boy, pointed to the banner, and asked "Ancient Order of Hibernians?"

The boy looked puzzled. He then looked up and saw what the confusion was all about. He flipped the banner back to its proper position. He pointed to two boys behind him who were supporting a much larger banner that read "Hebrew Orphan Asylum Cadet Corps."

The policeman let out a hearty laugh, looked up to heaven and said, "Dan that was a grand joke you played on me. Wait till the men hear this one."

Silence gripped the onlookers as the hearse appeared, coming down the street. A police officer, leading Dan's horse, preceded it. Empty boots were placed backwards in the stirrups, the universal symbol of a fallen comrade in arms. The hearse stopped and an honor guard carried the casket into the church, preceded by the Emerald Society's bagpipers playing "Amazing Grace."

The bishop, himself, officiated at the Solemn High Requiem Mass, assisted by Msgr. Quinn and the Police Department's Catholic chaplain. Msgr. Quinn gave the eulogy. He based his talk on a quotation from John15:13, "Greater love hath no man than this that a man lay down his life for his friends."

When the mass ended, Msgr. Quinn announced that he was honoring a request from his good friend, Rabbi Kattler, who wanted to pay his own personal farewell tribute to the man who had saved his life and who had done so much for the Hebrew Orphan Asylum.

Rabbi Kattler, wearing a green yarmulke, strode to the front of the choir loft at the rear of the church. He said, "Over the years that I had the privilege to Know Daniel Patrick Gallagher, I learned that he loved music. There was one song that was his particular favorite. He told me that it was written about a father watching his only son sail away from Ireland to America. I would like to sing that song to Dan now."

As the Police honor guard raised the casket to their shoulders and walked very slowly down the aisle, Rabbi Kattler, who had also been trained as a Cantor, raised his tenor voice in this haunting refrain:

Oh Danny boy, the pipes, the pipes are calling,
From glen to glen, and down the mountain side
The summer's gone, and all the roses falling
'Tis you, 'tis you must go, and I must bide.
But come you back when summer's in the meadow
Or when the valley's hushed and white with snow
'Tis I'll be there in sunshine or in shadow
Oh Danny boy, oh Danny boy, I love you so.

But if you come, and all the flowers are dying
And if I am dead, as dead I may well be
You'll come and find the place where I am lying
And kneel and say an "Ave" there for me.

And I shall hear, tho' soft you tread above me
And all my dreams shall warm and sweeter be
If you will bend and tell me that you love me
Then I will sleep in peace until you come to me.

When he finished, there was not a dry eye in the Church. Even the priests and battle hardened honor guards had tears streaming down their faces.

The cortege to the gravesite was something the neighbors talked about for years. It seemed that every police car and motorcycle in the city was in the funeral procession.

At the cemetery, the honor guard fired a twenty-one-gun salute over their fallen comrade in arms as a bugler played "Taps." The bagpipers played the Irish national anthem as Dan was lowered into his grave.

"Dan should be very proud of himself in heaven", thought Kathleen to herself, "he's getting a grand sendoff".

Rosa and Vito rode back from the cemetery in the limousine with Kathleen.

Rosa said to Kathleen, "I got a message last night from Frank Costello. He told me that Dan's death has been avenged."

"What in God's name do you mean by that?" she asked in astonishment.

"I honestly don't' know", replied Rosa. "Time will tell."

As they neared their apartment house, Kathleen suddenly cried out in pain, "Oh my God, the baby's coming!"

Rosa told the driver to proceed immediately back to the church since Knickerbocker Hospital was directly across the street from it.

The driver floored the accelerator and soon pulled into the Emergency entrance. Kathleen was immediately wheeled into the hospital and, within an hour, Sean Patrick Gallagher entered the world on the same day his father left it.

One of her first visitors to the hospital was Rabbi Kattler.

"Kathleen, I want to wish you congratulations on the birth of a fine boy. Words can't express how sad I feel that Dan isn't alive to see him."

"Rabbi, don't feel guilty about Dan. He was doing his duty and we both knew that he faced this possibility every day. I don't blame you. If Dan had to die, I'm glad that it was for a friend who is doing so much good in this world. His dad died in much the same way. I just hope and pray it's not something hereditary."

"You have no idea how much your words mean to me, Kathleen. Now, I have a proposition for you. I've given it a great deal of thought and I hope you will accept it. I know that the Police Department will give you a widow's pension, but it probably won't be quite enough for you and Sean to live on. I want you to come to work for me at the orphanage."

"You must be daft, Rabbi, how could I do that? I don't have any education or training for that kind of work and, besides, I'm nursing little Sean and I can't be away from him for more than a few hours for many months to come."

Rabbi Kattler continued, "Please hear me out. I have recently had a large turnover in personnel. Because I have been so busy attending other problems in the Orphanage, I neglected to address some serious problems with my employees. I really need someone I trust to help me and free up some of my time. You don't really need any experience. I only need someone with common sense and I know that you have that in abundance.

"You would be working with other women from the neighborhood, some of whom you probably know. Over the years, we have hired a number of women from your parish that Msgr. Quinn has recommended. As a matter of fact, I've already talked to him about my idea and he is heartily in favor of it. Furthermore, most of the children already know and love you due to your helping Dan with his self-defense courses.

"As for Sean, you can bring him with you to work. I can make arrangements so that you can have the privacy to care for him when necessary. We have a large number of girls there who would love to help you with him. I guarantee you he would not be neglected.

"Please think it over. You would be doing me a great favor."

Kathleen said, "Rabbi Kattler, I'm in no condition to think straight right now. When I get out of the hospital I'll call on you and you can show me what you're talking about."

The Rabbi's eyes brightened over the fact that she had not flatly turned him down. "I look forward to your visit."

The following day, the headline of the New York Daily News read "Cop Killer Found Floating in Harlem River." The lurid photographs showed the mutilated body of Lincoln Jones stretched out on a bank of the river.

Two days later, a plain brown package arrived in the mail at Dan's precinct. It contained Dan's gold shield, his ID card, and his police revolver. Captain O'Neill stared at the contents and sighed. Then, he pulled the file on Dan's death and marked it "CLOSED."

A few weeks after Dan's death, the Emerald Society created a scholarship fund for Sean's education. Soon after the fund was started, a rather large man lumbered into Dan's precinct and approached the desk sergeant, who said, "Well, if it isn't Two Ton Tony Mafucci. What are you doing here? Did Frank Costello send you?"

Tony held up a brown paper bag and answered, "I'ma here to give you dis. Itsa for dat Irish kid."

The sergeant said, "You mean the Sean Gallagher Educational Fund?"

"Yeah, dis is for him."

The officer took the bag and looked inside. It was filled with a large number of bills.

"Tony, who is this money from?"
"From friends of da kid's family."
"What are the names of these friends?"
"Dey said dey wanna remain unanimous."
"You mean anonymous?"
"Yeah, dat's what I mean."

The sergeant took the bag and said, "Tell your friends that we appreciate the donation."

"Yeah, arrivederci."

The money in the bag amounted to ten thousand dollars. The sergeant thought to himself that Sean would have an interesting academic future ahead of him.

Chapter 10

Two weeks after Kathleen left the hospital, she entered the heavy oak doors of the Hebrew Orphan Asylum to see Rabbi Kattler. He warmly welcomed her to his office. "You are looking well, Kathleen. How is your son doing?"

"Sean's fine. I'm very pleased with how he's behaving. Mrs. Morelli is looking after him right now."

"Good, I'm so glad to hear that."

Kathleen sat down and looked around the office. "Even though I've often been to the Orphanage grounds, I spent most of the time in the gym. I seldom visited the main building. I really don't know much about the place. How did it all get started?"

The Rabbi nodded his head, "Well, let's see where to begin. Members of the New York Jewish community originally funded our orphanage many years ago. Our main building was built in what is called the Renaissance style. It opened in 1884 to house 600 boys and girls. As you know, the building is shaped like a large capital E, with its spine fronting on Amsterdam Avenue. The main building, and two wings, are four stories high, while the smaller center wing is three stories high.

"The dormitories and infirmary are located on the upper floors. The main floor, where we are, contains a Synagogue, which we also use as an assembly hall, plus a dining room, reception rooms, offices, classrooms, and a library. In the basement, we have the laundry, bakery, kitchen, and storerooms. We are pretty much a self-contained community.

"We have a relatively small staff for so large an institution because the older girls work as unpaid housekeepers. Before leaving for school every morning, they make all the beds, including those in the boys' dormitories, and sweep and dust as well. After meals, the girls clear the tables, sweep the dining room, wash the dishes, and set the table for the next meal.

"Everybody goes to school about 8:30 AM. Half the children stay here to attend our very own Public School 192, which is located in this building. It's a primary school set up, with city approval, for the youngest children of our orphanage as well as the neighboring community. The older children, as you know, attend Junior High at P. S. 43.

"When the children return from school, they attend Hebrew classes from 4 to 6 PM. After the evening meal, the children are required to study and complete their homework assignments. Because of this discipline, the students attending P.S. 43 win most of the prizes and honors for scholarship. Not only are they well prepared, but also punctual and well behaved. The teachers at the school, who, by the way, are mostly Irish, are very fond of them.

"On Saturday morning, we hold religion classes for those boys and girls who are preparing for their confirmation classes. Saturday is also devoted to teaching the children various arts and crafts.

"I'm sure you realize, Kathleen, that we have had a close, warm relationship with the Irish Catholic community. It all goes back to the very beginning. You may not know this, but the original property for our institution was purchased from two Irish farmers named Devlin and Donnelly, between 1880 and 1882. These two men were members of your parish.

"In 1928, we built the gymnasium where you and Dan taught your self-defense course. It was a very generous gift from the Warner brothers, the motion picture producers. When not in use for athletics, the Warner Gym serves as an entertainment center. The large stage can easily be converted into a theater, movie house, or auditorium for meetings and dances. The roof has a fenced-in tennis court.

"A few years ago, your husband met with me and asked if we would consider making the gym available to the students from the Annunciation school. It seems that the boys had some pretty good basketball teams but no gym. They were forced to practice on the outdoor courts in the local park. I thought it was a wonderful idea. We owed a debt of gratitude to the parish for welcoming us when the home decided to locate here. I talked the idea over with Msgr.

The Almega Project

Quinn. Your church, as you probably also know, uses it for dances as well as for a gym. Your husband's suggestion has proven to everybody that a spirit of comradeship and cooperation can exist between people of different religious faiths. As a result, our neighborhood has become a much better place.

"Dan once told me, 'We Irish have a lot in common with the Jews.'

"I asked him, how?'"

"He replied, 'We both think we are God's chosen people, we hate religious persecution, we are both as stubborn as mules, and, we're not overly fond of the English'. I'll always remember that remark, it's so true."

Kathleen laughed at the story and interrupted the Rabbi by asking, "That sounded like Dan. By the way, are all the children here really orphans?"

"No, as a matter of fact, only about five percent are true orphans, about thirty five percent have one parent, and the balance have both parents Since the depression started a few years ago, many families have fallen apart and we have experienced a large influx of children. Currently, we have about 1,800 children under our care, the most ever. But only 600 actually live here, the rest are boarded out with foster parents. We normally don't accept children under five or six years old, they are turned over to another agency. We keep most of the children here until they graduate from high school or their parents take them back."

"How do you get the money for this huge operation?"

"We get some funding now from various government agencies. The rest comes from charitable contributions from the Jewish community in the city. We have a very prestigious and influential Board of Trustees that always seems to raise enough money to meet our budget requirements."

"What is it you would want me to do here?"

"Well, as I mentioned earlier, we have the largest group of kids ever, and we are shorthanded. We run on a very tight budget and I can't afford to add much more staff. I really need someone to assist me in a few areas, a jack- of all- trades, so to speak. As the Superintendent, I am stretched so thin that I can't get around to everything I want or need to. I need someone to be my eyes and ears and let me know if there are any problems that I need to look into. A new person, such as yourself, will not be encumbered with the attitude that 'We've always done it this way'. You'll see things with a new perspective.

"I also need someone who can do some administrative work, run errands and so forth. I know you are well organized. Dan told me you know how to type and you obviously get along well with people. Most of the children already know as Auntie Kate and they love you. You would fit right in."

"But what about Sean? I'll be nursing him for quite a while and I can't be away from him for more than a few hours at a time."

"You can bring Sean with you. Right now he's young enough to stay in a basinet. When he outgrows that, we'll fix up a playpen. There is lots of room for privacy when it's feeding time. Also, we have a number of girls who live here that would like nothing more to do than help you with him. Many of them have younger brothers and sisters that they had to take care of before they came to us. Trust me, they will be fighting for the privilege of watching and playing with Sean. It will also help them to relieve their loneliness. You would be doing them a big favor. Does that answer your question?"

"I think so."

"Great. Now, let me show you around so that you get an idea of what I'm talking about."

At the end of the tour, they returned to the Rabbi's office. Kathleen told the Rabbi, "I can understand what a difficult job you have but I'm not sure that I could do everything you want."

"I think you can. I'm reminded of another piece of wisdom that Dan gave me. He said that Irish women are like Irish tea bags, you don't know how strong they are until you put them in hot water."

Kathleen smiled. "That sounds like my Dan, alright. He always did have a way with words. I guess I'll have to prove him right. I'll take the job."

Rabbi Kattler's eyes lit up with genuine pleasure. "I'm so glad you said yes. I just know that it will be a good experience for you and the home.

"To start, I know that we have some problems in our kitchen. We've had a large turnover of personnel and things seem to have gotten out of hand. We have gotten a lot of complaints about the food and, quite frankly, I agree. Perhaps you could start there first. It opens at 5 AM."

The following Monday, Kathleen reported for work and spent the entire day in the kitchen to get a feel of how it operated. She deposited Sean in a small pantry where he could readily be seen and still be out of the way. She observed the kitchen routine and saw how disorganized it was. She tasted the food and was appalled by it. She wasn't sure what could be done to improve things since she had no experience in this area. After all, trying to feed six hundred people in a short amount of time, three times a day, was not something she had encountered before.

She remembered that a fellow parishioner, Maureen Flannigan, was a dietician who ran the kitchen at Knickerbocker Hospital. Kathleen made an appointment to meet with her.

When Maureen heard Kathleen's problem, she agreed to visit the HOA for a day, to get a first-hand look at the operation.

She subsequently invited Kathleen to visit her at the hospital to see how a kitchen should be run. She walked Kathleen through each step of the preparation of the food, explaining why certain things were done in a certain way.

She also discussed selecting the food to provide a well-balanced menu at an affordable price.

"Look, Kathleen, you don't serve gourmet food at institutions such as mine or yours. We really don't need experienced chefs. We select food that is simple to prepare and nutritionally well balanced. Almost anybody can cook it. I wrote a manual on how to create and cook well balanced menus, with a few options, to make the meals a little different and more interesting each time they are served. I'll give you a copy. I call it my bible. If you follow it, you can't go wrong."

She also gave Kathleen a list of the vendors that had proven to be honest and reliable over the years.

As Kathleen left, Maureen told her, "I know that I gave you an awful lot of information and I wouldn't expect you to remember all of it. Just consider it as an overview. When you need more information please feel free to get back to me. I'm more than glad to help you in any way I can. After all, we colleens have to stick together, now, don't we?"

"Yes, Maureen, we certainly do. I can't thank you enough for all the help you have given me."

Kathleen discussed some ideas for changes in the kitchen with Rabbi Kattler. "Rabbi, I worked for a Jewish family some years ago, and they had certain foods that they couldn't eat. Is that true here?"

"No, Kathleen, we are Reformed Jews. Our dietary laws and rituals are different from the Orthodox Jews. We do not keep a kosher kitchen. You have a great deal of leeway in planning the menus. Go right ahead and do whatever you think is necessary."

She proceeded to organize the kitchen staff along the lines that Maureen had suggested, assigning each person specific responsibilities. She noticed that the workers seemed to consult one particular woman when they encountered a problem. Kathleen made her the supervisor.

She looked over the current vendor list and noted their costs of supplies. There seemed to be a number of small vendors supplying the same food items at varying prices. She contacted the vendors recommended by Maureen and got their prices, which were invariably cheaper. She could understand this, since they shipped larger quantities and, therefore, their expenses were lower. She negotiated with them to get even lower prices by guaranteeing them continuity of purchases as long as their quality was acceptable. After all, there weren't too many customers in the city that had to feed six hundred people, three times a day, seven days a week.

Over the next few weeks, Kathleen's changes pleased almost everybody. The menu became more appetizing and the efficiency in the kitchen was upgraded. Rabbi Kattler was well pleased.

As the days went by, she spent more time assisting the Rabbi with the office routine. When she answered the phone, first time callers were startled when they heard a female voice with a decided Irish brogue saying "Hebrew Orphan Asylum." Rabbi Kattler and the entire staff had to laugh when Kathleen told them of the confusion she was causing since some of the callers hung up because they thought they had the wrong number.

She quickly adjusted to her new routine, getting to the Orphanage at five and leaving around three, having put in a ten-hour day. On Saturdays, she left at noon. She still managed to hold her citizenship classes with her friends. She spent Sunday mornings attending early mass and then spent the rest of the day relaxing with Sean. She got into the habit of singing Irish lullabies and speaking to him in Gaelic. She was still homesick, and this made her feel still connected to her native land.

Rabbi Kattler was right when he said that she would have more help with Sean than she could shake a stick at. The first time that Sean's diapers were changed by one of the girls, she giggled and immediately called some of the other girls over to take a look.

They also giggled. Kathleen noticed this and came over to ask, "What's so funny, girls?"

One of the older girls told her, "We've never seen a boy baby that wasn't circumcised. It just looks strange to us, like a little frankfurter."

Kathleen had to laugh too. "Well, you girls will just have to get used to it. The Irish don't have the same customs as you do."

As Sean grew older and learned to walk, he had the run of the place. He never lacked for companionship. The girls treated him as a beloved younger brother. They would sing lullabies and talk to him in their native tongues, mostly Hebrew, German, Russian, or Yiddish. Sean soon realized that he could really please the girls and make them smile if he made an effort to repeat their own words. Due to this total immersion experience, over a period of years, Sean developed a remarkable ability to understand and speak these languages. This delighted the girls and they took great pains to teach him more and more of their vocabulary. He had them wrapped around his little finger.

When he came of age, Kathleen enrolled him in P.S.192, rather than Annunciation, because of the in-house convenience. She was concerned about the religion classes he was missing, so she met with Sister Euphemia, the principal of Annunciation Boys School, and explained her situation.

The nun said, "Don't worry about it, Kathleen. Under the circumstances, you are making the right decision to let Sean stay there. I know that it's a good school. I will give you a copy of the catechism we use. You can just as easily teach him his religion at home. You can bring him by here occasionally and I will test him on his knowledge of the subject. If you decide to transfer him later on, just let me know."

Sean proved to be a very bright student. His outgoing personality attracted the friendship and respect of his fellow classmates.

During summer recesses, Sean spent his early mornings with his mother at the orphanage. The afternoons with spent with Joe. Rosa loved him as a second son. She told Kathleen that it was easier to look after two boys than one. "They keep each other amused and busy. Sean is so bright and polite. He is a pleasure to have around the house.

After a few summers, Rosa said to Kathleen. "I have to tell you a funny story. I am in the habit of talking in Italian to Joe at home. I forget that Sean is also there. The other day, I overheard Sean carrying on a conversation with Joe in fluent Italian. I was utterly amazed."

Kathleen nodded her head. "I know what you mean. His brain is like a sponge when it comes to languages. He seems to have acquired a special talent for that at the Orphanage."

Rosa continued. "When I told Vito about this, he decided to play a game with Sean. He would only speak to Sean in Italian. Sean realized what Vito was doing and then would only answer him in English. They wound up teaching each other new words and grammar. We all get a big kick out of it."

Sean's next door neighbor was Ivana Semenova. She gave English lessons to fellow Russian émigrés. She was also an accomplished pianist. When she discovered that Sean and Joe would sit outside her door and listen to her playing, she invited them inside. She told them they were more than welcome to visit her anytime. She had lost a young son to influenza when she lived in Russia and she still grieved for him. She looked upon the two boys as surrogate sons. She taught both of them how to play the piano as well as sing. She was pleased that they were fast learners and thoroughly enjoyed their time there.

When she learned that Sean was able to speak Russian, she was ecstatic. She went out of her way to improve his grammar and vocabulary. She read Russian stories to him and talked about Russian history. She gave him books to read. Sean proved to be a willing student.

Chapter 11

A Board of Trustees governed the Orphanage. They were required by the bylaws to attend a weekly meeting at the HOA, on Sunday. Reserved solely for their use, the Trustee's room was large, ornately decorated, and furnished with long tables and heavy chairs. Around 10:30 every Sunday morning, the trustees would begin to arrive in their limousines. Meetings usually lasted an hour. Rabbi Kattler gave them a weekly report and answered any questions they had.

One day, he mentioned to Kathleen that the Trustees seemed to get bored quickly, and absenteeism was a problem.

"Well, then, "she said, "You have got to make them feel more at home. About eleven in the morning, they are probably feeling a wee bit hungry. Why don't I prepare some refreshment for them? Maybe nice pots of tea and coffee, together with a little something to 'nosh' on, as you say."

"Whatever you think will work, Kathleen."

For the next Sunday meeting, Kathleen prepared one of her favorite recipes, Irish soda bread. It contained caraway seeds and raisins and it provided a nice in-between meal snack. Since Sunday was her day off, she told the rabbi to serve it with plenty of butter and freshly brewed Irish tea or coffee.

The following Monday, the rabbi said, "Kathleen, that Irish soda bread was delicious. The trustees were crazy about it. They all wanted seconds, but we ran out. Next time you'll have to make much more."

Kathleen smiled and said, "I'm so glad it went over well. Let me tell you what I'll do in the future. I'll make enough for everyone to have two pieces and then I'll provide an extra two pieces which I'll wrap in tissue paper and tie with a ribbon. They can take home a package and share it with their wives and families.

The future Trustee meetings seemed to have fewer absentees and, upon leaving the meetings, each trustee could be seen walking away with a small package wrapped in a bright Kelly green ribbon.

When President Roosevelt took office, he enacted a number of social legislations, one of which, the Aid to Dependent Children Act in 1935, foreshadowed the end to all orphanages in America. Government funding would now make it possible for widowed, deserted, and divorced mothers to care for their children at home.

Toward the end of 1939, an announcement was made that the HOA would be closing within the next two years. Throughout 1940, the last full year the HOA would be in operation, most of the children were discharged. The economic climate had improved. The depression was nearing an end and America was gearing up its defense efforts. More jobs were available and more families were able to take their children back.

In June of 1941, the last group of children ended their religion instructions. Rabbi Kattler held their confirmation ceremonies in the synagogue. June was also the month that the remaining children graduated from high school. At that point, all the children were discharged.

The HOA had been in existence for nearly 83 years. It had cared for about thirty five thousand children. Sep. 20, 1941 was the last day the HOA was officially open. On that day, its graduates held a farewell dinner in the dining room. Nearly a thousand alumni attended. Kathleen and Sean were invited and were named honorary alumni.

P.S. 192, however, remained open to continue to serve the neighborhood children.

Late in 1942, the HOA was sold to the city for $1.5 million, but the city never used it. Instead, it turned the building over to the U.S. Army, which needed it for the war effort. They renamed it Army Hall and converted it into barracks for soldiers studying at CCNY, under the Army Specialized Training Program.

Chapter 12

When the Orphanage closed, Kathleen decided it was time to enroll Sean at the parish grammar school. She met with Sister Euphemia who quickly completed the transfer paperwork.

The nun said, "By the way, Kathleen, if you have a little time to spare, someone you know wants to meet you."

"Sure", said Kathleen, "I have all the time in the world, now."

She led Kathleen out of the school and across the street to Manhattanville College. There, she introduced her to Mother Cronin, president of the school, as well as Mother Superior of the Sacred Heart nuns.

"I'm so glad to see you, again, Kathleen. Your husband was one of our dearest friends. He was a wonderful man and we really miss him. He would often ride his horse onto our grounds, at break time, and let him romp and play in the grass for a little while. The nuns and students would feed him an apple or some other tidbit. We all felt so safe, knowing that Dan was patrolling the neighborhood.

"My staff and I couldn't attend his funeral. As a cloistered order, we are not allowed to leave these grounds. However, all of us did watch the funeral procession from behind our gates, directly across the street from the church, and we prayed for him. We still do."

Kathleen replied, "Yes, I saw you and the other nuns. I certainly appreciated your concern and prayers."

"As you well know, we operate three schools on these grounds. At Manhattanville College, we teach our young ladies the liberal arts, with a strong emphasis on music, as well as proper social behavior. Our students come from some of the finest Catholic families in America, as well as Europe. We are training women who will eventually have it within their power, or influence, to help change the world for the better.

"For example, one of our graduates is Rose Kennedy, the wife of Joseph Kennedy, the ambassador to England. Their daughter, Eunice, is scheduled to enroll here next year. She has a sister, Jean, who will eventually follow her. They also have a few brothers. Two of them, Joseph Jr. and John, are currently in the service."

Kathleen said, "I've heard of them. I have seen their names in the Irish Echo newspaper quite often. That's quite an interesting family."

Mother Cronin continued, "In addition, to the college, we also operate two schools for your parish, Father Young's Academy, a high school for girls, as well as the grammar school for girls."

Kathleen interjected, "That's a terribly large responsibility. I don't know how you can do it all."

"I can do it because I have a very dedicated and able staff of nuns and lay people to assist me. However, I recently learned that I would soon lose someone who has been a valuable assistant for many years. Her name is Megan Cunningham."

Kathleen said, "Oh, I know Megan. Is she sick?"

"No, her husband is being transferred out of town. I am looking for a replacement and Msgr. Quinn told me what you have been doing for the past few years at the Orphanage. I think you have the ideal skills and experience to replace Megan. Are you interested?"

Kathleen asked, "What would you expect me to do?"

"I need someone with administrative and secretarial skills, which I'm sure you have. I prefer to have my nuns concentrate on their teaching duties and other assignments. Since we are a cloistered order, I also need someone who can travel outside the campus to perform some shopping and other tasks. I know that you have done all of these things and done them well. I would be grateful if you took this job."

"I am flattered that you considered me. I am interested, but I do have a small problem. My son, Sean, is still too young to be left alone at home after school."

"That problem is easily solved. We can work your hours around Sean's school schedule. He can always stay in our library before or after school, if necessary. He can read or do his homework. Some of the girls from our grammar school come over here to earn some money by waiting on the tables at meal times so he'll have a chance to meet a number of young girls his own age I'm sure he knows some of them already.

"We start early here, at 6 AM, but you can end your day in the afternoon when Sean gets out of school. By the way, you won't have to work weekends, except for special occasions."

"That sounds just grand. I accept your offer. "

When Sean told Joe about the transfer to Annunciation, he was very happy. "That's great. You'll like the school. The teachers are strict, but nice. You already know a lot of the kids there. We will have a good time together."

Kathleen's routine actually didn't change much with her new job. She and Sean would walk the four blocks to the school campus and arrive in time to attend the 6:00 AM mass in the nun's private chapel. Joe accompanied them because he was an altar boy and assisted the priest at those early masses. Sean soon became an altar boy, as well, and joined Joe for the daily services. Learning the Latin prayers was a snap.

They wound up staying in the college library before and after school. They spent most of that time either doing homework assignments or browsing through the large selection of books.

The nuns took an immediate liking to these two bright and well-mannered boys and went out of their way to make them feel comfortable in the all-girl environment.

Manhattanville had a unique program called the Pius X School of Liturgical Music. It had developed teaching methods for Gregorian Chant. Its graduate students practiced their skills on the high school girls at Father Young's Academy. The practices took place in the late afternoon, after regular school hours.

The nuns introduced the boys to one of these practice sessions. They were fascinated with this ancient and hauntingly beautiful form of singing. The nuns were delighted to take them aside and teach them how to sing the Latin chants. Their singing voices become even more developed.

Chapter 13

One of the things that Sean enjoyed about summer recess was the opportunity to relax and play games with the other boys in the neighborhood. Stickball was always a favorite way to pass the time. They played it in the street, with a sawed off broomstick and a pink-colored "spauldeen" rubber ball, which they also used to play another popular game, stoopball.

If they wanted to play basketball or softball, there was always the park, just two blocks away.

To cool off on hot, muggy days, they opened the corner fire hydrant. They would get a wooden milk carton case, the kind with steel bars on the bottom opening, and hook it over the hydrant's spout. The result was a wonderfully cool, rain-like shower. If a convertible car wanted to drive through the street, the driver would stop and ask the boys to unhook the milk case. If the driver was a stranger, or if he was obnoxious in his request, the boys would start to take off the carton to stop the spray. When the driver started to drive by, the boys would quickly slam the case back on the hydrant thereby spraying the car's occupants. If the driver dared to pull over to the curb, everybody would run like crazy in all directions. No one was ever caught.

They would continue to revel in the spray until the police inevitably came by and shut it off.

There were no organized sports clubs so the kids used their ingenuity and inventiveness to amuse themselves. Life was good.

Two or three times during the summer, Sean and Joe would reward themselves by spending a day visiting the Palisades Amusement Park located across the Hudson River in Cliffside Park, New Jersey. Loaded with a dollar in change, they would walk down ten blocks to the 125th St. Ferry Terminal for the ride across the river. The fare was five cents per person.

Sean was always conscious of the opportunity to save money. The ferries also accommodated fifty automobiles. Each car was charged a flat rate, regardless of the number of occupants. This gave Sean an idea.

He would walk by the cars as they lined up to board the ferry. When he spotted a lone woman driver, he approached her and asked if she would be kind enough to allow Joe and himself to hop in the back seat until the car was on the ferry. He explained that they were trying to save their money for the amusement park. They always found someone to accommodate them.

Once the ferry arrived on the Jersey shore, they faced a trolley ride up the steep road to the top of the bluff. This, too, cost a nickel. When it arrived at the gate to the amusement park, they faced an entrance fee, a dime.

Sean had learned from some of the older kids in the neighborhood of an alternative way to gain entrance to the park, and it was free.

The park boasted that it had the world's largest salt-water swimming pool. It obtained the water from the Hudson River via massive pipes that ran down the steep cliff. The boys would climb the rocky hill alongside the pipes until they reached the top of the hill. There, the pipes entered the park through a large hole in the park's security fence. The hole was large enough to allow the boys to slip through. They always experienced a thrill when they felt they had outfoxed the park's security forces.

Unbeknownst to them, Irving Rosenthal, one of the brothers who owned the park, was well aware of this worst-kept secret. The park's admission fee did not entitle a person to any rides, each attraction had its own price. Rosenthal loved children and reasoned that children, who had very little money to start with, would be more than willing to spend all of it, once inside. He instructed his security personnel not to close the hole and pretend not to notice anyone sneaking through it. It was a win-win situation. Everyone was happy.

Chapter 14

Sean's apartment house had no air conditioning. Occasionally, when it when it got too warm in their apartment, he would tell his mother that he was going to visit "Tar Beach". That was New Yorkese for the roof. Sean and his friends would spread newspapers or towels on the roof's hot tar and work on their tans. There usually was enough of a breeze at that height to cool them off a bit.

It was on summer evenings that Tar Beach became even more popular with Sean, Joe, and other residents of his building. From that vantage point, they had an unobstructed view across the street onto the stage of Lewisohn Stadium, the multi-purpose athletic stadium and amphitheater that was part of the City College of New York.

CCNY was founded in 1847 to provide the education to children of the poor and new immigrants that could give them access to the American dream. It was originally located at 23rd Street and Lexington Avenue in Manhattan. In 1907, the College moved to a new campus centered on Convent Avenue and 138th Street. The noted architect, George Browne Post, designed its distinctive neo-Gothic buildings. Over the years, eight CCNY alumni won the Nobel Prize, placing it among the top ranks of public colleges and universities, nationwide.

In 1915, the college built a multipurpose stadium on its campus, taking up two square blocks, from 136th St. to 138th St., between Amsterdam and Convent Avenues. It was named after businessman-philanthropist, Adolph Lewisohn, who played a major role in financing its construction by contributing $300,000.

The stadium was modeled on one found in the Trastevere section of Rome. It contained a sprawling athletic field, a grand amphitheater with nineteen rows of concrete seats, and a Doric colonnade of sixty-four columns, each fifteen feet high. It seated six thousand people for sporting events but could add enough seats in the infield to double its capacity for its extremely popular summer concerts.

During World War I, Minnie Guggenheimer, a wealthy New Yorker, was approached to join a committee to support good music at Lewisohn Stadium. Her participation grew until she was ruling the concerts single-handedly. Every year she raised money for the concert season because she wanted the tickets to be moderately priced, so that working people could afford to attend. The cheapest seats were priced at fifty cents. The season lasted for seven weeks, and featured the world's leading symphonies, conductors, and soloists. Some of the featured performers were Marian Anderson, George Gershwin, Oscar Levant, Eugene Ormandy, Ethel Merman, and Nelson Eddy.

Sean had a wonderful view of the Stadium stage from his rooftop. He, and some of the other tenants, would bring folding chairs up to the roof and spend many joyful hours listening to the finest music and singers in the world, free of charge. When the concerts featured Italian opera stars, Vito Morelli always made an appearance. He knew many of them personally. He also knew all of the operas by heart, and would sing along, softly, to the music. He took these opportunities to impart his love and knowledge of the operas to Joe and Sean. After a few seasons, the boys, both of whom had very good voices, could sing almost every aria along with Vito and the performers.

The college was a commuter school. There was plentiful public transportation, so there was almost no provision made for parking. Concert patrons had to park their cars on the street.

One evening, in the summer of 1942, Sean and Joe were standing on the stoop of their building after the concert had ended. A formally dressed couple, and their daughter, were about to enter their Cadillac, which was parked directly in front of the boys, when the man noticed that he had a flat tire. He was clearly annoyed. Joe immediately went over to the man and said, "Gee, mister, it looks like you've got a problem. Do you need some help?"

"I certainly do. Do you know someone who can change a flat tire?"

"Yes, sir, I can. My dad has a car and I've helped him change many a tire. I'd be glad to change yours. I wouldn't want you to get grease on your good clothes." He motioned to his friend, "Hey, Sean, come over here and give me a hand."

As they worked on the tire, Sean kept glancing at the young girl, whom he guessed was about his age. She was the prettiest girl he had ever seen. He was quite smitten. She was as tall as he was, maybe even taller. Her smooth, creamy complexion stood in stark contrast to her jet-black hair and her dark green eyes. She wore a long, navy blue skirt, atop which she wore a cardigan and shell sweater set in Kelly Green, his favorite color.

As he worked, he tried to strike up a conversation by asking her how she liked the concert, but she merely smiled and said, "Fine."

Sean asked her a few more questions, which she also answered in monosyllables. Sean couldn't figure out if she was extremely shy, or if she was a snob, and not in the habit of talking to strange boys, especially those who lived in this kind of neighborhood. Sean gave up trying to make small talk and concentrated on the job at hand while stealing furtive glances at her. He knew that he would be dreaming about her for many a night.

Joe knew what he was doing and the two boys completed the job in about thirty minutes.

The man was very grateful and said to them, "I really appreciated your help, boys. How can I reward you?"

In a moment of inspiration, Sean immediately piped up and, in what he hoped was his most innocent voice, said, "We didn't do it for a reward, sir. We were taught in school to act like the Good Samaritan in the bible. We were glad to be in a position to help."

The man arched his eyebrows and said, "It's refreshing to hear those words from one so young, but I am a firm believer that good deeds should be rewarded. Here's five dollars, have some fun, and thanks again."

When the man drove off, Joe said, "Holy mackerel, Sean, five whole dollars just for changing a tire! That was great. If we could do that every night, we'd be rich."

Sean thought for a while and then his eyes lit up and he said, "Joe, we can do this every night."

"How? We can't expect someone to have a flat tire every night."

Smiling, Sean replied, "Oh, yes, we can. All we have to do is let the air out of a tire on one of those big, expensive limos and conveniently be around when the owner comes back to his car, just like tonight."

"But that would be a sin", replied Joe.

"I'm not sure about that, but, if it is, it's only a venial sin. We're not destroying any property, and it's not like we're extorting money from the people. All we would be doing is inconveniencing them for a little while. We just put on the old Good Samaritan act and let them feel guilty. I think most of them will pay us something, not five bucks, but something. God wouldn't send us to hell for something like that, would he? What do you say?"

Joe took a few seconds to wrestle with his conscience. He quickly pinned his conscience to the mat and said, "OK, let's do it."

Sean worked out a plan with Joe. They watched every expensive car as it parked on their street prior to the concert. They took careful note of the age and attire of the occupants. Elderly, well-dressed couples became their marks. They were invariably well rewarded by the grateful car owners. Their scheme worked nicely for the balance of that summer season and for a few more.

Sean once said to Joe, "I think I like being in business for myself."

Chapter 15

When Joe Morelli was in the eighth grade, Sean talked to him about the future. "You have visited a number of Catholic high schools in the past few months and taken their entrance exams. Have you decided which one to attend?"

"Yes. I have decided to go to Fordham Prep."

"Isn't that in the Bronx?"

"Right. Do you remember the time that we went with our parents to visit the Bronx Zoo and Botanical Gardens?"

"Yeah, I do. It was really a pretty place."

"Well, Fordham University originally owned that land. They sold about five hundred acres to the city of New York, under the condition that the land only be used for a zoo and garden area. The University kept around one hundred acres for itself. This guaranteed them that Fordham would have a nice, wide-open space in the heart of the largest city in the world.

"The Prep shares a small part of the university campus. It has the best facilities of all the schools I have visited."

"Is that why you want to go there?"

"It's one of the reasons, but not the most important one. Jesuits run the school. All the nuns have told me that the Jesuits are among the best educators in the world. They have been doing it for over four hundred years. They run schools all over the globe. They know what they are doing.

"An added attraction is the fact that my father's restaurant is only a few blocks away, on Arthur Avenue, which dead ends right at the campus gate. That part of the Bronx is also known as 'Little Italy'. I can probably hitch a ride to or from school with my dad or mom on some days."

"That sounds great, Joe. If it turns out that you like it, I think I'll go there too."

The following year, Sean did join Joe at the Prep. The Emerald Society's fund paid for his tuition and expenses. He learned that, since 1841, when New York's Archbishop Hughes founded the school in the Rose Hill section of the Bronx, young men have studied Latin, Greek, English, Math, Science, and Religion there. Its rigorous curriculum fostered academic discipline and the pursuit of excellence.

The Prep was a relatively small school; the total enrollment was around four hundred boys. He knew that many of them came from well-to-do and well-educated families. Their fathers were doctors, lawyers, and successful business executives. They tended to live in nearby wealthy enclaves such as Scarsdale and Bronxville. Sean was initially apprehensive about fitting in with these upper-class boys. After all, his primary experience was with poor Jewish orphans and neighborhood kids from blue-collared families.

Joe told him, "Don't worry about that. We have kids from all over the spectrum. It doesn't make any difference what your background is. I'm living proof of that. You will do just fine."

Sean soon realized that the school's reputation for high academic standards was well founded. A minimum half hour of written homework was assigned every day, in each subject. Daily quizzes further prevented anyone from slacking off. There was a mandatory dress code. Coats and ties were required at all times. Transgressions in any area were met with swift punishment by Father Shea, the Dean of Discipline.

The Jesuits believed that one of the most important skills a person could have was the ability to communicate clearly in both the spoken and written word. Consequently, they placed great emphasis on language skills. In addition to the mandatory four years of English and Latin, Sean was required to take two years of two elective languages. He chose Greek as one of them.

One of his friends in his building was Tom Sakell whose parents came from Greece. Sean was able to practice his new language skills with him. This enabled him to pick up the language quickly.

His second choice was Spanish, a language that was becoming very prevalent in his neighborhood due to an influx of families from Puerto Rico. His fluency in Latin and Italian were a great help in easily mastering this subject.

Sean soon gained a reputation as the language "brain". Some of his fellow students sought him as a tutor. The parents were more than willing to pay for his efforts. Occasionally, they invited him to spend a weekend at their homes for a combination of work and play.

These invitations gave him the opportunity to see how the other half lived. For the first time in his life, he stayed in homes that had large manicured lawns and yards. Some even had pools. He visited some exclusive country clubs, featuring golf courses and tennis courts.

The mothers were invariably impressed with this tall, blond and handsome young man and his good manners. He was often invited back, especially if they had a daughter who needed a date for a country club dance.

Sean was quite impressed with these experiences. He made a promise to himself to do whatever was necessary to provide this kind of lifestyle for his mother and himself. He felt that the key to achieve that goal was to overcome his somewhat disadvantaged background with knowledge. Knowledge leveled the playing field. Knowledge was power, and he now yearned for that power. His mantra became "If it is to be, it is up to me."

Chapter 16

In his sophomore year, Joe started to work as a waiter at his father's restaurant, on Friday and Saturday nights. He talked Sean into working there as well. He started by busing tables and helping the chef in the kitchen.

The restaurant attracted an interesting and eclectic clientele. In addition to Mafia capos like Frank Costello, Carlo Gambino, and Paul Castellano, opera stars frequented the place. They were attracted by its reputation for good Italian food and interesting characters.

The mob leaders loved opera. Many held season tickets to the New York Met. They treated the opera performers like movie stars whenever they entered the restaurant. The performers seldom had to pay for their own meals. This, of course, encouraged them to keep returning to "Vito's Ristorante". They befriended Vito and provided him with tickets for their performances. As a result, Joe and Sean were regular visitors to the Met and Carnegie Hall.

The week after Sean started at the restaurant, Joe said, "The sharp dresser that just sat at my table is Frank Costello, my mother's cousin. He owns this building and is a part owner of the restaurant. Make sure you give him and his friends extra special attention and service."

Sean nodded and went over to the table to add some additional silverware. Frank Costello said, "Hey, kid, you're new here. You don't look Italian, you're blond. What's your name?"

Sean decided to answer him in Italian. "My name is Sean Gallagher, Mr. Costello. I'm Joe's friend. He and I go to school together."

Costello smiled and answered him in Italian. "Oh, an Irish kid who speaks Italian. That's a good one. Say, your name, Gallagher, sounds familiar. Wasn't your father the cop who saved Rosa's life many years ago?"

"Yes, sir," said Sean.

"Well, I'm glad to meet you. I was real sorry that your father got killed. I owed him a big favor for what he did for my favorite cousin and Vito, but he wouldn't take me up on it. I like to square accounts, so, if I can ever do you a favor, let me know."

"Thank you, sir."

The following year, Sean was promoted to waiter. Word had gotten around that he was a personal friend of Frank Costello. The Mafia guys never failed to give him the most generous tips for his service.

Early, one Saturday evening, the restaurant was barely half-full. As Sean was waiting for some of his tables to be occupied, he started to sing a few Italian opera songs, softly, to himself. Some of the people at a nearby table heard him and beckoned him over. They asked what he was singing. He told them he was singing an aria from The Barber of Seville. They asked him to sing louder and they applauded when Sean finished the song. They asked him if he could sing some popular Italian songs, and Sean obliged them. Soon, the whole table joined in. At the end, they were all laughing, and rewarded Sean with a very nice gratuity. The singing lessons from Semenova and the nuns really paid off.

This gave him an idea. He persuaded Vito to buy a piano and hire a piano player on the weekends so that he and Joe could become singing waiters, and periodically serenade the customers with Italian songs during dinner. Vito agreed. The customers loved it and the boys raked in big tips. Visiting artists often got into the spirit of things and wound up giving impromptu performances. The restaurant's reputation grew to the point that every table was booked weeks in advance.

Chapter 17

When Sean graduated from the Prep, he followed Joe to Fordham College, also an all-male school with a strict academic and dress code. There, he continued his education in the liberal arts. The Jesuits were fond of saying that the purpose of such an education was to teach a person how to make a life, rather than a living. If an individual knew how to think logically and communicate clearly, he would be a well-rounded individual who could be successful in any endeavor in life. If necessary, he could specialize in a particular field later, in graduate school, or on the job.

To fulfill their goal, the Jesuits required all students to take four years of Philosophy. The word philosophy, they said, just means "the love of wisdom". Sean avidly embraced the various philosophic subjects. There was Epistemology, which investigated the origin, nature, methods, and the limits of human knowledge. Ontology was concerned with the study of the nature of existence, or being. Cosmology dealt with the origin and general structure of the universe, with its parts, elements, and laws, especially with such of its characteristics as space, time, causality, and freedom. Eschatology revealed the doctrines concerning the ultimate or final things, such as death, the destiny of humanity, the Second Coming, or the Last Judgment. Of course, there was also the study of Logic.

Philosophy became his favorite subject. The courses cultivated his ability to analyze complicated problems and untie mental knots. They showed him how to peel away peripheral issues and penetrate to the heart of the matter.

Over the years, he spent many enjoyable hours with Joe and other classmates arguing and discussing how to deal with the ultimate issues of life.

Sean decided to pursue his love of languages by choosing to major in Russian. The college had recently established an Institute of Russian Studies, which was primarily staffed by Jesuits who had been expelled from Russia. Russian émigrés rounded out the rest of the faculty.

He already had a good command of Russian due to his experience at the HOA and the help of his neighbor, Ivana Semenova. He felt that Russia was going to remain a major military and economic power in the international scene. That would provide good opportunities for people with knowledge of its language and culture.

Since everyone was also required to take two years of a foreign language, regardless of his major, he chose French, a language to which he had not been previously exposed.

While at the Prep, he had seen the college's Army and Air Force ROTC cadets, in their uniforms, marching in military formation in front of his school every Wednesday in an area known as Edwards Parade. He knew that they were paid for their participation in the corps. Since he could always use some extra money, he enrolled in the Air Force program. He figured that, since there was no war, the chances for being called to active duty after graduation were rather remote. If a war did come, he would have the advantage of entering the service as an officer and not as a draftee.

He was also able to earn extra pocket money by continuing to tutor. The University had an excellent School of Pharmacy that had a very large percentage of Jewish students. Due to his knowledge of Yiddish, Hebrew, and Latin, Sean had a long list of budding Pharmacists who needed his help.

Between his studies, tutoring and his restaurant job, Sean was so busy that he had a very limited social life. However, this sacrifice didn't bother him very much. His primary goal in life was still to reward his mother by becoming financially successful and provide her with the economic security that she had lacked, and so well deserved.

Chapter 18

In the summer of 1947, Joe's parents took him on a trip to Italy, to visit their relatives.

In Sicily, Joe saw the ravages of the recently ended war. He also saw that the Mafia still controlled Sicily despite Mussolini's efforts to eradicate it. He felt sorry for his relatives.

When they visited Rome, however, Joe was pleased to learn that one of his close relatives was a bishop who worked in the Vatican, a member of the Curia. He arranged a private audience with Pope Pius XII.

The pope said to Joe, "The bishop has told me about you. You are an American, going to college, is that right?"

"Yes, your holiness." replied Joe. "I'm attending Fordham University."

"Ah, yes," said the pope. "I have been to your school. I was the papal nuncio in your country many years ago and I remember visiting your campus. The Jesuits run a fine school. They have always been considered the intellectual elite of the church. You are very fortunate to be in their hands."

"I think so too, your holiness."

"What is your impression of our country?"

Joe replied, "I had no idea of the destruction and poverty caused by the war. I had only seen some photos in the newspapers, but I was not prepared for what I actually saw."

"Yes", sighed the pope. "Our country has been badly wounded, both physically and spiritually. The Church has many challenges in the future to heal the suffering caused by the war. We, unfortunately, have lost many of our priests due to the outrages perpetrated by the Nazis and Communists. As Jesus said, 'The harvest is great, but the laborers are few.' We need more priestly vocations in order to fulfill our mission. Tell me, Joseph, have you ever thought about becoming a priest?"

"Not really, I think most young boys in a Catholic grammar school have entertained the notion of becoming a priest. But, they also dream of becoming a movie star and president of the country. I guess that I was no different."

"I have a feeling that you may have a vocation. The church needs new, young blood from other countries. The Vatican has too many Italians. If the Church is to be truly universal, it requires more leaders from other countries. America has become the dominant military and economic power in the world. It is now the world's greatest hope for peace and moral leadership.

"Before the war, I traveled extensively in the United States. I marveled at the optimistic spirit that all you Americans have. Nothing seems impossible to you people. You always come up with innovative answers to old and new problems. The Church desperately needs such talent. Will you seriously consider a vocation to the priesthood and pray for guidance in this matter?"

Joe replied, "I will do as you ask your holiness."

When the audience concluded, Joe spent some time with the bishop, asking him about his daily life and work. He said that he found working in the Vatican to be an exhilarating experience. He genuinely believed that he was fulfilling the Lord's work. He told Joe that if he eventually decided he had a vocation, he could easily arrange it for him to be posted to the Vatican.

Chapter 19

In June of 1950, Joe graduated from Fordham. Sean asked him, "What are you going to do now? Are you going to join your father full time in the restaurant business?"

"No. I have been giving a good deal of thought to that question and I have recently reached a decision which will surprise both you and my parents."

"Well, what's the big surprise?"

"I have decided to become a priest."

"What? Are you kidding me?"

"No, I'm deadly serious."

"What made you decide that?"

"Well, as you know, I had a private audience with the pope a few years ago. He made a deep impression on me. He sensed that I might have a vocation and asked me to think and pray about it, and I promised to do so.

"After that meeting I was talking to one of my relatives who is a bishop in the Vatican. I asked him why he had decided to become a priest. He answered by taking his wallet from his pocket. He fished out a small, round piece of a mirror, about the size of a quarter. Then, he said, 'When I was a young boy in Sicily, I found this broken piece of a mirror in a vacant lot and began to play with it. I became fascinated that I could reflect light into dark places where the sun would never shine, deep holes, crevices, dark closets and the like.

'I kept this little mirror, and, as I became older, I grew to understand that this was not just a child's game but a metaphor for what I might do with my life. I am a fragment of a mirror whose whole design I do not know. With what I have, I can reflect light, truth, understanding, and knowledge into the black places in the hearts of men and change some things in some people. By becoming a priest and working in the Vatican, I have the opportunity to shine the divine light on many people all over the world.'

"This statement made a profound impression on me. The more I prayed, and the more I thought about it, the more I became convinced to follow his example. I want to shine some of that same light."

Sean shook his head and said, "That's quite a story. I can almost understand how it might have influenced your decision. I know that you will be a very fine priest and I wish you the very best."

Joe enrolled at St. Joseph's Seminary, located in the Dunwoodie section of Yonkers, New York, just a few miles from Fordham.

One day, Joe visited Sean. "I've been invited to a small meeting to hear a talk by Fr. Pierre Teilhard de Chardin, the Jesuit philosopher. He just moved to New York. You know who he is, don't you?"

"Of course, he's mentioned prominently in some of our philosophy classes. If I remember correctly, he's also a paleontologist, theologian and mystic. But, isn't he viewed as some sort of maverick by the church?"

Joe nodded his head in agreement, "Yes, I guess you could call him a maverick. He's not too popular with the pope or the people in the Vatican. That's why we didn't get to study much about him in school. They've prohibited him from publishing his works. However, I recently was able to obtain an underground copy of a manuscript that he wanted to publish as a book, titled 'The Phenomenon of Man'. It's one of the most fascinating things I have ever read. My professors think his theories will revolutionize the field of theology.

"Would you like to come along with me?"

"I would love to. Most of the other philosophers we've studied have been dead for many years. They make for pretty dull reading. I think it would be interesting to meet and hear a live one."

Since he really didn't know much about Chardin, Sean decided to do a little research prior to the meeting.

Pierre Teilhard de Chardin was born in France in 1881. His mother was the great grandniece of Voltaire. He entered the Jesuit order in 1899 and was ordained in 1911. He received a doctorate in paleontology from the Sorbonne in 1922. For a few years, he lectured at the Institut Catholique in Paris.

In 1926, his Jesuit superiors, and Rome, forced him to abandon teaching because of his controversial attempts, among other things, to reconcile the Church's traditional view of original sin with his concept of evolution. At that same time, Rome also decided that his publications should be limited to purely scientific materials, a limitation that was to continue throughout his life.

His superiors eventually exiled him to China where he was named adviser to the National Geological Survey. There, he collaborated on research that resulted in the remarkable discovery, in 1929, of Peking Man, an extremely important link in the evolution of man.

While in China, he also completed the manuscript of "The Phenomenon of Man", in which he outlined his concept of cosmic evolution and his conviction that belief in evolution does not entail a rejection of Christianity. He remained in China until 1946.

He spent the next few years traveling to various countries. Eventually, he accepted a position with the Wenner-Gren Foundation, which supported anthropological research. The foundation was located in Manhattan, on Park Avenue, just a short distance from his residence at the St. Ignatius Church, which was also on Park Avenue.

Chardin presented his talk in the private apartment of a wealthy couple in downtown Manhattan, not too far from where Teilhard lived and worked. He was a thin, ascetic man with a prominent nose. He spoke with a noticeable French accent. In his presentation, it was obvious that he was very passionate about his subject. He said his purpose was an attempt to marry Christianity with his theory of evolution. Whereas Darwin's theory concerned only the physical evolution of man, Chardin added the element of a spiritual evolution.

He explained that evolution follows a cosmic natural order of things. He called this the law of increasing complexity-consciousness. By this, he meant that the degree of consciousness of an organism varies according to that organism's complexity of structure. Man is the most complex organism in the evolutionary scale and, therefore, has the highest degree of consciousness.

Men unite with other men to form increasingly more complex societies, or organisms. These societies grow more complex, becoming super-organisms with super-consciousness. He called this super-consciousness the "noosphere", which he defined as a thinking layer circling the earth.

He further stated that the universe is evolving not only in the direction of greater consciousness, or spirituality, but, at the same time, in the direction of greater unity. The point of maximum unity he called the Omega Point, where man eventually becomes united with Christ, the son of God.

After the meeting, the two boys discussed their impressions of Chardin's presentation.

Sean said, "I think I grasp the idea of his law of complexity-consciousness but he lost me with his idea of a thinking layer enveloping the earth. I visualized a Hollywood science fiction movie depicting this huge pulsating global brain surrounding our planet, bent on enslaving us to its evil will."

Joe laughed. "I kind of got that same feeling. But the thing that really confused me was his idea of the Omega Point. I don't understand how he eventually expects mankind to unite with Christ. He didn't explain that concept very well and I was afraid to ask any questions. After all, you and I were by far the youngest people there.

"Let's face it, he is a mystic and has a great deal more experience in the world than we do. Perhaps when we get older we will understand a little better."

Sean nodded, "I hope so. His ideas sound much more interesting than those of Thomas Aquinas and St. Augustine."

Chapter 20

At the end of his junior year, in June of 1950, Sean was required to spend six weeks in an ROTC summer camp for some military training. He was posted to Langley Air Force Base, Virginia, just outside of Newport News. On the twenty-fifth of that month, the Korean War erupted and the military draft was immediately re-instituted. Those in the ROTC program were allowed to continue in college until they graduated and received their commissions. Sean congratulated himself on having made the right decision to join the program.

The CIA also happened to be headquartered near there. Some of their agents often shopped at the Langley PX and Commissary.

On his first Saturday at Langley, Sean, dressed in his khaki cadet uniform, visited the PX, and wandered through the book section. He found a small section of foreign language books that attracted his attention. There was one other customer in that section, a man who appeared to be in his fifties. He was dressed in a white sport shirt and navy slacks.

Sean spotted a biography of Fyodor Dostoevsky, written in Russian. The older gentleman was standing in front of that shelf and was browsing through a book.

"Excuse me, sir" said Sean, "May I step in front of you to get a book?"

The man said "Of course. I'm sorry that I was blocking your way. I was preoccupied with reading this book."

"Thank you," replied Sean. He took the book and started to page through it, stopping occasionally to read long passages.

The man looked at Sean for a few minutes and then asked, "Say, soldier, I see that you're interested in Dostoevsky. He's one of my favorite authors. Have you read any of his works?"

Sean turned around and replied, "Yes, sir, I've read all of his works, in the original Russian."

The man's eyes widened with interest and then he started to speak to Sean in Russian, "I assume you can also speak Russian if you can wade through some pretty tough reading like Dostoevsky".

Replying in Russian, Sean said, "Yes, sir, I can."

"I see by your name tag that your last name is Gallagher, so I also assume that you are not of Russian descent. Where did you learn the language?"

"I major in Russian language and literature in school. But, when I was growing up in New York City, my neighbors were a Russian Jewish couple. They had been university professors in Moscow. They immigrated to the USA when the Communists started their pogroms. The husband taught Russian at CCNY. His wife couldn't get a teaching post, so she stayed home and gave private English lessons to other Russian émigrés.

"She had no children of her own and took a liking to me. I visited her apartment often and, while there, she taught me Russian. She was a very nice lady.

"Over the years, I became fluent and decided to pursue a study of the culture and language at the University level."

"That's interesting. You speak Russian better than the average Muscovite. By the way, my name is John McCooe."

He extended his right hand to Sean and they shook hands. He continued in English, "I'm head of the Russian Desk at the CIA, the Central Intelligence Agency. Do you know what that is?"

"I think I remember reading that your agency was a successor to the OSS after World War II, and that you essentially work on gathering intelligence regarding the security of the United States."

"That's about the size of it. Look, I really would like to have a long talk with you but I have an appointment back in my office. If you are free tomorrow, I would like to take you to my office, off base, and continue our conversation. Are you interested?"

"Sure, I don't have much to do on Sunday except go to church. Oh, wait a minute, I just remembered we're supposed to be confined to base for our first weekend."

"No problem, I'll get you permission. Suppose I pick you up here at the PX at ten o'clock. OK?"

"Yes, sir. I'll see you then."

"By the way, don't mention this conversation to anybody."

Sean was surprised by this remark but said, "Yes, sir, mum's the word."

The following morning, McCooe met Sean and drove him to the Agency headquarters. During the ride, he made small talk. Sean told him that he was a student at Fordham.

John said, "Good school. I graduated from Georgetown, myself, and went on to their Law School. The Jesuits sure do a good job of teaching students how to think. Their graduates all seem to come away with a strong sense of devotion to God, family and country. I guess that's why the CIA and the FBI recruit so many of them. We both seem to get a lot of Irish Catholics from their schools. As a matter of fact, the joke going around is that FBI stands for Full Blooded Irish."

Sean smiled. "Am I being recruited, Mr. McCooe?"

"Do you want to be?"

"Well, sir, I really don't have enough information at this point to give you an intelligent answer. I don't know what my options are."

"That's a good answer, Sean. I also need to know more about you before I decide if I want to recruit you. Let's just play it by ear for a while and see what happens. We will both have ample opportunity to gather enough information on which to base our decisions. Maybe we'll have a meeting of the minds, maybe not. We'll find out in due time."

When they arrived at CIA headquarters, McCooe led Sean to a small, sparsely furnished interview room. "Sean, here's a background questionnaire that I'd like you to fill out. When you finish it, give it to my assistant. His office is just next door. Then wait in this room for me. I'll return after I have had a chance to review your form."

Sean spent the best part of an hour filling out a lengthy list of questions and then gave it to the assistant.

Another hour passed until McCooe returned to the room. "Sean, am I reading this correctly? Do you really speak all these languages you've listed?"

"Yes, sir. I speak ten languages: Russian, as you know, plus Hebrew, Yiddish, German, French, Italian, Spanish, Latin, Greek and Gaelic."

"Fluently?"

"Yes, sir. I consider myself to be very fluent in most of them, and reasonably fluent in the rest."

"That's remarkable. I'm more than twice your age and it took me many years to become proficient in only five languages. You're barely old enough to shave. How could you possibly have accomplished so much in such a short time?"

"Well, sir, it's a long story." Over the next hour, or so, Sean described, in great detail, his upbringing at the Hebrew Orphan Asylum, and the eclectic composition of the playmates in his neighborhood.

"One of my psychology professors told me that, if a person is immersed in a new language before he reaches the age of thirteen, he will pick up that language in a matter of a few months. I was in a very unique situation while growing up. I was immersed in a number of languages since the day I was born, and I adapted to them quite readily. I didn't know any better. The other languages I acquired in school. I seem to have an ear for language."

Shaking his head, McCooe said, "That's quite a story and it will certainly be easy enough for us to test you on your fluency. I have a few more questions to ask you."

When McCooe was finished his interrogation, he said, "Sean, based on this interview I am interested enough to want to proceed by ordering a thorough background investigation. This will take a couple of weeks, which is just as well, since I'll be in Europe during that time. While I'm gone, I'll have one of my agents pick you up on a few weekends and bring you back here for further testing. You'll also get the opportunity to tour our facilities and question our people about what we do. How does that sound?"

"It sounds like it would be very interesting. I look forward to it."

"Good. When I get back we'll get together again."

Sean nodded his head in agreement and then inquired, "Mr. McCooe, do you mind if I ask you a few questions about yourself and how you got started in this business?"

"No, Sean, I don't mind at all. I was a young lawyer in private practice when World War II broke out. In July of 1941, President Roosevelt appointed William 'Wild Bill' Donovan to draft a plan for a new intelligence organization. That organization came into existence in June, 1942, as the Office of Strategic Services. Donovan was one of the most decorated officers in World War I and, afterwards, had become a very successful New York lawyer. He assembled a staff that had a large number of lawyers, and I was lucky to become a member. I worked hard and eventually became one of Wild Bill's top assistants.

"The OSS played a very important role in the war. We had a number of successful covert operations. When the war ended, President Truman disbanded the organization in October of 1945. Many of us were transferred to the State and War departments. "Two years later, Truman felt the threat of Communist Russia and the need for a new intelligence organization. The OSS was essentially reborn with a new name, the CIA, and a new director, Rear Admiral Sidney W. Souers. I was one of the midwives.

"So, you see, Sean, I've been in this agency from its very inception. Like any proud father, I want to see it grow stronger and better. I firmly believe that the very existence of our country is at stake if we fail to do our job properly. Communism is a cancer that is determined to eat away at the very core of democracy. I view our confrontation with Russia as a classic biblical example of the battle between good and evil. That's why I stay on this job and that is why I try to recruit people who share certain strong core values.

"Based on your background, I think you and I share the same values. You also have the added advantage of having mastered the language of our very determined enemy. That's why I'm interested in you.

"But, we still have to verify everything. I'll see you in a few weeks."

Over the next few weekends, Sean was driven to the CIA offices and met with a number of different people. Foreign language specialists talked with him at length to determine if he was truly as fluent as he claimed. He was given a tour of the facilities and learned a good deal about the Agency's mission and how it operated.

When McCooe returned from his trip, he met with Sean. "I have the results of your security background investigation. We talked to some of your teachers, friends, pastors, and other people you referenced on your questionnaire, and some of whom you didn't. You seem to have some very unusual acquaintances."

"What do you mean by unusual?"

"People who have a lot of vowels in their last names."

Sean smiled and said, "You must mean the Morellis. They are my neighbors, and their son, Joe, is my very best friend. He's studying to be a priest."

"Yes, I know about the Morellis, but I wasn't referring to them. I was referring to people like Frank Costello, Paul Castellano and other mafia types. How do you know these people and, more importantly, how do they know you?"

Sean went into an in-depth explanation of his family's relationship with the Morellis. He talked about his working in their Bronx restaurant and his unexpected warm reception by Frank Costello and other reputed Mafia leaders. "Mr. McCooe, if you want to know more about my relationship with the people you mentioned, all you have to do is talk to the police captain in charge of that Bronx precinct."

"We have, Sean. He pretty much verified what you said. I just wanted to hear about it in more detail from you, personally. I'm fascinated by the experiences that you have encountered in your short life. It's like the stuff of fiction.

"I also talked to the agents who interviewed you and, I don't mind telling you, they were impressed with your language capabilities and how well you handled yourself. They said you were a good listener and that you asked very intelligent questions."

"I'm glad to hear that, sir. I was hoping that I wasn't wasting your time."

"Quite the contrary. I am impressed with you and I want you to join the Agency. This cold war with Russia is going to last a long time. With your language skills, you would be a valuable asset to your country and to me. Are you interested?"

"I'm not sure, sir. My immediate goal is to finish college. Then, I'll be receiving my Air Force commission and will have a two year obligation to go on active duty. Right now, I'm fairly certain that I don't want to make a career out of any government position.

"You mentioned once that we Jesuit trained grads have a devotion to God, family and country, in that order. My mother is all the family I have. She has sacrificed so much for me over the years that I vowed to make it up to her by giving her the financial security that she has never experienced. I've done a lot of serious thinking in the last two weeks and I don't think I could make that kind of money working in any government job. I hope you're not offended."

McCooe nodded his head. "Sean, I'm not offended in the least. I understand your position. But suppose we compromise."

"What do you mean by compromise?"

"Suppose you give me at least three years of your life. That's only one year more than your two year military obligation. The government is desperate for men with your kind of talent. We are actively trying to recruit and train as many qualified people as we can but it takes years to train someone with anything near your talent. You can be an effective agent in a matter of a few months.

"Sean, I'm going to lay a guilt trip on you and appeal to your sense of patriotism. We are living in dangerous times and your government really needs your help. Your mother can spare you for an extra year, and I guarantee you that the experience you get from us will be invaluable in civilian life. And, believe me, we are not without friends in the business world if you decide to leave us after three years."

"What exactly are you proposing?"

"Try this scenario on for size. Finish your senior year and get your commission. You will then receive orders to report back here to active duty at Langley Field. This will be your cover. You will actually also become a CIA agent. We will put you through an accelerated training program. Part of that training will include a study of Arabic, since this is one major language I need and which you don't have. With your unique background, I can send you to almost any Embassy in the European and Middle East region under cover as a military attaché.

"I need someone who can give me first hand, unbiased reports on situations in certain countries. I've found that I can't completely rely on the reports that I get from the diplomatic bureaucrats stationed in some of our Embassies. I need a set of fresh, unjaded eyes to get a better perspective on things. Your reports would be sent directly to me."

One further thing, when you report for active duty, you will do so with the rank of captain."

Sean was surprised at this, "Is that possible? I thought you had to be in the service for a number of years to get to that rank."

"That's true for most people, but there are exceptions for people with special skills. Doctors, dentists, lawyers, some scientists, etc. automatically enter the service with the rank of captain. Your special skills will allow me to place you in that same category.

"A captain's pay, together with a dependent's subsidy for your mother, will come close to the typical entry level salary you could expect in civilian life. I promise you that no civilian job will be able to give you the kind of experience you would get with me. That would be an invaluable asset on your resume in the civilian world. Who knows, you might even change your mind about a government career.

"How does that sound to you?"

Sean paused for a long time, and then answered, "That's an intriguing offer. You certainly pushed all the right buttons. This is such a life changing decision that I need some time to think this over."

"Of course you do, Sean. I would like to have your answer next week. That way, if your answer is yes, we can get your ROTC instructors to give you some special tutoring in areas that would be important to us. We can also have some of our agents talk to you during vacations and semester breaks."

"That sounds fair. You'll have my answer by then."

"Good. I must remind you that our discussions are highly confidential and you cannot reveal them to anyone who doesn't have the proper clearance."

The following week, Sean accepted the offer."

McCooe was pleased. "May I ask what influenced your decision?"

"Now that we are at war, I feel a strong obligation to serve my country in whatever way is best. I also realized that, in an emergency situation, my country could keep me on active duty for whatever length of time it wanted. I thought that, if I acceded to your request, you would honor your promise to let me go at the end of three years, if I wanted to."

"Sean, that's a fair assessment of the situation. If you perform as well as I think you will, you will have my support and friendship for life."

Sean graduated from college and received his commission as a second lieutenant in the U. S. Air Force, along with his fellow ROTC classmates. He got his orders to report to Langley.

Shortly after arriving there, he was issued new orders to report to the military language school at the Presidio of Monterey, California. He also received his promotion to captain.

He spent a number of weeks studying Arabic, which he mastered easily. He was also given intensive training in the art of espionage. When he completed his studies, he was assigned to the U. S. Embassy in Rome as a military attaché.

Chapter 21

Sean flew to Rome via military transport and reported to the U. S. Embassy. His immediate superior was General John Nicholson who welcomed him aboard.

"Captain Gallagher, John McCooe has told me that you are on special assignment and are using your military attaché position as a cover. That's fine with me. John and I are old friends, as a matter of fact, we were college roommates. If you need any help, or run into trouble, just let me know.

"Meanwhile, I have assigned you living quarters in a nearby BOQ. Good luck."

When Sean settled in, he called Joe Morelli who had been transferred to Rome, in 1951, to study at the Pontifical North American College in preparation for his ordination. Joe invited him to dinner at his apartment. The two friends stayed up until the wee hours of the morning, catching up on each other's activities.

Both had busy schedules. For the next two years, Sean was constantly on the road visiting and revisiting embassies throughout Europe and the Middle East. He spent a number of weeks in each country. He met with local embassy employees and undercover agents. He read the local newspapers and magazines and talked to ordinary citizens. He wrote comprehensive reports to McCooe after each stop. Some of his observations and conclusions did not seem to coincide with those of the local embassy staffs. This was exactly the type of information that McCooe wanted.

Sean did spend some leave time to return home and visit his mother and the Morellis. After that visit, he decided that he would treat his mother to a vacation trip to Europe during the summer of 1953. He wrote to her about his plan. They would meet in Ireland, in August. There, they would spend some time visiting relatives that he had never seen. Then, they would continue on to Rome, where he and Joe would give her a very personal tour of the city and the Vatican. He had also secretly arranged for Joe to get a private audience with the pope. His mother would be ecstatic.

On June 24, 1953, General Nicholson called Sean into his office and said, "There's no easy way for me to tell you this, Sean. The Red Cross just called to tell me that your mother died of an apparent heart attack yesterday, while at work. The nuns at Manhattanville College asked the Red Cross to arrange an emergency leave for you."

Sean was momentarily stunned by this news. When he recovered his senses, he said, "How much time do I have, sir?"

"I'm issuing you orders for a two week emergency leave. I think that should be enough time to settle your affairs. Call me when you are ready to come back, just in case something comes up. Meanwhile, I've arranged passage for you on our next courier plane to New York. It leaves tomorrow morning. I wish to extend my personal condolences to you, Sean, I know how close you were to your mother."

"Thank you, sir," said Sean. "I appreciate your consideration in this matter."

He tried to get in touch with Joe, but was told that he was on a spiritual retreat in Spain and could not have any contact with the outside world. He sent a telegram to Rosa.

Sean arrived in New York in the late evening and went directly to his mother's apartment. Rosa Morelli was waiting for him. They tearfully embraced each other.

Rosa related what had happened. "Your mother was doing some paper work in her office, at the school, when she suddenly collapsed at her desk. Mother Cronin heard the noise and rushed into the office. She thought your mother had a heart attack. She immediately called Knickerbocker hospital and the medics were there in less than three minutes. However, they were too late. It seems that your mother had died instantly of a brain aneurism. If it's any comfort to you, she suffered no pain.

"The nuns took the liberty of calling the funeral parlor. They prepared your mother's body and brought it back to the convent.

The nuns are holding the wake in their chapel. They hope you approve."

"Of course I do. My mother loved those nuns. I couldn't think of a better place for her to be. I won't try to disturb the nuns at this time of night, so I'll wait until morning to walk over there. Thanks for all your help, Rosa, I really appreciate it."

"Sean, you know that I've always regarded you as a second son. I feel fortunate to have known you and your parents. I might not be here now if it weren't for your father. I'm so glad that you and Joe are together again in Rome. He has written to us and told us all about your travels and experiences. Your mother and I would share our letters from you boys. We were both very happy for you two."

The following morning, Sean went to the convent and talked with Mother Cronin. She asked him if he would permit them to hold the funeral mass in their chapel so that all of the nuns could attend.

"Of course, I wouldn't have it any other way. I would prefer to keep the whole affair somewhat private. Mom didn't like people to make a fuss over her when she was alive. I think I should make arrangements to have her buried next to my father."

Mother Cronin replied, "I want to talk to you about that. Your mother once told me that your father had promised to take her back to Ireland, someday, for a visit, but he died before he could fulfill that promise. She had always wanted to see her relatives again. She was so excited when you made plans to bring her there later this summer. That's all she could talk about. Then, last week, as if she had a premonition, she told me that if something happened to her before that trip, she would like to be buried in Ireland along with Dan. She said that Dan never broke a promise to her in his life and she wanted to make sure that his promise would be fulfilled, even in death."

"That's just like her," said Sean. "I can understand her saying something like that and I'll certainly do as she wished. Do you know what I have to do?"

"Yes, I do. I took the liberty of having the funeral home check on the necessary paperwork to have your father's casket removed from his grave and flown to Ireland along with that of your mother's. All you have to do is sign the papers I have here. We have a convent in Dublin and I can call them to make the necessary arrangements on that end. Would that meet with your approval?"

"Of course." replied Sean. "That was very thoughtful of you. Please make whatever arrangements are necessary. I'll sign the papers and leave myself in your hands."

The funeral mass was a beautiful affair. The chapel was crowded with all of the nuns and parish priests, along with the college staff and close neighbors. Rosa had discovered that Rabbi Kattler was in town and she invited him to the ceremony. At Sean's request, while the casket was being carried out of the chapel, the choir sang, "I'll Take You Home Again, Kathleen."

Sean spent the next few days taking care of his mother's personal affairs. He terminated the lease on the apartment. He only took his parents' wedding and engagement rings as keepsakes. He donated everything else to a Catholic charitable organization. He spent almost a full day talking with Rabbi Kattler, who was getting ready to go to Israel on a teaching assignment. Finally, he bade farewell to the Morellis, and the nuns, boarded the plane to Ireland that contained the two caskets of his parents.

When he arrived in Dublin, Dermot Riley, the owner of a local mortuary, met him. He informed Sean that the nuns had arranged for the burial to take place on the following day, at noon. Dermot had made a reservation for him at a nearby hotel and arranged to pick him up in the morning to bring him to the cemetery.

When Sean arrived at the cemetery, he was surprised to see a crowd of people there. He was even more surprised to see a military guard of honor.

Sean asked Dermot, "Why are all of these people here and who are they?"

Dermot pointed to a tall, thin man approaching them and said, "Ask the Long Fellow."

The man addressed Sean, "Captain Sean Gallagher, I'm pleased to meet you. My name is Eamon de Valera."

Sean replied, "It's an honor to meet you, sir. My mother always spoke highly of you. May I ask why the Prime Minister of Ireland is here?"

"You may indeed. Your grandfather, PJ Gallagher, saved my life during our aborted Easter uprising in 1916. As you probably know, your father was a member of the IRA, doing intelligence work for us. After he killed the British officer who had just murdered his mother, he escaped to the United States. He became my bodyguard and traveling companion. He was my friend. I owe a debt of gratitude to your family, as does all of Ireland. When the good nuns told me about your trip here, I arranged to have your father buried with full State honors. Our country will never forget those heroes who helped set us free."

Sean said, "I'm overwhelmed. I don't know what to say, except thank you on behalf of my parents. This is a very proud moment for me."

When the ceremonies were finished, de Valera told Sean, "If I can ever do anything for you in the future, please let me know."

"Thank you, sir."

When de Valera left, Sean was introduced to some family relatives who had learned of the burial. He had never met any of them but he felt an immediate kinship. They were pleasantly surprised when he talked to them in Gaelic. He received many invitations to visit their homes, all of which he had to decline. However, he couldn't refuse an invitation to accompany many of them to a nearby pub where they regaled him with stories of his mother, father and grandparents. It was like a delayed Irish wake, and it made him feel good. It was a tired but thoroughly happy Sean that bade farewell to his new-found friends as he left the pub well after midnight.

On the following day, Sean called General Nicholson to report on his plans to return to Rome a few days early. The general told him that he was on his way to London for an important meeting, and he wanted Sean to meet him there, at the U. S. Embassy. Before he left, Sean visited the nuns who had given him so much help and thanked them for their efforts.

Chapter 22

Sean arrived in London on Friday, July third. He reported to the US Embassy where General Nicholson briefed him on the upcoming Monday meeting. He also told Sean of the party the Embassy was hosting the following day, the Fourth of July. Sean was invited to attend. He was also provided quarters in a nearby BOQ.

On Saturday, Sean donned his summer dress uniform and attended the Independence Day party at the Embassy. Upon entering the reception room, he looked around to see if there were any familiar faces. Finding none, he took a glass of white wine and strolled around. Eventually, he spotted General Nicholson and walked over to him.

"Well, Sean, what do you think of this affair?"

"It's very interesting, sir. I've never seen so many different types of people in one place, or so many different uniforms and clothing."

Nicholson replied, "The Fourth of July party is always the best attended social event of the year. All the diplomats look forward to it. Our Embassy always serves the best food and drinks in town. Also, it is one of the few times that diplomats from the smaller countries get a chance to cozy up to all of the world's leading nations in an informal way. Even some of the Russians come. As a matter of fact, I see one of them now."

Sean followed the general's gaze and saw a stocky man wearing a colonel's uniform. There was something vaguely familiar about him but Sean couldn't put a finger on it. "Who is he?" he asked.

"That's Colonel Dmitri Ivanovich, a highly decorated war hero. He's an important man in the Russian military and a very unusual guy."

"Why is he so unusual?"

"Because he is not a member of the Communist party. He is quite outspoken and doesn't toe the party line."

"How can he get away with that?"

"He can get away with a lot of things for two reasons. First, because he's a genuine war hero, with lots of medals. Secondly, because of his father who is a financial genius. He was a very prominent Russian banker before the war. His financial acumen was instrumental in helping finance the war, and he is now the most important man in the Finance Ministry."

"What's the colonel doing now, sir?"

"He's on staff at the United Nations. I understand he frequently visits the London Embassy to try to establish trade agreements with the British and other European countries. I've met him briefly on a few previous occasions and I like him. He's the kind of guy we could do business with. I would like to get closer to him because I believe that he will be playing a very important figure in Russia's future."

"When you mentioned the fact that he's with the United Nations I remembered something that could prove to be helpful. Can you introduce me to him?"

"Sure, come with me." They approached the Colonel and General Nicholson said, "Colonel, it's good to see you again."

In flawless English, the colonel replied, "General Nicholson, I am also pleased to see you again. I believe that it has been almost a year since we last met."

"Yes, that's about right. I would like to take this opportunity to introduce one of my staff to you. Captain Sean Gallagher, please meet Colonel Dmitri Ivanovich."

Speaking in Russian, Sean said, "It's a pleasure to meet you again, Colonel."

The colonel's eyes narrowed as he looked intently at Sean, trying to reach back in his memory about a previous encounter. He shook his head slightly and replied, in Russian, "I'm sorry, Captain, but I don't remember having met you before".

"I wouldn't expect you to remember me, sir. It was at the United Nations about three years ago. A mutual friend, my teacher, took a group of his Russian students to the UN building. You were gracious enough to give us a private talk on international finance and World War II. After the talk, there was a small reception and all the students were introduced to you. It was a very impressive occasion for me."

The Colonel smiled and said. "Ah, yes, I remember that time. The mutual friend you mentioned had to be Father Serge Maximov and you must have been a student of his at Fordham University."

"Yes, sir."

"I was wondering why you had such an excellent command of our language. You could easily pass for a Muscovite. Father Maximov has taught you well."

Sean turned to General Nicholson and said, "Excuse me, sir, I didn't mean to exclude you from our conversation by speaking in Russian."

The General replied, "Don't apologize. I gather from both your expressions that you were getting along very well."

Sean explained, "The colonel and I have a mutual friend, a college professor of mine, Father Serge Maximov. Father Maximov had told me how the colonel's family helped him escape from Russia prior to the war. Isn't that true colonel?"

"Yes, that's true. Father Maximov was my personal tutor for many years before the war. He lived at our house and taught me English and philosophy as well as many other subjects. He was more than a tutor, he became like a member of the family.

"My father learned that the extremists in the Politburo decided to ban most religions and arrest all the priests. My father and I helped him to leave Russia before things became violent. Even though my father is a high-ranking government official, he is a Russian Orthodox Christian, not an atheist. He did not condone the expulsion of some of the brightest intellectuals our country had.

"I regard Father Maximov as a dear friend and I still see him when I'm in New York."

General Nicholson smiled, "What a coincidence."

The colonel replied, "Yes. It's a small world and I think it is going to get smaller every year. Captain Gallagher, it has been a pleasure meeting you and I would like to continue talking to you but this is not the time or place. Perhaps we could meet again. If you are going to be in London for a few more days please call me at my embassy.

"Now, you must excuse me. I am trying to find my wife. We got separated shortly after arriving here and she gets lonely without me. She is very self-conscious about her inability to speak English well. Furthermore, we have another engagement to attend in a short while."

General Nicholson looked at the departing Russian and said, "That was an interesting meeting. It's obvious that he took a liking to you. You should take him up on his offer."

At this moment, an older and very distinguished looking gentleman approached them and said, "General Nicholson, my old friend, jolly good to see you again."

"Lord Thornton, it's good to see you. It's been a long time."

"Yes, too long, I might add. My present position is taking much more of my time than I would like."

Nicholson turned to Sean and said, "Captain Sean Gallagher, I would like to introduce you to Lord Thornton, a Member of Parliament and a distinguished banker."

Lord Thornton shook hands with Sean and said, "Gallagher, eh? That's a good Irish name. Were you born there?"

"No sir. My mother and father were both born in Ireland but they immigrated to the United States and I was born there."

"May I ask where exactly your father was born in Ireland?"

"He was born in Howth, a small town near Dublin."

"I see, and do you know what year he left Ireland?"

"My mother told me that the year was 1920."

"By chance, was your father's name Daniel Patrick Gallagher?"

Sean was taken aback by this question. "Yes it was. Did you know him?"

"No, but I knew of him. You see, he killed my father."

"What? Are you serious?"

"Yes, I am. Didn't your father ever tell you why he had to leave Ireland?"

"No, sir. He died a few days before I was born. But my mother told me that my unarmed grandmother was almost decapitated and killed by a British officer. My father then killed him. But I was told that the officer's name was Gordon, not Thornton."

"That's quite true."

Sean was so unnerved at this point that he started to stammer, "I, I, don't know what to say. This is such a shock."

The man smiled and said, "Please don't get upset, captain. I have no animosity to you or your family. As a matter your father did me a great favor."

Sean's face showed a puzzled look. "He did you a favor by killing your father?"

"Yes. You see, my father was a wretched man. He was a drunkard and a very sadistic person. He spent all of his money on liquor and mistresses. He often beat my mother and myself. We lived in dreadful fear of him.

"After he died, my mother met and married a wonderful man, Lord Thornton. He was an older gentleman, very wealthy. He had never been married and had no heirs. He doted on the two of us. He adopted me and sent me to the finest schools. After university, he took me into the bank that he owned and taught me all about banking.

"He and my mother died some years ago and I inherited his estate. So, you see, young man, I can harbor no hostility toward you. On the contrary, I feel deeply indebted to your father."

Sean shook his head and said. "I can hardly believe what I'm hearing. I had no idea about any of this."

Lord Thornton replied, "Of course you could not have known. But I'm glad to have met you. I was always curious as to what had happened to your father. I would like to hear more about him and yourself. Would you possibly be available to be my guest for lunch this week?"

Sean looked at General Nicholson, who nodded his head. "You still have some leave time left, Sean. Why don't you have lunch with Lord Thornton? Our business won't take long."

Sean turned to Lord Thornton, "Yes. I would be glad to."

"Good, here's my card. Please call on Monday morning and we'll discuss the time and place."

"Thank you, sir."

As Lord Thornton departed, General Nicholson turned toward Sean and said, "This has had to be one of the most intriguing hours in your life, Sean. It looks like you will have your hands full for the next few days."

"Intriguing is hardly the word for it, sir. I'm completely overwhelmed."

Laughing, Nicholson said, "I'm afraid to introduce you to anyone else right now, you might blow a blood vessel".

"You're probably right, sir."

"Well, Sean, it seems to me that the good lord has given you two wonderful opportunities to explore. These two gentlemen are extremely influential in their governments. I'm sure you will find a way to turn their friendship to your advantage and to ours."

"I'll certainly try, sir."

"I have no doubt about that. Now, I am going to leave you to your own devices. I have some people I want to meet. By the way, I forgot to mention to you that you and I have been invited to a dinner that the Ambassador is holding immediately after this affair is over. I'll get hold of you later and show you the way."

"Right, sir."

The general smiled, saying. "And Sean, please try not to have any more intriguing encounters today."

Sean laughed and replied, "I'll try not to, sir. I think I've used up my allotment for the year, if not my life."

Sean walked around the large reception hall, soaking up all the sights. Eventually, he spotted Colonel Ivanovich talking to a tall, dark haired woman whose back was toward him. As he passed close by, he heard them talking in Russian. He walked over to them and said, in Russian, "Colonel Ivanovich, I see that you have found your wife."

The Colonel smiled and replied, "No, Captain, this charming young lady is not my wife, she is a dear friend".

At this point, the young lady turned toward Sean. Her cool gaze quickly examined him from head to toe. She evidently liked what she saw because the beginnings of a smile formed on her lips. Sean was equally impressed with her.

Her raven colored hair was cut in a simple pageboy style. His initial impression was that her eyes were black, but when he got a closer look, he realized that they were actually an unusually dark green. They sent a small shiver inside him. Her face was the color of cream. The only evidence of makeup was the dark red lipstick that was applied to her full, somewhat sensuous, lips. There was one minor flaw that dropped her from the stunningly beautiful category to the merely beautiful. It was her slightly aquiline nose. Sean thought that the gods gave her this one blemish so that she wouldn't be perfect, and thus be tempted to indulge in overwhelming vanity.

The most noticeable thing was her height. She stood a little over six feet tall while wearing low heeled shoes. In his experience, many young teenage girls were so self-conscious about being taller than the slower developing boys that they developed a permanent habit of slouching. Not so with her. She stood tall and square-shouldered, as if to tell the world that she was proud of her height. This gave her an almost regal bearing. Sean wondered if her father had nicknamed her "Princess".

She wore a simple sleeveless black cocktail dress with a neckline that showed just a hint of décolletage. Around her neck, she wore the almost de rigueur strand of pearls, which fairly glowed due to the warmth of her skin. Sean was immediately captivated by her elegance.

"As a matter of fact," continued the colonel, "she is a fellow countryman of yours. Captain Sean Gallagher, allow me to introduce you to Miss Sarah Goldman."

"I'm pleased to meet you, Sean", she said, extending her hand.

"I assure you, the pleasure is all mine," he replied. Her hand was soft, but the handshake was remarkably firm. It wasn't the limp wrist kind of handshake that so many women proffered on social occasions. Sean got a message that here was a woman who was very self-assured and who considered herself an equal to any man or woman.

"When I heard you and the Colonel speaking in Russian, I naturally assumed that you were his wife. May I ask how you came to speak Russian so well?"

"Well, both sets of my grandparents were born in Russia and immigrated to the United States many years ago. My parents were born in New York City, and are bi-lingual. They taught me to be the same.

"Now, it's my turn to ask you some questions. How come you also speak Russian so well, and are you stationed here in London?"

"As I recently told the Colonel, I studied Russian in school. In answer to your second question, I'm not stationed here, but in Rome. I was on leave in Ireland when my Commanding Officer asked me to stop here on my way back to Rome. And, I might add, now that I have met you, I will be eternally grateful to him."

Her face lit up. Reverting to English, she remarked, "That sounds suspiciously like Irish baloney to me, but I'm very flattered".

"Oh, let me hasten to correct you, Sarah. That was not Irish baloney, it was Irish blarney."

"Oh? What's the difference?" she asked, while flashing a broad smile, showing a perfect set of teeth. Sean imagined that some orthodontist had been able to send his child to college because of them.

Sean replied, "Well, baloney is flattery cut so thick that it is hard to swallow. Blarney, on the other hand, is flattery sliced so thin that it is easily swallowed and leaves you wanting more."

Sarah gave a hearty laugh. "That's a good one. I'll have to remember that anytime I'm around Irish boys."

Colonel Ivanovich also smiled at this exchange. He turned to Sarah and said, "I just met Sean a few minutes ago. We learned that we have a mutual friend in New York. I wanted to talk to him some more, but I have an urgent appointment soon, and I must find my wife. Wait a minute. I have an idea. Sean, my wife and I are celebrating her birthday tomorrow. Some weeks ago, Sarah agreed to join us as our only guest. Would you also be available to join us? This would be a good opportunity to continue our conversation."

Sean looked at Sarah who smiled and arched her eyebrows, expectantly. He said, "I would be delighted".

"Good. I really must go now. Sean, perhaps you would be kind enough to escort Sarah to my place. She has all the details. I'll see you two tomorrow."

When the colonel departed, Sean said, "Well, you two must be very good friends."

"Yes. We met about a year ago when he was taking a tour of Cambridge University. I'm a graduate student there, and, since I speak Russian, I was appointed to be his guide. We talked about many things. He's an interesting man. He mentioned that his family had been in the banking business before the war. I told him that my father was also in the same field. A week after the tour, he invited me to lunch. He told me he had contacted his father and discovered that he knew my father. They had done business together before the war. Dmitri and I became good friends after that.

"I get invited to dinner when he is in town. I have met his wife, Raisa, and their children. I like him. He's not your typical Russian military man."

"That's quite a coincidence. By the way, what are you studying at Cambridge?"

"Biology. I graduated from Columbia with a biology major and am now working on a PhD degree in genetics. I came here because I wanted to be around two people at Cambridge, James Watson, and Francis Crick."

Sean said, "Those names sound familiar. Where would I have heard of them?"

"They were in the news in February of this year. They discovered the double helix structure of DNA. They literally uncovered the secret of life. That was a monumental achievement. All of our lives will be profoundly affected by the results of their work. There's no question that they will receive a Nobel Prize. And, they're so young. Watson is an American and is only twenty-five years old. Crick is British and is thirty-seven. I still get goose bumps when I think of it. I was there when it happened! What a wonderful experience."

Sean smiled at her enthusiasm. "That's great. It sounds like you had a ringside seat at an historic moment."

"I did, I really did" she gushed. "By the way, both of them are here at the party. They are the honored guests. Would you like to meet them?"

"I certainly would. It's not every day that I get a chance to meet a future Nobel winner."

Sarah soon spotted the men. She escorted Sean over to them and said, "Doctors, I would like you to meet a friend of mine, Capt. Sean Gallagher."

Sean shook hands with both of them saying, "Sarah has told me about both of you and how much you helped her discover the secret of DNA."

Sarah turned beet red and poked a finger in his chest. "Sean, I said no such thing. Tell them you're lying."

Watson burst out laughing and said, "Come on Sarah, everyone knows we couldn't have done it without you. It was a group effort. I mean, after all, you were the one that kept us supplied with coffee and tea so we wouldn't fall asleep during the day. You were the best gofer we had."

"Gofer?" fumed Sarah. "I worked my tail off for you two guys, and this is the thanks I get? Gofer?"

Crick chimed in, "Come on Sarah, Jim is just pulling your leg. You know what a tease he is."

Watson hastened to add, "Sarah, I apologize if I embarrassed you in front of your friend. You ought to know by now how much Frank and I appreciate all the time and hard work you did for us in the lab."

Now mollified, Sarah said, "I'm sorry for flying off the handle. Both of you have been very kind to me this past year and I appreciate the tremendous experience you gave me."

Crick turned to Sean and said, "Sarah is a remarkably bright young lady. I would be willing to bet that we will see her name in the scientific journals someday."

Watson agreed. "Sean, you are a lucky man to have a woman who has so much beauty as well as brains. I envy you. Now, if you will please excuse us, we have to go to a press interview."

After the two departed, Sean said, "They seemed like very nice people."

"Oh, they are. I'm so happy for their success."

At that moment, Sean spotted General Nicholson across the room. The general motioned him to come over. "Sarah, I'm afraid I have to leave now, as well. My commanding Officer just gave me the nod to join him in a previously scheduled meeting with our Ambassador. Now, about tomorrow evening?"

"I'm staying in a hotel in downtown London for a few days," said Sarah. I'll write down the phone number. Call me and I'll tell you how to get to my hotel so you can pick me up about five o'clock. I know how to get to the Dmitri's place."

"Great," said Sean, "I'll see you tomorrow."

Chapter 23

Promptly at five the next evening, Sean knocked on Sarah's hotel room door. She opened it and greeted him with a big smile.

"Hello, Sean. Come on in and take a seat. My mother called just before you knocked. I should be finished soon."

Having said that, she picked up the phone and said "Sorry for the interruption, mom, I had to let someone into the room. Who? Just a friend I met yesterday at the Embassy. He's a captain in the Air Force."

At this point, Sarah glanced at Sean and continued, in Hebrew, "I don't want him to understand our conversation, so let's talk in Hebrew... Is he good looking? He's gorgeous... Oh, he's about six feet four, blond hair, blue-green eyes, and built like Michelangelo's statue of David in Florence... No, of course I don't know if he's circumcised like that statue ... Oh, mom, you're making me blush. Please don't tease me like that when the guy is right in the same room. I'm trying to make a good impression on him... No, he's not Jewish, he's Irish, and his name is Sean."

While Sarah continued her conversation, Sean pretended to read a magazine that he found on the coffee table. He decided, then and there, that it might prove interesting if he did not tell Sarah that he understand Hebrew, or reveal to her his background at the Hebrew Orphan Asylum.

Sarah continued, "No, unfortunately, he's not stationed here in London. He's stationed in Rome ... Mother, I just met the guy. Of course I'll be careful. You forget that I'm over twenty-one and have traveled all over the world and have managed to survive. I've got to go now, we're on our way to a dinner at Dmitri's place. I'll tell you all about it tomorrow... I love you too. Goodbye."

Sarah turned to Sean and said, disingenuously, "Please excuse me for talking to my mother in Hebrew. I studied it in school and my mother doesn't want me to get out of practice while I'm over here."

"I can understand that," replied Sean, smiling. "What did your mother have to say?"

Shrugging her shoulders, Sarah replied, "Oh, just the usual girl stuff. How's the weather? Where did I go shopping? What did I have for lunch? My mother is very protective and insists on keeping in close touch with me. I'd hate to have her phone bill. I don't suppose your mother tries to smother you the same way."

"As a matter of fact, my mother died in New York City last week. I buried her beside my father in Dublin, just two days ago. My CO asked me to join him here for a few days before returning to Rome."

Sarah gasped, "Oh, no!" She stepped forward, hugged him and whispered huskily in his ear, "Oh, you poor boy. I'm so sorry, so very sorry."

Sean was momentarily taken aback. He put his arms around her and held her tightly. His lips gently brushed against her face, and he was surprised to taste a salty tear running down her cheek. He had barely known her for twenty-four hours and here she was, being genuinely sorry over his loss. His initial impression was that she was a very self-disciplined person. He hadn't guessed that she could be this emotional.

He felt the warmth of her body, as it seemed to melt into his. He detected the scent of her freshly washed hair and the subtle trace of what was probably a very expensive perfume. He breathed in deeply, as if trying to inhale the very essence of her being. He felt a tranquility that he had never experienced before. He wished that this moment wouldn't end. He held her even more tightly. After a few minutes, they let go of each other and Sarah said, "We don't have to go to the dinner. I can call Dmitri and cancel."

"No, I insist we go. I want to be around people now, especially with you. My mother was a good person, very religious. I'm sure that she's in heaven. I like to believe that she's reunited with my father who died a few days before I was born. I'm sure they are both very happy now and wouldn't want me to be sad for very long."

They proceeded to dinner, which was held at Dmitri's hotel. Sean felt an instant rapport with him and his wife, Raisa. They had some stimulating conversations in English as well as Russian. The evening was a great success.

Toward the end, Dmitri informed them that he was going to leave the military at the end of the year and return to Moscow. There, he would take over the family bank for his father. His father was spending more and more time in his government position and the bank was too important to allow someone else to be in charge.

"I extend an invitation to each of you to visit me in Moscow sometime. I would like to keep you two as friends."

Sean said, "I have visited the American Embassy in Moscow on assignments a few times in the past and I will probably be there again, someday. If so, I promise to pay you a visit."

When they left, Sean escorted Sarah back to the door of her hotel room. He had learned that she was planning to stay in London for the balance of the week. "Sarah, I'll be here until Saturday when I have to return to Rome. I'll find out, after tomorrow morning's meeting, if my CO wants me to do anything else in London. Would you be interested in being my tour guide around London during my free time? I've never been here before."

"I would be glad to. Call me tomorrow and we'll work around your schedule.

Sean agreed, shook her hand and left.

The Monday morning meeting turned out to be very brief. General Nicholson told Sean that he wouldn't need him any further and that he could spend the rest of the week using up his leave time.

Sean called Lord Thornton who invited Sean to lunch that very day. He was to meet at the Thornton Bank.

He also called Sarah and told her that he would be free from that afternoon and the rest of the week. She said that she would set up an itinerary for them.

Sean met Lord Thornton in his office. Thornton greeted him warmly and told him that they would have lunch at his private club, which was only a block away.

The club looked like something right out of a Hollywood movie set. The walls were paneled in dark wood. Large oil paintings of kings, queens, politicians, war heroes, etc. lined the walls. Richly upholstered chairs were strewn around on thick oriental rugs. The waiters were attired in formal wear; the tables were adorned with fine china and silverware. Sean had never been exposed to such opulence. He tried not to be awed by all of this.

When they were seated, Lord Thornton said that he had taken the liberty of having a bottle of champagne ready at the table. When the waiter popped the cork and poured two glasses, Thornton proposed a toast, "Sean, here's to your health and a friendship that I hope will be established from this day forth."

They clinked glasses and each took a sip of the wine.

Sean said, "I'm flattered by your toast but at the same time I am very confused as to what you mean by it."

"I'll explain in due time. But now, I would dearly like you to tell me about you and your family."

Over lunch, Sean began a lengthy recitation of what had happened after his father had fled Ireland. Lord Thornton seemed to be paying rapt attention to every detail.

"To tell you the truth, Sean, I talked with General Nicholson last night. He and I became good friends during the war. We both served in our countries' intelligence service. He told me a little bit about you, but I wanted to hear the full story in your own words. I am fascinated by it.

"By the way, General Nicholson holds you in high regard."

"I'm very flattered to hear that. He's a fine officer and I have the utmost respect for him. Now, since I have bared my soul to you, would you think it impertinent if I asked you to tell me a little bit about yourself, and your family, after your father died?"

"I don't think it impertinent at all, Sean. Turnabout is fair play, as they say.

"My mother was an only child. Her father owned a small local newspaper, here in London. She worked there and learned all the jobs: interviewing, writing stories, editing, printing, etc. She was a beautiful young lady and eventually was swept off her feet by a dashing young army officer, named Jonathan Gordon. He came from a good family but had the reputation of being somewhat reckless and irresponsible.

"After they were married, they were posted to various parts of the empire. He eventually wound up gambling and losing a good deal of money. He started to drink excessively, and became physically abusive to my mother and myself. The beatings got worse when we were posted to Ireland. She feared for our safety. Mother did not want to expose him then, for fear of jeopardizing his career. She thought she would wait until they returned to England where she would have close family support to help resolve the problem.

"However, her parents died during an influenza epidemic. Because of the confusion during the war, and bureaucratic bungling, she was not told about this until many weeks after their deaths. She was devastated and felt very alone.

"When my father died, the British army commander covered up the truth about the incident of the death of your grandmother. He called my father a hero who had been assassinated by an IRA terrorist. He gave my father a posthumous medal and a hero's burial.

"Lord Thornton was sent from London to attend the funeral as a representative of the British government. He held the rank of colonel.

"As I said, my mother had been a beautiful woman when she was married, but after so many years of abuse, her beauty had started to fade. She had lost a good deal of weight, her eyes were sunken in her head, and she always looked sad.

"Lord Thornton visited us after the funeral to offer his personal condolences. My mother accepted them gracefully. She never mentioned my father's abusive behavior or the truth about his death. She didn't want to embarrass our family or the government.

"He said that the government wanted him to provide extra assistance to a hero's widow and son. The government would return us to England and provide a small pension for us. He would make the necessary arrangements. When she got settled in, he wanted her to visit him at his office.

"After a few weeks, we arrived in England and stayed at the home of my mother's cousin. The lady had been a widow for many years and was glad to have our company.

"Shortly after we had settled in, my mother called Lord Thornton's office. He told her that he was in the process of being mustered out of the army and returning to civilian life as the head of Thornton Bank. He invited her to visit him at his new office the following week.

"My mother's health and appearance had improved tremendously in the weeks since my father's death. She had regained the same beauty of her youth, but her maturity and newfound confidence had added an indefinable something to her bearing. Men noticed her.

"Lord Thornton was an older gentleman, who had never been married. His father had founded an investment bank in London, which did quite well. Thornton was an only child and had been doted on by both his parents. He received the best education. He eventually joined his father in the bank. He was very astute and quickly became an integral part of the business.

"When World War I broke out, he was asked to join the army's intelligence branch, with the rank of colonel. Due to his banking background, he had extensive personal contacts throughout Europe that would prove useful.

When mother entered Lord Thornton's office at his bank, he greeted her warmly. He couldn't get over the remarkable transformation that had taken place in her. They had a long chat. He was interested in her current situation. She told him we were sharing living quarters with a relative, but she needed to find a job to supplement her pension.

"He asked if she had any experience in the business world. She told him that she spent a number of years at her father's newspaper.

"This seemed to excite Lord Thornton and he asked many questions as to what exactly she did at the paper. The reason he asked so many questions about her experience was because his private secretary was pregnant and was planning to leave her position within a few weeks. He was looking for a replacement and thought that my mother had some excellent credentials and skills that would be perfect for the job, if she were interested.

"My mother was extremely interested, and wound up with the position.

"She proved to be more than a secretary and became what I would call his executive assistant. She impressed everyone who met her. She particularly impressed Lord Thornton. Their relationship turned to love. He proposed marriage and she accepted. That was the start of a whole new life for me.

"Lord Thornton dearly loved us. He adopted me. He proved to be a wonderful father. He sent me to the finest schools. The three of us traveled extensively throughout the world. When I graduated university, he brought me into the bank and taught me everything he knew.

"When he and my mother died, I inherited his estate. I became a very wealthy man.

"So, you see, Sean, your father was the cause of my good fortune. I think you can understand my interest in meeting with you."

"That was a fascinating story, sir. I'm glad you told me."

"Sean, I want you to know how impressed I am with what you have accomplished in your young life. You have done it on your own. You had no father, and no close-by relatives to help, as I did. You had no safety net. You must have felt awfully alone, especially now that you have so recently lost your mother."

"Yes, sir, at times I envied some of my friends that had both parents and extended families close by. But my friends became a kind of substitute family."

"That's a commendable attitude, Sean."

Thornton was quiet for a few moments, seemingly lost in thought. Then he perked up and said, "That gives me an idea. How would you like me to be a part of your substitute family?"

"What do you mean?"

"I would like you to consider me as the uncle you never had, sort of a mentor, someone you could rely upon for advice, someone who could give you the benefit of a different, long range perspective on things."

"Sir, that is a very generous offer but why would you want to do such a thing for me? You shouldn't feel guilty about anything. You don't owe me anything."

"No, Sean, I don't. But I do feel indebted to your father for my good fortune, and I would like to do something about it. Maybe some people would call it an attempt to expiate a guilt feeling, but that's not quite the case. Let me try to explain my philosophy.

"You are a Catholic and I am a member of the Church of England. Our two churches share the same basic beliefs. We both believe that the greatest commandment is to love God and to love our neighbors as ourselves.

"My wife and I were never blessed with children, but we do have a few nieces and nephews. I love them as if they were my own children. It gives me great joy to be with them whenever possible and to help them however I can. It's a wonderful vicarious parental feeling for me.

"We are active in various charities. I firmly believe that we are all stewards of the gifts that God has given us, and that He will judge us on how well we have utilized them. God has blessed me, and I feel obligated to show my love for my fellow man by sharing some of my gifts.

"As far as having a guilt feeling, I have none concerning you. After all, I had nothing to do with my father's death, and neither did you. However, I believe that our meeting the other day was due to more than pure chance. I feel that there is an invisible bond that exists between us, and I have an odd feeling that the Good Lord wanted us to finally meet, and our destinies to be intertwined. Does that make sense to you, Sean?"

"Strangely enough, it does. You see, after meeting you on Sunday, I also had the oddest gut feeling that our meeting was not accidental. I guess some people would call it kismet. I don't know how to explain it any better than you did."

"My dear boy, sometimes we should leave logic behind and act according to our gut feelings. I believe that this is one such time. Do you agree?"

"Yes, sir, I do."

"Excellent. Here's what I propose. Let's start off by doing away with formalities. I know you Americans don't like titles and, frankly, neither do I. If I am to be your surrogate uncle, I insist that you call me Uncle Jim. Is that agreeable with you?"

"Yes, sir, I mean Uncle Jim," said Sean laughing. "Excuse me but it will take me a little while to get used to that."

"Good. As your newly acquired uncle, I am going to exercise my prerogative by asking a few personal questions."

"What more do you want to know?"

"Are you planning to make the military a career?"

"No. I like what I'm doing and I know it's important work for my country, but I dislike the bureaucracy that goes along with it.

I'm not cut out to be a follower. I want to have more control over my destiny."

"I don't blame you Sean; I've felt the same way. Have you thought about what you want to do after you leave the service?"

"Yes. I want to go back to school and get an MBA degree. You see, my prior school experience was what you would call a classic liberal arts education. The Jesuits were fond of saying that a liberal arts program teaches you how to make a life, rather than a living. And, they are right. My education taught me how to think logically and independently and to communicate effectively. I want to round out my education by applying my analytical skills to the more practical aspects of making a living."

"I like your thinking, Sean. Now, I would like you to offer you my very first piece of avuncular advice. I would like you to consider majoring in international finance."

"Why is that, Uncle Jim?"

"Because the post-war European economy is going to grow enormously in the next decade or so. You have a most unusual command of all the major European languages. You will have traveled to most of the major capitals and seen, firsthand, what needs to be done. These countries will need a great amount of outside financing to fill their needs. Your background would give you a tremendous advantage with the right company. Right now, I wish I had ten such people."

Sean was quiet for a few minutes, digesting what had just been said. He replied, "That makes a lot of sense. I don't think I would have thought of it on my own. From this point on, I will pay more attention to the business and economic situations in the countries I visit.

"I sincerely thank you for that advice. I'm really excited about it. I'm going to enjoy being your nephew."

Lord Thornton smiled and replied, "And I'm going to enjoy being your uncle. I am going to insist that you stay in close contact with me by mail or phone. Whenever you visit England, you must meet with me. Is that agreeable with you?"

"Of course, Uncle Jim."

"That's a deal, as you Yanks would say. If you are to be part of my extended family, I would like you to meet my wife, your newly acquired aunt."

"I would love to, but my time here in London is limited, I have to leave on Saturday and I have no idea when or if I can return to London."

"I understand. Why don't we plan to have dinner at my house on Friday evening, before you leave town. Is that possible?"

"Absolutely."

"Very good. Call me on Thursday and I will give you directions."

Chapter 24

After the lunch with Uncle Jim, Sean called Sarah and arranged to meet her later that day.

Sarah proved to be a knowledgeable and entertaining guide. She laughed easily as they spent their week visiting the traditional tourist attractions, as well as operas and plays.

As they discussed their backgrounds, they found they had a good deal in common.

Sarah told him that her grandfathers, Saul Goldman and Isaac Silverman, had worked for their parents, who were partners in a diamond and jewelry company in Moscow. In 1895, both their parents were killed during a pogrom. The boys managed to escape the country and immigrate to New York.

When they arrived, virtuously penniless, a Jewish Aid agency found them jobs in the diamond district. Jewish merchants, who transacted their business primarily in Yiddish and Hebrew, dominated the New York diamond industry. They made deals on the basis of a handshake. Any dealer, who reneged on a deal, found himself ostracized from the industry, as well as the Jewish community. Since the boys spoke both languages, and had extensive experience in the trade, they did well. They also learned to speak English.

After a few years, they followed in their fathers' footsteps and formed their own company. They were shrewd businessmen. They prospered and became quite wealthy.

They were very happy when their only two children decided to marry each other.

Sarah's father, David, opted not to join the family business. He chose, instead, a career in finance. He graduated from Columbia, received an MBA from Harvard, and joined JP Morgan. He attracted a large clientele from the jewelry industry, due to his family's connections, and his ability to speak Hebrew and Yiddish, as well as Russian.

She grew up in a co-op apartment in midtown Manhattan, and attended private schools. Her parents wanted her to be proud of her Jewish heritage, so she took religion classes at the local Reformed temple, and made her Bat Mitzvah.

She learned to speak Russian, Yiddish and Hebrew from her parents and grandparents. She studied Latin to prepare herself for her biology major at Columbia University. While there, she also took Italian as one of her electives. She was very proud of her linguistic abilities.

Sean was impressed. She seemed to share a love of language much as he did. However, he decided not to reveal all of the languages he knew. He also decided to be a bit more circumspect in talking about his past. He told her about growing up on Vinegar Hill, only a short distance from Columbia, but avoided mentioning his, or his mother's, involvement in the Hebrew Orphan Asylum. He talked about the father he never knew, and his death in attempting to stop a holdup. He discussed his schooling at Fordham, particularly his Philosophy and Russian courses.

He told her of his friendship with Joe Morelli and his family, and that their restaurant was the source of free tickets to Carnegie Hall, the Metropolitan Opera, and Broadway plays. They discovered that each of them had seen many of the same performances.

They learned that they also shared a love of art museums. Each had spent many hours at the Guggenheim and the Museum of Art, both on Fifth Avenue.

Sean said, "I wouldn't be surprised if we were in some of these places at the same time and, might even have brushed against each other."

Sarah smiled, "That's funny, I was just thinking the same thing. We lived in the same area for many years and visited the same places, yet we had to travel over three thousand miles to finally meet face to face. It must be kismet."

Sean mused to himself, "I've had a lot of kismet happen to me this week."

The Almega Project

On Thursday, Sean called Uncle Jim. "Uncle Jim, may I ask a favor of you?"

"Of course. What can I do for you?"

"May I bring a guest to dinner tomorrow? I met this wonderful girl at the Embassy party. She is an American student at Cambridge and she has acted as my guide to London this week. I would like you to meet her."

"My dear nephew, I would be delighted. My wife will enjoy the company of another woman at dinner."

On Friday evening, Uncle Jim entertained the young couple in his home. He and his wife were enchanted with this beautiful young woman and, by the time dinner ended, Sarah felt that she, too, had gained a surrogate uncle and aunt. It was the start of a beautiful friendship.

When they left the Thorntons, Sean took Sarah back to her hotel. This was their final evening together. Typically, Sean would escort Sarah to her room, open the door for her, say goodnight, and leave. Tonight, Sarah insisted that he come inside.

Sean took her hands and said, "Words can't express how much I've enjoyed spending the past few days with you. It has gone much too fast and I'm really sad to see it end."

Sarah said, "I feel the same way. I'm also sorry that there is one thing that we failed to do."

"What's that?"

"This." She threw her arms around his neck and smothered him with a series of passionate kisses.

When Sean came up for air, he gently pushed her back a half step, and said, in a husky voice, "I think I better leave right now."

"Sean, I've practically thrown myself at you and you want to leave right now? Any other boy would grab this opportunity to try and take advantage of me, but you want to go? Right now?"

"Yes."

Her face suddenly became contorted. She looked up at Sean and gasped, "Oh, god! Oh, no! Please don't tell me.

"Tell you what?"

"That you're queer."

Sean's eyes widened in surprise. He shook his head and laughed loudly. "No, no, no, I'm as heterosexual as can be."

Sarah sighed, "Thank god".

"The truth is, I'm afraid to stay longer. My adrenaline is pumping so hard that I'm actually trembling. My hormones are urging me to grab you and, as you said, try to take advantage of you. But, that's not the way I was raised.

"I have to admit that I have not had much experience with women. I feel so overwhelmed and awkward right now. This emotion is so new to me that I'm not sure how to handle it. The last thing in the world I want to do is something that would ruin the best experience I have ever had."

Sarah hugged him tightly. As she looked up, tears started to form and run down her face. She nuzzled her head against his chest and said, "I'm so glad you told me that. I have dated a lot of men. None of them would have had the courage to bare their souls the way you just did. I think I understand what you are going through.

"I have never been the aggressor with any guy before. But, with you, I had to try something different. You have been so damned polite this past week that I had to find out if you were as attracted to me as I am to you. Now I know."

They clung to each other for a while, reflecting on their newly confessed feelings for each other.

Finally, Sarah asked, "Where do we go from here?"

Before he could answer, the harsh ringing of the telephone interrupted their conversation. Sarah answered it and said. "Hi, mom. I'm fine, only..." then, switching to Hebrew, she continued, "You called at a very inopportune moment. I was just saying goodbye to Sean....Yes, I am crying. He has to return to Rome tomorrow morning and I'm going to miss him so much....Yes, I was kissing him...No, he did not try to take advantage of me. It was almost the opposite... No, he wouldn't let me. Can you imagine that? All my other boyfriends kept trying to get into my pants, but not him. .... Believe me, mother, you have nothing to worry about. Hey, I've got to hang up now. Call me tomorrow.... I love you, too, goodbye."

Sean smiled to himself while eavesdropping on the conversation.

Sarah went back to Sean and gently hugged him. "Now, where were we?"

"We were just starting to talk about what happens next."

She asked, "Do you have any suggestions?"

"I know that I very much want to see you again, and as soon as possible. However, I have a serious problem. I have a number of travel assignments coming up for the rest of the year. My missions are classified. I can't tell anyone where I'm going, or what I am doing. I have no control over my time."

Sarah replied, "They have to give you leave at some time, don't they?"

"Yes. The Christmas holidays are usually pretty slow for everyone. That would be my best bet. Would it be possible to get together at that time? I'm sure that you have a school break for the holidays."

"Of course I do. That sounds like a great idea."

"Could you meet me in Rome? Rome is such a great place at Christmas. I would love to show it to you then."

"Sean, that sounds great. I love Rome. Let's plan on it. It will be so exciting."

Sean said that she could write to him in care of the Rome Embassy. The letters would then be rerouted to him wherever he was.

Sean gave her a big hug and a gentle kiss on her cheek. As he started to leave, he paused at the door for a moment and said, "By the way, for your information, an Irish queer is a guy who prefers alcohol to women."

Despite the tears in her eyes, Sarah laughed.

When Sean returned to Rome, he and Joe had dinner together. He told Joe about his mother's funeral and burial.

Joe said, "I am truly sorry that I could not attend the funeral, but I was on a spiritual retreat at the time, as part of my studies for a doctorate in Theology. I was not allowed to have any communication with the outside world."

Sean said, "I know. There's no need to apologize." He proceeded to talk at great length about meeting Sarah and the wonderful time they had spent together.

"It seems to me that you are quite smitten with her."

"You're right. I have never met a girl quite like her. We have only been away for one day and I can't stop thinking about her.

"Sean, I've never heard you talk about any girl this way. She must be quite a woman. I'd like to meet her."

"I'm sure you will, Joe. She's planning to come here at Christmas time. She and her family have apparently traveled extensively. She said Rome is one of her favorite cities. I would value your opinion of her. Do me a favor, though, when you do meet her, don't tell her about the HOA. She doesn't know that I understand Hebrew. It's proven to be quite useful when she talks to her mother on the phone in that language."

"Sean, you rascal, you, I really shouldn't, but I will do as you ask. But I'm not going to lie for you."

"I'm not asking you to do that. All I'm asking you to do, is to omit any mention of my stay in the HOA if she starts to question you about my background. I see no problem with you compromising that overly scrupulous conscience of yours."

Joe started laughing at his friend's needling and said, "All right, Sean. I got the message."

Chapter 25

Sean travelled extensively during the latter part of 1953, without being able to return to Rome.

Sarah wrote to Sean, telling him that she would have a long break in her school schedule during the year-end holidays. She felt obliged to spend part of that time visiting her parents in New York. Afterwards, she would fly to Rome for the Christmas season. She gave him her dates of arrival and departure.

When her letter caught up with him, Sean made arrangements for leave at the same time. He wrote to Sarah, confirming the dates. He also notified Joe.

When he finally arrived in Rome for the Christmas holidays, he met with Joe.

Joe smiled, "I'm anxious to meet this gal who has so enchanted my closest friend. I promise not to embarrass you too much. Let me remind you that I will be ordained the week before Christmas. My mom and dad will be here. I, of course, expect you to attend. After that, I will have a month off for myself. I would love to hang around with you two to make sure that you avoid the temptations of the flesh. And, if you don't avoid those temptations, I will have the opportunity, for the first time, to act as your confessor. I want to hear all the juicy details."

Joe laughed as he said this, and Sean did too.

"Joe, you've got a deal. We will have a great time."

Sean attended the elaborate ordination ceremony along with Joe's parents. The pope presided over the event, which was held in St. Peter's Basilica.

Rose and Vito left for home shortly after.

Two days after Christmas, Sean met Sarah at the airport and greeted her with a warm hug, saying, "You look as beautiful as ever. I have really looked forward to seeing you again."

Sarah smiled, "I feel exactly the same way. Now, pray tell, what do you have in store for me?"

"Well, now it's my turn to return a favor and play tourist guide for you. I'll take you to your hotel and let you rest up for a while. Then I'm going to take you to a place where they serve the best Italian food in the city. I'll come back for you at five."

When Sean picked her up at five, he took a scenic route around Rome. He finally parked the car in front of an apartment house. He ushered her up two flights of stairs, and knocked on the door of an apartment.

"I thought you were taking me out to the best dinner in Rome," said Sarah.

"I am," replied Sean. "Just be patient."

Joe Morelli, dressed in casual attire, opened the door, and welcomed them to his apartment.

Sean made the introductions. "Sarah, I'd like you to meet my best friend, Joe Morelli. Joe, this is Sarah Goldman. Joe shook her hand warmly and said, "I'm probably telling tales out of school, but Sean hasn't stopped talking about you since he returned from London. Now I can see why. Please come in and take a seat."

Sarah smiled and said, "Thank you for the compliment, kind sir." As she walked to a chair, she had a chance to look over the apartment and said, "This is a lovely place and it's so conveniently located to some of the best tourist spots in Rome."

"Thank you. Would you like a drink before dinner?"

"A glass of wine would be fine."

Sean said, "I'll get a bottle and three glasses."

While he was gone, Sarah asked, "Joe, are we waiting for your date?"

Joe smiled, "Didn't' Sean tell you?"

"Tell me what?"

"That I'm a Catholic priest."

Sarah furrowed her eyebrows and looked over at Sean. "No, he never mentioned it. I'm sure I would have remembered something like that."

Sean returned with the wine and said, "I didn't tell you because I wanted you to meet Joe first, and feel comfortable with him. Joe and I are best friends, almost like brothers. We grew up together and he doesn't stand on formality with friends."

"That's right, Sarah. Just call me Joe. Sean may have mentioned that my father owned an Italian restaurant in New York. He and I worked there part time while attending school. We both learned to cook up some mean pasta dishes. Sean and I have prepared our favorite dish, Osso Buco Morelli. I hope it becomes yours as well."

Some fine Italian wine accompanied the meal that Sarah said was outstanding. "This is, without doubt, the best Italian meal I have ever tasted. You guys missed your calling."

Joe smiled, "Thank you ma'am. Now why don't we relax in the living room?"

"After some postprandial brandy, a warm glow enveloped the trio.

"Joe," said Sarah, "I have to ask you a few questions. When Sean and I were in London, he didn't talk too much about himself. I poured my guts out to him. I told him things that I never told anyone else, except my mother. Since he seems to have a serious problem of memory lapse, I want to ask you to fill in some details that he might have left out. I know you won't lie to me."

Joe smiled and said, "Go ahead, shoot. I'll answer all your questions as long as it doesn't violate the seal of Confession."

She smiled. "OK. Tell me your version of how you two met, and all about your backgrounds."

Joe proceeded to tell her about the Morelli and Gallagher families being neighbors in the same building, and how Sean's father saved his parents' lives. "Sean followed me to the same schools as we grew up. I regarded him as my younger brother. He spent so much time with me and my folks that he learned to speak Italian fluently.

"We lived across the street from Lewisohn Stadium, and we used to listen to all the summer concerts from our rooftop. My father would sing along with all the Italian performers, and he taught us all the operatic arias.

"All the visiting Italian singers ate at our restaurant and we always had free tickets to the Metropolitan Opera and Carnegie Hall. We had a great time growing up there."

Sarah said. "How interesting. My parents had season tickets to the Lewisohn Stadium concerts. I will always remember the first, and only time, I went with them. When we left the concert, we discovered that our car had a flat tire. Then, two young neighborhood kids came by and offered to change the tire for us. They didn't want to accept any money but my father gave them a generous tip for helping us out."

Sean was in the process of sipping his brandy when Sarah said that. He laughed so hard that the brandy started to spurt out his nose. Joe also started to go into convulsions.

Sarah looked at the two of them with a frown on her face. "What's with you guys, did I say something funny?"

Joe was the first to gain control of himself and said, "You may find this as hard to believe as we do, Sarah, but those two kids were Sean and myself."

"That's not possible", she said. "You're pulling my leg, now, aren't you?"

Sean added, "No, honest to God, it's the truth. Your father drove a black Cadillac, and he was wearing a tuxedo. Your mother wore a blue cocktail dress. You wore a navy blue skirt with a Kelly green sweater set. When I tried to make conversation with you, you refused to talk to me. I thought you were a stuck-up snob."

"You're right, I remember that. I can't believe this."

Sean said, "When I first saw you in London, I had this strange feeling that I had met you once before. It was your eyes. Now the mystery is solved."

Joe then proceeded to tell her about how that incident inspired the two of them to run their parking scam. "So, it was you and your family that started Sean and myself on the road to perdition."

"And, for that, we are eternally grateful. It was an interesting road to travel" said Sean, still laughing.

Sarah continued to shake her head and said, "My god, what a small world. To think I had to travel three or four thousand miles to meet up again with you two rascals."

"God works in mysterious ways, Sarah", said Joe.

"He sure does," she replied, "He sure does."

Joe continued to regale Sarah about other experiences that he and Sean had while growing up in the Vinegar Hills neighborhood.

He was taken aback when she asked, "Wasn't the home for Jewish orphans across the street from the stadium?"

"Yes, it was" Joe answered. "It was called the Hebrew Orphan Asylum. Sean and I played basketball in their gym all the time. It closed down in 1941. Why do you ask?"

"It was both of my grandfathers' favorite charity. They really empathized with the orphans. As a matter of fact, my paternal grandfather was one of their trustees. Whenever he came home from Sunday meetings there, he always took back with him a loaf of Irish soda bread, tied up with a green ribbon. I guess the cook was Irish and she made it especially for the trustees. I remember that it tasted delicious. I think I ate most of it."

Joe looked at Sean, whose mouth had fallen open in disbelief and his eyes started to cloud over. Sean abruptly arose from his chair and went into the kitchen, in order to hide his astonishment and emotion from Sarah.

Joe covered his friend's hasty exit by shouting, "Sean, as long as you're up, please bring back another bottle of brandy. This soldier's about dead."

The remainder of the evening passed without any further startling revelations. Joe told them that, since he was also on vacation for a few days, he would be honored to show them around parts of Rome not seen by the ordinary tourist.

He asked Sarah what she wanted to see.

"I was in Rome some years ago with my parents and we visited St. Peter's, but I never got the chance to see the Sistine Chapel. Could we do that?"

"Absolutely. As a matter of fact, if we get an early start, I can get us in there before it opens for the tourists."

Early the next morning, the trio entered the Sistine Chapel. They would have it all to themselves for two hours. Sean had already been there a few of times. Sarah was enthralled by the magnificence of the place. Joe gave them a running commentary as they slowly walked around.

They paused before the magnificent Throne of St. Peter, a huge Baroque composition of marble with white and gilt stucco. A large stained glass window rose above it.

Sean stared at the window for quite a long time.

Sarah inquired, "Why are you stopping here for so long?"

Sean grasped her hand and said, "Sarah, I'm in awe of this stained glass window."

"I admit it is beautiful, but I'm sure you've seen many other such windows in the various cathedrals you have undoubtedly visited."

"That's true. However, being here with you, contemplating the beauty of Michelangelo's work, and the work of all the other artists, has suddenly made me very emotional and has heightened my awareness of things. All of a sudden I'm beginning to understand what the architects and the stained glass artists were trying to convey to us."

"And what, pray tell, would that be?"

"Well, the architects obviously needed as much light in the church as possible, so they incorporated a goodly number of windows. They placed many of them, such as this, toward the ceiling, forcing us to look up toward heaven to remind us that God is the light of the world, and that His light shines through to illuminate our souls with His love. I see each of the shards of colored glass as different experiences and impediments in our lives. The mosaic, created by all these pieces of glass, distorts and colors the divine light, thus robbing it of its purity. We humans cannot fully understand and appreciate His brilliance and love because of this diffusion."

"Whoa, big guy. That's pretty heavy stuff. Are you some kind of philosopher?"

"As a matter of fact, anyone who graduated from my college could rightfully call himself a philosopher since we had four intense years of philosophy. Joe and I used to spend many hours arguing over philosophical concepts. We still do, but I don't think this is the time, or place, for you to be bored to death by us."

Sarah nodded her head and said, "I'm just a scientist. I never studied philosophy and don't have the kind of insight you guys do, but now I know that I'll never be able to look at another church or synagogue without thinking of what you said. I'm glad you told me."

"Sarah, I'm sorry I got on such a serious subject. We're supposed to have fun."

"Please don't feel sorry. I've never met a guy who could express such sensitivity without being embarrassed. Most men try to impress women by attempting to be macho, or by flaunting their expensive cars, or other possessions. You're a refreshing change."

"I wasn't trying to impress you. I'm surrounded by so much beauty, both yours, and the art, that I just got carried away by the moment."

"Sean, that's the sweetest thing anyone has ever said to me. I think I'm going to cry."

And, she did.

Sean wiped away her tears and hugged her until she calmed down. Joe looked on at the scene and smiled.

When they finished their tour of the Sistine Chapel, Joe took them on a walk through the Vatican. Sean had seen it all before, but Sarah had not. She was fascinated by the experience.

For the next few days, the trio visited the various historic spots in Rome. They spent their evenings eating in the apartment or at one of the finer restaurants. They also managed to attend a few operas

Toward the end of Sarah's stay, Joe said, "I've saved a special treat for both of you tomorrow."

"And what may that be, my dear tourist guide?" asked Sarah.

"I'm going to show you something that few people have seen in this century. It's located in the Cathedral of John the Baptist."

Sean said, "I don't remember seeing that one here in Rome."

"That's because it's not here. It's in a town a few hours' drive from here."

"What is it you want us to see?" asked Sean.

"I want it to be a surprise, so, you will just have to wait until tomorrow. We will leave at dawn."

The following morning, Joe drove them north to the town of Turin. The cathedral was surprisingly large for the size of the town. Joe walked them through the church and into a large chapel at the rear. They proceeded to an adjoining room and entered it.

There, they saw a long table that contained a linen fabric runner down the middle. The cloth was about thirteen feet long and about three feet wide. It appeared to be quite old and covered with brown stains. A few nuns on either side of the table were examining the fabric.

Sean asked, "Is this what you wanted us to see?"

Joe nodded.

"What is it?" inquired Sarah.

"This is what many people believe to be the actual burial shroud of Jesus Christ."

Sean shook his head, "Are you serious?"

"Absolutely."

"But how is that possible. How could it have existed for two thousand years?"

"That's a good question, and I have been asked to do some research in the Vatican Library, and elsewhere, to see if I can come up with some answers.

"My research, thus far, shows some written historical evidence that the shroud existed in the sixth century, in the town of Edessa, Turkey. Some sources believe that the cloth was brought there from Jerusalem, in the first century, by the disciple Thaddeus. However, I cannot yet verify that. It has had an interesting journey and it has been here, in Turin, since 1578.

"The shroud is normally folded and locked up in a special reliquary box behind the altar. Periodically, it is taken out and examined, like today. It's a rare treat for anyone to see the shroud laid out to its full length like this.

"Take a good look at the image on the cloth. It's very blurry, you can't see much detail. However, you can see that it's the front and back image of a man about six feet tall, who bears the marks of crucifixion and scourging.

"Let me show you some unusual pictures of the shroud, taken by a photographer named Secondo Pia, back in 1898. When he was developing his photographic plates, he saw something amazing. The black and white negatives showed much sharper details of the image on the cloth. They jump off the page. Look."

Sean said, "Yes, I can see that. When I compare the pictures, side by side, with the actual cloth, I can easily make out wounds in the man's forehead, as if made by a crown of thorns. I see a wound in his right side, consistent with a spear thrust. There are also wounds on his wrists and feet as if made by large nails. Everything is consistent with the biblical accounts of the crucifixion of Jesus."

Turning to Sarah, he asked, "What's your reaction to all this?"

She answered, "As a Jew, I was taught to recognize the historical existence of Jesus. We regard him to be a prophet, but we don't regard him as the Messiah, or the Son of God.

"As a biologist and geneticist, I'm fascinated by this cloth. I would love to examine it more closely with scientific instruments, especially the stains that appear to be blood. I could learn a great deal from that."

Joe said, "I, too, would love to have it examined scientifically, but the prevailing opinion is that science does not yet have the equipment to analyze the entire cloth without doing irreparable damage. Perhaps, some day in the future, we will have the proper tools."

Sean looked at Joe, "Do you believe it to be the true shroud?"

"Yes, I do."

"What's the official attitude of the Church?"

Joe said, "The Vatican is not willing to issue an official opinion. It's naturally wary of verifying its authenticity and then be proven wrong. That would be devastating to the faithful. How could we then expect them to believe in the truth of any further Vatican decisions? No, the Vatican will wait until science can unequivocally prove it to be the true shroud or a fraud."

Sean said, "Science may be able to prove the age and the manufacturing point of the fabric, but how could it prove that it actually covered the body of Christ?'

"You are absolutely right, Sean, that's why it will probably always remain a matter of faith. But wouldn't it be wonderful if it were true?"

When the tour was finished, it was time to return to Rome and they arrived there just in time for dinner.

They had an after dinner drink and felt very relaxed after such an exciting day.

Sarah said to Joe, "I want to thank you so much for such a wonderful week, and, in particular, for today. It was fascinating to see the shroud that might belong to Jesus.

"My short experience with the two of you has made me realize that I have been missing something important in my life. I have spent so much time on my scientific studies that, since my Bat Mitzvah, I have almost completely ignored anything pertaining to religion.

"Let's face it, the scientific community seems to consist almost exclusively of atheists or agnostics, and the subject of religion rarely comes up for discussion.

"But, now, since we are discussing religion, I have a question that has been lurking in my mind for many years."

Joe said, "What question is that? Perhaps Sean and I can help answer it."

"Why did God create us? Your religion and mine teaches us that God is a perfect being and we are imperfect creatures. He didn't need us, did He?"

Joe replied, "No, He certainly did not need us. Yours is an excellent question, and one that philosophers have wrestled with for centuries.

"I look at it this way. We think of God as a perfect, and a loving pure spirit, and the creator of all things. We know that the essence of love is sharing. Since God had an overabundance of love, He decided to share it by creating other beings such as angels and men, who could experience this wondrous gift.

"Man was unique in that he was given a corporeal body and a spiritual soul, that part of him that is God's image. We could rightly call ourselves God's spirit children.

"Included in the gift of a soul, was an intellect and free will. Man could use these gifts to know God's magnificence, and to thank Him for sharing His love by loving Him in return. Like any good father, God promised a reward for such a child.

"On the other hand, man could use the gift of free will to reject God by sinning. A father would be expected to punish such ingratitude."

Sarah said, "I like that analogy. It makes a lot of sense to me."

Joe continued, "I have another interesting view on this subject. Aristotle, some three hundred years before Christ, wrestled with this same question. He noted the fact that everything, which existed in the world was contingent, that is, dependent on something else for its existence. From the contingent nature of everything in the world, he argued that there had to be a non-contingent or self-existent entity, a God, to account for those contingent things. In our philosophy, we call it the uncaused first cause argument for the existence of God.

"Aristotle reasoned that God could not love man. He had analyzed various types of love, and he concluded that the only true love was between beings that were similar and equally good. Therefore, God could only truly love another being, another entity, which was similar to God. He also concluded that God had to be perfect. However, the world was obviously imperfect, and so was man. This ruled out man as a being that God could love.

"Why would a perfect God make an imperfect world? Aristotle could not find a satisfactory explanation for this because he believed that ours is a static world, things didn't change. He, of course, did not know about the Big Bang theory and the theory of evolution."

Sarah interrupted, "So, what you're saying is that Aristotle believed that a self-existent and good God could only love another self-existent and good entity, in effect, another God. However, that's not logical. How could there be another God? God could not create another God. A created entity would not be self-existent and, therefore, not be perfect."

"You're absolutely right, so, we have a serious quandary. I belong to a school of thought that may offer a solution. It's based on the writings of the theologian, Teilhard de Chardin.

"Chardin believed that, from the moment of creation, 'a certain mass of elementary consciousness was originally imprisoned in the matter of the earth, a cosmic natural order of things.

"Teilhard explained this cosmic law as the trend toward complexity–consciousness', which stated that increasing complexity is accompanied by an increased consciousness. At some point in time, man will arrive at the ultimate stage of super complexity and super consciousness.

"While God could not create another God, He could initiate an evolutionary process in a being that could possibly lead to the self-creation of a somewhat similar entity. A process involving self-creation, resulting from super-consciousness, could lead to the emergence of an entity that was essentially both self-created and good.

"At this pinnacle of evolution, man's super-consciousness would lead him to be fully aware of the grandeur of God and His love for us and, consequently, be consumed with a corresponding love for Him.

"Man would then have fulfilled the greatest commandment: to love God with his whole heart, and to love his neighbor as himself. In other words, he would have become more god-like and, therefore, worthy of God's love and unity. Chardin termed this union of God and man as the Omega Point."

Sarah furrowed her eyebrows and replied, "That's an interesting explanation. I don't fully understand all of it. However, I think if I hang around you guys long enough, I'll get the equivalent of an advanced degree in Philosophy and Theology."

Joe and Sean laughed. Joe said, "I don't think that's such a bad idea."

Sean chimed in "I agree and I hope that you do hang around us for a long time. You seem to enjoy our company and we, obviously, enjoy yours."

"Thank you, sirs. Thanks for everything. It's been a long day and you have more than boggled my mind. I need time to unboggle it. I think it's time for Sean and me to leave. I have to get up early to pack and get to the airport."

Sean escorted Sarah to her hotel and entered her room. He took her in his arms and held her tightly. "This vacation was the very best time of my life. I feel so comfortable and happy when I'm with you. I wish it didn't have to end."

Sarah melted further into him and whispered, "I feel the same way." They remained silent for a while, reflecting on their emotions.

Sarah broke the silence by looking up to Sean and asking, "So, again, where do we go from here?"

"That's a good question. We probably won't be able to see each other for quite a while. I have a full travel schedule until my tour of duty is up in June.

"When I get back to New York, I want to get an MBA degree. You will probably be there to finish your PhD at Columbia. That's probably when we can get together again. I'll enroll there too.

"I guess we will get a chance to test the old adage that absence makes the heart grow fonder."

Sarah nodded her head. "I'm afraid you're right, darn it."

Sean said, "I don't like it any more than you do, but I don't see any alternative. All we can do is bide our time and see what the future has in store for us.

"I better leave now, before my emotions get the better of me. You have to pack and get a good night's rest. I'll pick you up in the morning and drive you to the airport."

Sarah gave him a long kiss before he left.

The following day, Sean and Joe, dressed in his clerical garb, drove her to the airport. At the gate, Sarah gave Sean one last passionate kiss, then turned to Joe and asked, "Is it OK to kiss a priest?"

Joe replied with a grin, "Yes, as long as you don't get into the habit".

"Huh?" replied Sarah.

Joe explained, "That was just a feeble attempt at religious humor."

"Oh, now I get it. That's funny, really funny." Then she made a big production of giving him a noisy, sloppy kiss on his cheeks. "Now, try to explain those lipstick marks to the pope."

They both laughed. "I can't tell you how much I enjoyed meeting you. Sean is lucky to have you as his friend. I hope you will consider me as a friend, too."

"Have no fear of that, Sarah. I look forward to seeing you again."

Sean said goodbye. They promised to write each other frequently.

As they watched Sarah's plane depart, Joe said to Sean, "I can see why you're so infatuated with her. She is a remarkable woman. She is not only intelligent and beautiful but, most important of all, she has a great sense of humor. You would be a fool not to marry her someday."

"Yeah, I know, Joe. We both have a few years to accomplish our goals. Any thought of marriage will have to sit on the back burner for a while. If we do wind up getting married, I want you to do the honors."

"That goes without saying, little brother."

Chapter 26

For the next five months, Sean was sent on a series of secret assignments away from Rome. One such trip took him to Moscow. He called Dmitri, who invited him to dinner at his home where Raisa greeted him warmly. They spent a number of hours catching up on their activities.

Dmitri told Sean that he was very pleased to be out of the military and back at the bank. "I think that I can be more valuable to my country in the financial field. There is so much potential to develop our economy after the disastrous effects of the war. Obviously, I don't have the freedom to do all the things that are allowed in your country, but I, and a few others, are working on trying to get some small changes made by our government.

"The communists are starting to realize that some compromises have to be made. It is a slow process, but we are beginning to see some progress. I wouldn't be surprised if my government eventually is forced to reach out to the west for more trade agreements and technological assistance. It would certainly help to thaw out our relations."

Sean said, "I hope you're right. If you are, then maybe you will have to visit America and we can see each other more often."

"That's a deal, Sean."

When the evening was over Sean bade goodbye to his friends.

Sean wrote to Sarah and told of his visit with Dmitri. He also apologized for the fact that he was not able to get back to Rome or England in order to see her. He told her that he was on an extended assignment to various Eastern countries.

A letter from Sarah eventually caught up with him, in late April, when he was in Saudi Arabia. She informed him that her studies in England were about to end and that she would be returning home shortly, to finish her pursuit of her PhD. "I changed my plans. I am not going to continue at Columbia. I decided to enroll at Harvard because my old friend, James Watson, recently joined the faculty there. Why don't you enroll there also? Harvard has one of the best MBA programs in the country. We could see each other all the time.

"Call me as soon as you can get back to the U.S. By the way, I recently had dinner with Lord Thornton and his wife. They are such a lovely couple and they both expressed their hope of seeing you soon again."

When his assignments were finished, Sean flew back to the CIA home office, in June, to meet with John McCooe.

"Well, Sean, your commitment to the service is almost finished. I'm sorry that you have decided not to re-up. You have done an outstanding job for me. Is there anything I can say to make you change your mind?"

"No, sir. It has been an invaluable experience. You were absolutely right when you told me that I could not have duplicated it in the corporate world. I am truly grateful to you for giving me that opportunity.

"You have been so good to me that I feel somewhat guilty by not staying on. However, I find the bureaucracy in government positions to be stifling. It's very frustrating. I guess I'm just too damned independent. I would like to have more leeway to think and act on my own initiative.

"Another important reason is the fact that I have met a wonderful woman, that I never would have met if I hadn't accepted your offer and been posted to Europe. I want more time to see her and get to know her better. So, I also owe you for that. The role of being an active field agent is not conducive to thoughts of marriage and raising a family."

"Well, Sean, I can't argue with you there. I'm sorry to lose you. You have exceeded my expectations and I want to express my appreciation for a job well done.

"What are your plans after you get out?"

"I want to get an MBA degree in international finance. I was accepted at Columbia where my girlfriend was supposed to be, but she changed her mind and enrolled at Harvard. When I tried to enroll there also, they informed me that I was too late.

"I see", said McCooe. He then picked up his phone and told his secretary to get the dean of the Harvard Business School on the line.

After a short pause he said, "Hello, Ben, Jack here. I wanted to tell you how much my wife and I enjoyed dinner at your house last week. Next time you're in the Washington area I insist you visit us. Good, we have a deal then.

"By the way, I have a favor to ask of you. I have a young Captain in my office by the name of Sean Gallagher. He will be leaving me shortly. For the last three years, he has been an outstanding officer. He graduated from Fordham with honors. He speaks eight or nine languages and has traveled extensively throughout Europe and the Middle East. He wants to attend your school but, apparently, his application was too late. He was turned down for this coming semester. Do you have any suggestions?"

McCooe listened for a few minutes, furrowed his brow and said, "I see. Great. Thanks a lot. Hope to see you soon. Bye."

McCooe looked at Sean and said, "You have just been accepted at Harvard. Forward your application to the Dean at the address I am going to give you. The Dean and I have been good friends for many years. You'll enjoy meeting him."

Sean shook his head and said, "That's amazing. I can hardly thank you enough for what you have done for me."

"Well, Sean, I once told you that we have extensive contacts in the civilian world. There may be some time in the future that I need your help and I hope that I can call on you to return the favor."

"That's only fair, sir. All you have to do is ask. I owe you."

Chapter 27

When Sean received his discharge, he went directly to Harvard. He finally rejoined Sarah and had an emotional reunion. The deep attraction for each other was still there.

He was fortunate to have found a small room above the garage of a private home, not far from the school. Sarah was sharing a nice apartment with a fellow classmate on the other side of town. Sean used his GI Bill to pay for his school expenses. He had saved enough money from his service time for his living expenses. He earned additional money by tutoring some of the graduate and undergraduate students in foreign languages. Life was good.

Their heavy workload at school kept them quite busy during the week but they managed to get together on weekends and holidays. There was much to do and see in the culture-rich Boston area. Their strong attraction to each other blossomed into a deep love.

Sarah worked so hard on her studies that she opted not to go home on school breaks. Her mother became so frustrated at her absence that she came up to Boston to visit for a few days in December. Sarah invited Sean to meet her mother over dinner one Saturday night.

Nancy Goldman was cordial and polite, but Sean sensed a certain aloofness on her part.

The following day, Sean asked Sarah, "Well, what's the verdict?"

"Mother told me that she thought you were a nice young man, and very handsome, but that there were a lot of Jewish boys studying medicine and law at Harvard and she was hoping that I would get involved with one of them."

Sean laughed. "I can understand your mother's position. My mother probably would have had a preference to see me with a nice Irish Catholic colleen. But, she would have respected whatever decision I made. Knowing her sense of humor, she would have called you Seanie's Jewish Rose."

It was Sarah's turn to laugh. "That's funny. I'm sorry that I never got the opportunity to meet you mother. I can see where you got your sense of humor.

"By the way, mother told me that both of my grandparents are going to celebrate their golden wedding anniversaries this coming June. It's just going to be the family at our summer cottage on Long Island. I'm inviting you. Will you come?"

"Of course. I look forward to meeting the relatives that you have talked so much about. They sound like very nice people."

"They are."

Chapter 28

On the appointed day, Sean drove from Boston to Southampton, Long Island, and checked into a local hotel. He called Sarah for directions to the cottage and proceeded to that address. He found the "cottage" to be a magnificent estate, right on the water. Sarah had been anxiously watching for him and ran outside to greet him.

Sean took hold of her extended hands and said, "You told me that this was your summer cottage. That's the understatement of the year. This is not what I would call a cottage. I'd call it a mansion. I had assumed from our past conversations that your family lived comfortably, but I never imagined that they lived this comfortably."

"Sean, I know what you're feeling. But I really didn't mislead you. Notice the U shape of the house? My parents actually co-own the house with both grandparents. We each use a separate wing. My father hates ostentation, so he prefers to call our wing 'the cottage'. It makes it feel homier to him. So, you see, I was telling you the truth when I used the term cottage.

"From what you told me when we first met, I gathered that your family didn't have much money. I didn't want to tell you everything about my family's financial status for fear you might be intimidated, or feel obligated to spend a lot of money on me in order to impress me. I didn't want that. I wanted you to accept me for who I am and not because of my family's wealth.

"When I got to know what kind of a guy you were, I knew my family's situation didn't mean a thing to you. But, I took the coward's way out and decided to let you find out about my family at a more opportune moment, such as now. Are you mad at me for that?"

"Oh, you know that I couldn't be mad at you for very long. I think I understand. I'm sure that you had attracted your fair share of gold diggers in the past. I appreciate your thoughtfulness in trying to protect my male ego. But what will your father think of me? After all, I don't even have the proverbial pot to piss in."

"Don't worry about him, it's my grandparents you really have to worry about. I'm their only grandchild. They're worse than my mother in thinking that a nice Jewish girl like me should only date and marry a nice Jewish doctor or lawyer and have a bunch of nice Jewish children they can spoil. Just use some of your Irish charm, or should I say, blarney, on them."

'I'll do me best, lassie," said Sean, affecting an Irish brogue as Sarah giggled.

Sarah introduced Sean to her father who welcomed him warmly. "Sarah reminded me that we met many years ago. You were that very polite little boy that fixed my flat tire and didn't want a tip."

"Yes, sir. I remember that I gave you that old reliable Good Samaritan story."

Sarah smiled and interjected, "That, dad, was what I now know as Irish blarney."

Sean laughed, "She's right, sir."

Mr. Goldman also smiled. "Well, it sure worked. I was very impressed with your ability to act so innocent and sincere. You showed great poise and initiative for one so young. Welcome to our home. Let me introduce you to our guests of honor."

He met the grandparents, Saul and Ruth Goldman, and Isaac and Molly Silverman. As expected, they were polite but somewhat reserved in their greetings.

After the family introductions, someone stepped behind Sean and softly started to sing, "Oh Danny's boy, the pipes, the pipes are calling."

Startled, Sean turned around and stared into the face of Rabbi Kattler!

The two men embraced warmly. The Rabbi greeted him in Hebrew, "Sean, it's so good to see you again after all these years. How have you been?"

"I've been great", answered Sean, also in Hebrew. "You look great, too. You're the last person in the world I expected to see here."

"I am more surprised than you are," replied the Rabbi. "I'm an old friend of the celebrants and their families. The two men were very generous benefactors of the HOA. Saul was also a trustee. They asked me here to celebrate their anniversaries and offer a blessing. What in the world are you doing here?"

"Sarah invited me. We met in London about a year ago, when I was on active duty with the Air Force. Now, we are both attending Harvard University and we have continued seeing each other. This is the first opportunity I've had to meet the whole family."

At this point, Sarah tugged at Sean's sleeve and inquired, in English, "How come you know Rabbi Kattler and, more importantly, why didn't you ever tell me you spoke Hebrew?"

Sean started to stutter a reply when Rabbi Kattler interrupted, and said to Sarah and the family, "Please let me explain my relationship with Sean. I'm afraid he would be much too modest if I let him tell the story."

Kattler proceeded to tell them how Sean's father had sacrificed his own life for him. He recounted the fact that Sean's mother came to work for him at the HOA as his assistant, and that Sean practically grew up with the resident orphans. "Although Sean was an only child, he always felt that he had six hundred brothers and sisters. He attended our on-campus public school and received very high marks. He also attended my Hebrew classes and became one of my best students. Visitors were always surprised when they saw this blonde-haired, blue-eyed Irish kid win some of the prizes in reading and writing Hebrew. When the HOA closed in 1941, the Alumni Association voted him in as an honorary member.

"He was exposed to so many languages during his ten years at the Orphanage, and in schools, that he became multilingual. I've lost count of how many languages he speaks. He has a fantastic God given talent in this area.

"I last saw Sean a few years ago, after his mother died. I attended her funeral. We have not seen each other since because I

The Almega Project

went to Israel to teach, and Sean was traveling in Europe with the Air Force.

"We write to each other once or twice a year. As you know, I returned to America just a few weeks ago and I hadn't yet gotten around to getting in touch with him.

"I'm honored to call him my friend. Sarah, you are a very lucky woman to know this young man."

Sarah, who had been looking daggers at Sean, said, "You're right, Rabbi. Thanks for telling us the whole story. It seems that Sean left out a few pertinent details when he was telling me how he grew up." Speaking under her breath, she whispered in Sean's ear, "Wait until I get you alone, I'm going to kill you."

However, Sarah didn't get the chance for murder that evening. Her parents and grandparents monopolized all of his time. They conversed with him, alternating between English, Yiddish, Hebrew and Russian.

"Tell me, Sean," said Grandfather Goldman, "Was your mother the one who baked the Irish soda bread for the trustees?"

"Why, yes, she was. Sarah told me that you were one of the trustees and that you frequently brought some back home with you."

"Ah, yes, indeed", he said, laughing. "Rabbi Kattler started that practice. He used it as outright bribery to get some us to attend the Sunday meetings more regularly and it worked marvelously well. The bread was delicious and Sarah, in particular, looked forward to it. I think she became addicted to it.

"I remember meeting your mother, once. As I recall, she was a beautiful, red haired woman."

"That she was," said Sean", and I still miss her."

After the meal, Sean spotted a piano in the living room. He sat down and started playing. He sang a few songs in Russian. Next came some songs in Hebrew. Rabbi Kattler whispered something in Sean's ear and he started to play Danny Boy, which the rabbi sung. After this extemporaneous performance, the family stood up and applauded. They surrounded Sean and the rabbi and hugged both of them.

Eventually, it was time to go. Sean thanked the parents for their hospitality, bade farewell to her grandparents and Rabbi Kattler. As he gave Sarah a goodbye kiss on her cheek, she whispered in his ear, "You and I are going to have a long talk tomorrow. Call me from your hotel in the morning."

Chapter 29

Sean called Sarah the following day and invited her to meet him at his hotel at noon.

When she arrived, she said, "I sat up all night thinking of all the nasty things I was going to say to you today. I wanted you to know how violated and exposed I felt when I learned that you knew Hebrew. You heard some of the most intimate conversations with my mother when I was telling her about you and our relationship. That wasn't right, Sean. That just wasn't fair."

She started to sob. Sean put his arms around her and held her tightly. He realized that he should allow her to vent her emotions before he said anything.

When she appeared to relax somewhat, he said, softly, "Sarah, you're right and I apologize. It's just that I had never met a girl like you before. We come from different faiths and backgrounds and, in the beginning, I wasn't sure where we were heading. When I overheard your early conversations with your mother, I realized that you felt about me the same way I felt about you. It gave me the confidence to continue pursuing you. I don't think you can accuse me of taking advantage of you because of this."

"No, I can't. Other guys might have, but not you. When I went to bed last night, I was so emotional and mad at you that, for a crazy, fleeting moment, I thought about breaking up our relationship. However, reason quickly returned. It's a good thing it did, because, otherwise, my parents and grandparents would probably never talk to me again. Your Irish charm, and the Rabbi's endorsement, made them fall in love with you, just as I have.

"My grandparents rationalized, as only Jews can, that since you were an honorary alumnus of the Hebrew Orphan Asylum, you automatically became an honorary Jew as well, and, therefore, not a real goy."

Sean laughed, and Sarah joined him. "Sean, I could never stay mad at you. I love you too much."

"Sarah, I love you, too, with every fiber of my being." He then lifted her chin and kissed her gently for a very long time. When he came up for air, he asked, "Sarah, let's not postpone the inevitable, will you make me and everybody happy by becoming formally engaged to marry me?"

"Oh, Sean, I never expected you to ask me that question today. For one of the few times in my life I'm almost speechless. Almost, but not quite. Yes, of course I will."

"Good. I hadn't planned on asking you today, but now the time seems to be right, since it appears that your whole family accepts me.

"I hope you agree with me that we shouldn't get married until we finish our degrees, and that's almost a year away. Then, I have to find a job. Is that all right with you?"

"Oh, my darling," she purred", I've waited this long, I can wait a little longer. Think how much fun we can have planning our future together. My mother is going to die when I tell her the news. She was afraid that I was on my way to becoming a spinster and, as you undoubtedly know, that's the worst thing a Jewish girl can do."

Sean smiled and said, "I can think of worse things. Now, there are a few important issues we should discuss.

Sarah nodded, "Right, where do you want to start?"

Sean replied, "Well, first off, how to be married?"

"Sean, I know how seriously you take your religion and I assume you would want to be married by a priest. As you know, my parents and I do not practice our religion as seriously, so I have no problem with that. However, I do have a question."

"And that is?"

"Would I have to convert?"

"No, but you would have to agree that our children be raised as Catholics. But, I would make sure that they are aware of and study their Jewish heritage."

"Again, that's not a problem for me."

Sean continued, "I am going to suggest something that would hopefully make your family happy. Let's have a small double ceremony, here, at your summer home. Let's ask Rabbi Kattler to marry us in a Jewish ceremony and have Joe marry us in a simple Catholic ceremony."

"Can you do that?"

"Yes. It's not very common but I'm sure that Joe can get the necessary dispensations for doing it. I know that in your religion, being a Jew is based on a matrilineal basis. If your mother is a Jew, you are a Jew. Your parents and grandparents can rightfully think they will have the Jewish grandchildren and great-grandchildren that you told me they want so badly."

She threw herself into his arms, kissed him, and said, "Oh, Sean, what a wonderful idea. You're such a sensitive soul and that's one of the many reasons why I love you so much."

"There's one more thing, Sarah. I want you to have an engagement ring but since I hadn't planned on asking you today, I don't have one.

"Hey, wait a minute. I just had a thought. The only mementos of my parents that I kept were their wedding and engagement rings. I always carried them in my travel bag. They helped me feel connected to them and less lonely when I had to travel so extensively to all those foreign countries. Would you be offended if I temporarily gave you my mother's engagement ring until such time as I can afford to pick out one that is more appropriate?"

"Of course not."

Sean went over to his garment bag and come up with his mother's engagement ring. He slipped it on her finger. It fit perfectly. The tiny diamond was almost lost in the golden band.

Sarah held it up and said, "Oh, Sean, I'd be honored to wear it. I know how much love is imbedded in this. But, I do have one favor to ask of you."

'Whatever it is, you've got it."

"As you know, both my grandparents are in the jewelry business. I'm their only grandchild. They told me a long time ago that, if I ever got married, they wanted to make me a gift of the engagement and wedding rings. I don't have the heart to turn them down completely. What if I let them provide us with the engagement ring and we use your parents' wedding rings? That way, maybe we will all be happy."

Smiling, Sean replied, "That's a solution worthy of King Solomon. Look, if it will promote family harmony, let's do it your way, but, with one proviso. I insist on paying for any ring they offer. An engagement ring is the symbol of my love for you. The essence of love is sharing things of value and a gift doesn't have the same value to me as something for which I have worked and sacrificed.

"You know my thinking. I'll trust you to work out the details. Why don't you pick out one you like and then I'll go with you and pick it up."

"I understand your feeling, Sean. I think I can work it out. The important thing is that we'll be married regardless of what rings we wear.

"By the way, my father and mother happen to be descendants of the House of David, whose father, as you probably know, was King Solomon. So, I come by my gift naturally. My parents are quite proud of that fact.

"Oh, Sean, I'm so excited. Can I call my mother right now?"

"Of course, go right ahead. Just remember, this time, you can talk to her in English."

Sarah picked up a pillow and threw it at him as they both broke up laughing.

When Sarah returned home, her mother immediately started to talk about planning the engagement announcement, the wedding, etc. She wanted to have elaborate parties and a large wedding reception, just as her friends had done in the past. "It's payback time", she had thought to herself.

She was almost heartbroken when Sarah said the marriage would take place after they graduated and she requested a small, intimate affair at home, with just the immediate family.

"Why can't we have a nice big reception at a fancy hotel like our friends the Millers, the Cohens and the Rosenblatts?"

"Mother", interrupted Sarah, "Look at it this way. Sean has no immediate family and just a few close friends. Almost all of the people you would invite would be your friends and Dad's business acquaintances. I don't think that would be right. Besides, Sean and I aren't trying to impress anybody. We have different values in life. I really would feel much more comfortable if you would indulge me on this.

"Sean said that he would rather see you take the money you would spend on an elaborate wedding and donate it to your favorite charity, and I agree with him."

Her mother screwed up her face and said, begrudgingly, "Oh, damn. I'm so disappointed. But, I'm not going to be a spoilsport and get off on the wrong foot with you and Sean. To tell you the truth, your father will probably be glad to hear this. He hates elaborate parties, too."

The following day, Sarah visited her grandparents at their jewelry office. She explained in detail to them what she wanted.

"All right Sarah, we will do as you ask."

Two days later, she took Sean back there. The grandparents excitedly took a ring from a small box and put it on Sarah's finger for her approval. They had taken the gold band of Sean's mother's ring as the basis for building a totally new design. In the middle, they had mounted a flawless four carat emerald-cut diamond and surrounded it with four small diamonds, one of which came from the original setting.

Sarah held her hand up and exclaimed, "My god, it's gorgeous."

Sean was equally impressed. "Is that what you want?"

"Oh, I love it. It is even more beautiful than I had pictured."

She paused and looked at Sean asking, "But, do you like it?"

"It's the most beautiful ring I have ever seen. I am in awe of the way they have transformed my mother's ring. How could I not like it?"

Looking at her beaming grandparents, she said, "We both love it, we'll take it."

Sean interrupted, "Wait a minute. I told Sarah that I insisted on paying for it and I won't leave with it until we come to some kind of arrangement."

Mr. Goldman replied, "Sarah told us about your conditions. Believe me, we have no intention of letting you leave with that ring until we have extracted a righteous payment. We know you can't afford to pay for the whole thing now, so we have agreed to offer it to you on an installment plan. We insist on you giving us one dollar now, the balance to be paid after you are married and settle down."

Sean was quite surprised. "That's more than reasonable. What is the final payment to be?"

The two men smiled, having anticipated this question, and they simultaneously said, "Great grandchildren."

He looked at Sarah, who had a big smirk on her face.

"Well, you did say that you left the details to me."

Sean shook his head and smiled. "I've been had. Once again you've proven to be a true descendant of Solomon."

He looked at the other two conspirators and said, "If my final payment is to provide great grandchildren, then all I can say is, it will be my pleasure."

"And mine too", said a giggling Sarah.

Everybody laughed. They wound up crying and hugging each other. Sean was so happy that he was so warmly embraced as a new member of the family.

During a subsequent trip to visit her parents, Sarah's father took Sean aside and said, "When you graduate, I would like you to work for my firm, JP Morgan."

Sean hesitated in replying, but then he said, "I appreciate your offer. It's very kind of you. I don't want to offend you but I don't think I can accept. You see, I don't approve of nepotism."

Mr. Goldman pursed his lips, nodded his head a few times and said, "I admire your independence, Sean. You kind of remind me of myself when I was about your age. I didn't want to go into the family business for much the same reason. But, believe me, this is not a typical case of nepotism. You could never be the proverbial schnook son-in-law. You are a uniquely qualified individual. You speak so many languages, and you have three years of military and diplomatic experience. You have traveled extensively throughout Europe where we have offices. You have a personal relationship with Lord Thornton's bank and with an important Russian bank

The Almega Project

and you will graduate with a prestigious Harvard MBA in international finance.

"As you know, I graduated from Harvard with an MBA degree. The current dean and I were classmates. I inquired about you and he gave me a glowing report. I also talked to the head of our college recruitment team and they gave me a list of five members of your graduating class that they intend to recruit. Your name was number one on their list. They plan on a full court press. They, of course, have no knowledge of your relationship with our family.

"Next year, you will be the most heavily recruited graduate in your class. The only problem you'll have when you get out of school will be to choose what company will be lucky enough to grab you, and how much you can get them to pay you. My company needs people like you. I know from your track record that you have the intelligence and ambition to succeed in anything you do. I'd like you to succeed with my firm rather than face you as one of my competitors. I know Lord Thornton has his eye on you and will undoubtedly make you an offer to join his bank. Am I right?"

"Yes, he has broached the subject with me."

"To put your mind at ease, you would not be working directly for me. You would start in a probationary training program with all the other new recruits, rotating throughout various departments. Each department head will write an appraisal on you. At the end of the trial period, the department heads will sit down together and discuss whether or not you will continue with the firm. I will not be involved in that process."

Sean thought for a long moment and then answered, "O. K. That makes sense. I'll do it on one condition, Mr. Goldman. If I don't perform better than any of your other recruits during the training program, I want you to let me know so that I can resign. I don't ever want to embarrass you and I don't want you to be accused of favoritism. I want to succeed on my own merits."

"You have my word on that, Sean."

Mr. Goldman was right. Sean was the most heavily recruited student at school. He listened to all the offers and was amazed at the starting salaries thrown at him. If he hesitated for any length of time, the recruiters upped the ante. He contacted Mr. Goldman and told him of his experience. When asked, Sean told him what the highest salary he was offered. David said, "We will beat that offer by a healthy amount."

Sean responded, "That's very generous but I wouldn't be comfortable with that. Everyone would eventually find out and deem that to be blatant nepotism."

"I see your point. Would you feel comfortable if we just matched it?"

"Yes".

"Very good, I'll tell our people to make the necessary arrangements."

A few days later, Sean called Uncle Jim and told him of his engagement to Sarah and that he had accepted the offer from JP Morgan.

Thornton said, "Congratulations. She is a remarkable woman. I wish that you could have joined my firm but I understand your position. I probably would have made the same decision if I were in your place.

"I want you to know that I wish to continue our personal relationship and I insist that you and Sarah visit me In London after you get married. After all, you two are my favorite surrogate niece and nephew."

Sean laughed and said, "Thanks, Uncle Jim. I promise that we will visit you as soon as we can, after our marriage.

The wedding took place at the Goldman's Southampton home in June, shortly after graduation. After Father Joe performed the simple Catholic rites, Rabbi Kattler followed with the more colorful Jewish ceremony. John McCooe acted as best man.

The couple spent their honeymoon in the Cayman Islands on one of Lord Thornton's estates. It was his wedding gift to them. In this paradise-like setting, they relaxed and enjoyed the intimacy that they both had longed for. The two truly became one flesh. Nowhere on earth, they felt, could there be a happier couple and they pledged to remain that way for the rest of their lives.

Lord Thornton maintained a branch of his bank on the island. He charged its manager with the responsibility of seeing that their stay was a comfortable one. He proved to be a gracious host. He gave Sean an extensive tour of the bank and explained the fact that the Cayman Islands banking laws guaranteed the secrecy of its banking customers via numbered accounts and other devices. Many of the wealthiest people in North and South America maintained healthy deposits there, safe from the prying eyes of governments and courts. In this respect, it was a worthy competitor of the famed Swiss banks. Sean was impressed.

Sarah's parents wanted to buy them a house on Long Island as a wedding present, but Sean, with Sarah's consent, turned down the offer. He insisted on paying his own way. The couple rented a small apartment in Greenwich Village, which was a convenient commute to both of their workplaces. Sarah became a researcher at her alma mater, Columbia University. Sean's office was on nearby Wall Street.

When Sean joined J P Morgan, he entered their one-year training program, spending time in the various departments. He learned quickly, worked harder than anyone else and impressed everyone he met. After the mandatory program ended, he received the highest appraisal ratings possible. All the department heads wanted him to work for them. As a result, Sean was given the unique opportunity to choose where he wanted to start. He chose foreign operations and specifically requested Rome. To no one's surprise, he got his request. Obviously, he had strong personal contacts in the area, but Rome would also give Sarah the opportunity to meet, and work with some of Europe's leading scientists in the field of genetics.

They bade a tearful farewell to her parents and flew to Rome.

Chapter 30

Sean and Sarah settled down in a Rome apartment that Joe found for them. It was only a few blocks from his place. This meant that they could easily see each other on a regular basis.

Over their first dinner, Joe told them he had completed his doctorate in theology and was now working at the Vatican. "I am very excited to be on the inside of such a unique global institution. I am grateful for the chance to be able to make a meaningful contribution to the Church."

Sean replied, "I know how you feel. I feel the same way about my new job."

Sarah raised her wine glass and chimed in, "I'm so happy for the two of you and I would like to propose a toast that I was told to be an old Irish one, 'May the hinges of our friendship never grow rusty'."

Joe said, "Hear, hear. I think it would be appropriate to oil those hinges right now." He then raised his wine glass and drained it. Sean and Sarah followed suit.

Jason Roth, a twenty-year veteran with the firm, headed the JP Morgan office. He greeted Sean, saying, "Welcome aboard, Sean. I've read your resume and it is quite impressive. I can really use someone with such a command of so many languages. You should fit in here quite nicely."

"Thanks, Mr. Roth. I'll try my best not to disappoint you. As you know, I lived in Rome for a few years. I love this City and I am glad to be back and to be able to see some old friends."

"Great. For the next few months, you will be my assistant. I will take you with me everywhere I go. You will get a chance to meet all our clients and see how we operate. Some of my clients don't speak English very well. I have a good command of Italian but I have a limited knowledge of some of the other European languages. You will be of great help to me in that respect.

"When I think you've gained enough experience, I'll assign you to a more specific job. How does that sound?"

"That sounds like a great way to start, Mr. Roth. I'm really looking forward to it."

Sarah found a position at the University of Rome, the largest university in Europe. It had been in existence for over seven hundred years. She taught one class in biology and, the rest of the time, she conducted research in the field of genetics. Europe was a leader in this area and she had a chance to meet a number of prominent scientists during the many conferences she had to attend in various countries. It would prove to be a learning experience that could not be duplicated in the United States.

Sean spent the first month becoming familiar with the office routine. Roth spent a good deal of time mentoring him as they visited some local accounts. Sean was a quick study. Roth was impressed.

When told that Roth had scheduled a trip to London, Sean phoned Uncle Jim and arranged to have dinner one evening.

After their first day in London, Sean approached Roth and said, "I have a good friend here whom I haven't seen in a few years. I would like to meet him tomorrow evening for dinner. Would you mind?"

"Of course not. I've been here a number of times and I know how to amuse myself for one evening.

Sean met Uncle Jim at his club and they warmly embraced. During dinner, they talked about their experiences since last they met.

After the pleasantries concluded, Thornton said, "Sean, I have something your bank might be interested in. A client of mine is one of the world's foremost oil drilling and engineering companies. They have been negotiating with the Russian government to drill wells in the Ukraine and other parts of the Soviet Union. They will need a good deal of financing but it's more than I am comfortable handling by myself. I would like to have a participating banking partner if the deal goes through. I thought that your bank might be interested."

Sean replied, "I'm sure that they would love to have the opportunity to evaluate it."

"If they are interested, I thought that you could contact your friend Dmitri Ivanovich in Moscow and arrange a meeting with myself and your bank. Dmitri and his father know everything of importance that goes on in their country. I would value their opinion on the project before I decide to proceed.

"How does that sound?"

"Uncle Jim, that sounds like a wonderful opportunity for my firm. Let me see my boss first thing in the morning and run it by him, then I'll get back to you."

The following morning, Sean had breakfast with Jason. Sean outlined explained his relationship with Lord Thornton and the offer to pursue a banking relationship.

Roth was fascinated by it and said, "That sounds like a wonderful opportunity. I've been calling on Lord Thornton for years, but haven't been able to get to first base on any collaboration. I'm anxious to see him.

Sean arranged a meeting with Lord Thornton the following morning.

"It's very nice to see you again Mr. Roth."

"The pleasure is all mine, Lord Thornton."

Thornton said, "I'm sure my adopted nephew has told you that I insist he call me Uncle Jim. Like you Americans, I hate formality. Would it be all right if I call you Jason and if you call me Jim? I hope that we will become good friends."

Roth smiled and replied, "That would be great. I appreciate the opportunity to discuss the business proposition you outlined to Sean. It appears to be just the type of thing we would be interested in. Tell me more about it."

They spent the next few hours going over the business proposal. At the conclusion, Jason said, "Jim, this looks like an excellent opportunity. Because of the size of the investment, I will have to get the approval of our Board of Directors at our headquarters in New York to pursue it further. I like the idea that Sean has a close tie to Dmitri Ivanovich and can get an appointment with him. He and his father are two of the few Russians that have credibility with the West. If Dmitri says that it's a good deal, then I'm sure that we will want in.

"I can't tell you how grateful I am to you for giving us this opportunity."

They shook hands while Thornton said, "You're quite welcome, Jason. I have always admired your firm for its business practices and I hope that this may be the start of an ongoing relationship."

As he shook hands with Sean, he said, "Now that you and Sarah are once again so close by, my wife and I would love to have you two spend a weekend with us in the near future. Could you please arrange it?"

"Of course. I promise you that we will get together soon. Sarah told me she is anxious to see you both again."

Back at the hotel, Jason wasted no time in writing up a formal proposal for the Board of Directors. Rather than trust it to the mail, he decided to fly back to New York and present it personally to the Board.

The Board examined the proposal very carefully. They had always held the Thornton Bank in high esteem and were pleased that they had their first opportunity to participate in such a large project. They authorized Jason and Sean to go to Moscow and return with an evaluation of the deal.

When the Board meeting was over, Jason met with David Goldman, and said, "Dave, I can't tell you how impressed I am with Sean. He was just responsible for delivering to us a potentially huge deal with the Russians. He is the hardest worker I have ever seen and he is so modest and unassuming. Your daughter is a very lucky woman and you are a very lucky father-in- law."

"Jason, you don't know how happy I am to hear you say that. I think he has a great future here."

"I agree. I'm going to be extra nice to him, because I have a feeling that we both will be working for him someday."

They both laughed.

Chapter 31

Sean Called Dmitri in Moscow and gave him a brief outline of the business proposal that the Russian government offered to the British firm to build oil wells in Soviet Union countries.

"Dmitri, I would appreciate it very much if Lord Thornton, my boss, and myself could meet with you soon to discuss this situation. In the past, Russia has not allowed western firms to do much work in their territory. We have some major concerns in proceeding on this deal and we would value your opinion."

"Sean, I would be glad to see you again, on one condition."

"What is that, Dmitri?"

"You must bring Sarah, or there's no deal."

Sean laughed and said, "Consider it done. I know your wife and she have been carrying on a good deal of letter writing over the past few years. She keeps asking me when she will be able to see you two again. She will be thrilled."

Good, now let me give you some dates when we can meet."

On the agreed upon date, Lord Thornton, Jason, Sean and Sarah flew to Moscow. While the men met with Dmitri, Sarah spent her time with Dmitri's wife, Raisa, and their children.

Dmitri told them that he had investigated the oil drilling proposal and found it to be legitimate. As a matter of fact, his father had instigated the whole thing. Russia was well behind the west in the technology of oil exploration and drilling, and was forced to extend its hand to the west for help. They desperately needed the revenue from oil to expand their economy and enhance their role as a major world player. Russia had too much to lose if it didn't play fair and square. When his father learned of the Thornton and Morgan banks potential involvement in the project, he arranged for Dmitri's bank to handle the financial details on Russia's end.

Dmitri said, "As you know, my father and I are not members of the Communist party. I am hoping that my country will become a democracy sometime in the future. Cooperation with western democracies in a project such as this could be a small step in that direction. I would like this partnership to be a model to the rest of the world to show that the Soviet Union can be a legitimate business partner with western companies. I will do everything in my power to ensure that this happens."

Lord Thornton said, "I couldn't have asked for a stronger endorsement."

Jason said, "Neither could I. I think that by working together we can make this happen for the mutual benefit of our companies and our countries."

That evening, Dmitri entertained his guests at an elaborate dinner and introduced them to his parents. The evening was a rousing success. A good deal of Vodka was consumed and a strong friendship was developed among them.

At the end of their stay, the travelers were given a warm sendoff at the airport by Dmitri and Raisa.

The deal was ratified by the JP Morgan Board of Directors and by Lord Thornton's bank.

The British company started on the project. After one year, everything was going more smoothly than anyone had anticipated. Dmitri was true to his word. Both sides were quite satisfied.

The Saudi Arabian government had followed the Russian project closely and was impressed by its success. They eventually approached Lord Thornton's bank to ask its assistance in putting together and financing a similar project in their country. Thornton was quite interested and asked Sean if JP Morgan would once again want to participate. The answer was an enthusiastic yes. Since Sean had travelled there and had a command of Arabic, he became an integral part of the negotiations. A deal was struck and the drilling was started. It turned out to be an extremely lucrative and long term relationship.

Sean's star was secure in the firmament.

Chapter 32

Fr. Joe had been out of the country when the Russian and Saudi transactions were taking place. He had been in Israel, teaching theology and doing research. When he returned to Rome he had dinner with his friends and heard all about the two oil projects. He said, "I'm so glad to hear that. It must be a feather in your cap, Sean. Your boss must be well pleased."

"Yes he is, Joe. I was so excited to be a catalyst in these projects. I'll never be able to thank Uncle Jim for giving me these opportunities."

"Speaking of opportunity, Sean, I may have another one for you."

"Really? What is it?"

"Yesterday, I was talking to an old friend, Msgr. Fellini. He recently took over as head of the Institute for Religious Works, more commonly referred to as the Vatican Bank. It seems that, in the past, the bank has only been investing in, and dealing with, Italian banks and companies. Their performance has not been very impressive. He believes strongly that he needs to diversify his portfolio. He also thinks that there is some hanky-panky going on with some Mafia affiliates. He is looking for other financial institutions to work with. How would you like to meet him?"

"You won't have to ask me twice. I'd love to meet him, just set it up. What kind of guy is he?"

"Well, he's kind of crusty. He's very intelligent and works hard. He has some experience in the financial field but is not yet really comfortable in this new job. However, he is a quick study.

"Needless to say, he has had a lot of people knocking on his door. At this stage, he's suspicious of everything and everybody. He doesn't speak English very well, so I think you should conduct your conversation with him in Italian. That should impress him."

"Do you want me to really impress him?"

"Certainly, but what are you thinking of?"

"Suppose we conduct the meeting in Latin?"

"Oh, my God. That would really blow his mind. What a great idea."

When Sean was introduced to Msgr. Fellini, he spoke to him in Latin saying, "I'm honored to meet you Monsignor."

The priest was surprised. "You speak Latin, Mr. Gallagher?"

"Yes. Father Joe and I grew up together. We were almost like brothers. He taught me Italian and he and I learned some Latin as altar boys. The Jesuit fathers also taught it to us for four years in high school and conducted some of our classes in Latin. I thought that as long as I was in the Vatican, it might be appropriate to use its official language."

"Young man, I'm impressed. You are the first American businessman that has ever been able to do that with me.

"Father Morelli has told me about his close association with you and has vouched for your character. I am well aware of your firm, JP Morgan. It has an excellent reputation. I would feel very comfortable in having a business relationship with you. Let me explain what I have in mind."

Msgr. Fellini essentially said the same thing that Joe had explained. He wanted to diversify his holdings on a global basis. The bank would set aside a certain percentage of its assets for this purpose. He asked Sean to prepare a proposal for his consideration. Sean, of course, agreed.

When he returned to his office, he met with Jason and told him about the meeting. "Msgr. Fellini would like to have a proposal. Are we interested?"

"Are you kidding me, Sean? Any bank would give their eyeteeth to have the prestige of being associated with the Vatican Bank. I'll get on it right away. Correct that, I mean you will get on it right away. I want you to be the lead man. I want you, personally, to make the presentation."

"Thanks, Jason, I appreciate the opportunity."

When they had put the final touches on their proposal, Joe set up the appointment with Msgr. Fellini.

Prior to the meeting, Sean told Jason that he would be doing the presentation in Latin.

"Latin? You've got to be kidding. You actually speak that dead language?"

"Well, Jason, it hasn't yet died in the Vatican, they have been using it for close to two thousand years. Msgr. Fellini told Joe he was bowled over that I could speak it fluently."

Jason muttered, "Well, I'll be damned."

The presentation went very well. Msgr. Fellini was impressed with Sean's proposal and arranged to sign an agreement with JP Morgan.

That evening, Jason treated Sean and Father Joe to dinner in one of Rome's finest restaurants. He lifted his wine glass for a toast, "Sean, here's to a job well done, my heartfelt congratulations."

"Thank you, but it couldn't have happened without Fr. Joe. I propose a toast of thanks to him."

With that, they clinked their glasses and took a deep sip of wine. They managed to consume two very fine bottles over the course of the meal and followed that with some large brandy snifters.

Jason, by then, was in a mellow and philosophical mood. "When I tell some of our associates in the home office what you did, Sean, they will probably say 'For such a young guy, he is really lucky.' Then, I will say to them that I define luck as that which happens when preparation meets opportunity and Sean Gallagher is the most prepared person I have ever met. And, he is not afraid of seizing opportunity by the throat and dragging it off with him. I wish our company had ten more like him."

Sean smiled. "That was very kind of you to say that, Jason, but you're embarrassing me. The good Lord was kind enough to give me certain talents and I try to use them to the best of my abilities and to the advantage of my family and friends. Now, everybody, I think it's time to go home before we all get too maudlin."

Sean was obviously regarded as a rising star by the home office. Over time, the company rewarded him well with hefty salary increases and bonuses. He repeatedly turned down offers to return to New York for promotions. Sarah and he were very happy to remain in Rome, for the time being. Sarah was getting the opportunity to meet and work with Europe's most outstanding genetic scientists. She published a number of scientific papers and was gaining an international reputation.

Jason Roth, on the other hand, did eventually accept an offer of a very nice senior vice presidential promotion in New York. The year was 1961. He called Sean into his office and said, "Sean, this particular promotion would never have happened, except for you. You really put this office on the map and I want to tell you how much I appreciate what you have done.

"I have a surprise for you. I hope you like it. I made a recommendation to the home office that you be named my successor. That is, if you'll accept it."

Sean shook his head in surprise. "Wow! I don't understand. There are a lot of people with more seniority and experience in the company. I think I'm too young. Why wouldn't they choose one of them?"

"Sean, your age is not a factor. You have proven that no one is more suited for this job. You know everything and everybody you need to know. You were born for this job. Everybody in headquarters knows about you. This is just the first giant step up the corporate ladder. Your future in the company is unlimited.

"I once told your father-in-law that we all should be extra nice to you because we will probably wind up working for you. He agreed."

Sean laughed. "Those are very kind words. If you feel that way, then I feel obligated to accept. Thanks."

Sean was given the title of a vice-president and relished the extra freedom he had. The office continued to flourish.

Chapter 33

During Christmas dinner with Joe, in 1963, Sean asked him, "Now that the Second Vatican Council has begun, what can you tell us about it?"

"Well, as you know, Pope John XXIII called this council for the purpose of updating and renewing the Church. There will be three sessions over the next few years. It's an ambitious project. There are over 2,500 bishops and other participants attending these meetings. I'm really excited about it. We theologians believe that we have many recommendations that can change and renew the Church.

Sarah said, "Joe, one thing about your church that has always bothered me is its reluctance to change even the smallest of things. Why is that?"

"The primary reason is that Church officials strongly believe in tradition. They argue that Christ promised us that the Holy Spirit would always be with His Church. That means that the Holy Spirit has personally been guiding its growth and development for over 2000 years of its history. No other man-made institution comes close to that time span. They feel, therefore, that the structures and practices of the church are not merely the product of chance or human intervention and, therefore, should not be changed.

"They are very reluctant to accept the idea that the Holy Spirit may be calling them to realize that the uncovering of new information may require a new approach to the interpretation of Scripture and tradition. This mindset creates a stifling environment over almost everybody in the Vatican and, in particular, younger theologians such as me.

"A contributing factor is the secular Italian environment and the custom known as 'bella figura', which, as you well know, means beautiful figure. To Italians it means that it is very important to maintain a good outward appearance at all costs.

That's one of the reasons why Italy has become a leading center of the fashion industry in men's and women's clothing and accessories as well as automobiles.

Sarah said, "I know what you're saying. When I look at the outside appearance of the typical city home in Italy, it invariably looks good. The Italians spend a good deal of money and effort primping up the outside even though they may have hardly any furniture inside. The plumbing and electricity may not even work. They make every effort to make sure that no matter what happens, they must keep up appearances. This is such a superficial vanity".

Joe agreed. "This attitude has become so ingrained in the psyche of Italian society that it easily becomes an excuse for not confronting inner rot as long as the surface looks good.

"It's one of the main reasons why church officials tend to sweep under the rug such problems as sexual misconduct, financial discrepancies and so on. They don't want to scandalize the laity by airing their dirty laundry in public. A good appearance often becomes more important than justice.

"However, the biggest problem, in my opinion, is the Curia."

Sarah interjected, "Exactly what is the Curia?"

"It's similar to the president's Cabinet in our country. Its members form the administrative apparatus of the Church. The major problem is the way they assign managers to oversee the various departments. Very often there is little relationship between the work performed by a given department and the qualifications of the person selected to lead it. Traditionally, churchmen have been assigned Vatican jobs not so much on the basis of their training or professional expertise, but on the basis of their loyalty, their ecclesiastical pedigree, and the compatibility of their vision with that of the pope or other top officials. Subordinates are not judged as much for their competence or expertise as they are for their loyalty to the pope or their Curia boss. There is a good deal of cronyism going on. This leads to bad decisions.

"Like bureaucrats the world over, they fear and resist change. Very few people ever get fired at the Vatican."

Sean said, "I heard a story that may or may not be true, apropos your comments. Someone once asked Pope John XXIII, 'How many people work in the Vatican?' He replied with a sigh, 'About half.'"

Joe laughed. "I think there's more truth than fiction in that answer. Let's face it, the Vatican is an institution that has been rooted in Italian culture for 2000 years, and cannot help but be profoundly influenced by it. The Vatican employees live in Rome. Roman news media, Roman virtues and vices all influence the Vatican officials who spend their working hours inside their little world. The gravitational pull of this environment strongly colors their decision-making process. They become extremely parochial in their thinking and, consequently, fail to understand the viewpoints of people in other parts of the outside world.

"I have come to the conclusion that the motto of the Vatican should either be 'We have always done it this way,' or 'We love benign neglect.'

Sean said, "I liken their approach to that of a driver who tries to drive his car by only looking through his rearview mirror."

"I agree with you, Sean, and I have to admit that I am becoming increasingly frustrated with this situation. The idealism and enthusiasm I had when I first became a priest has been slowly eroding away. I am hoping that this Council will change things for the better."

Sean patted Joe's arm. "I am getting the distinct impression that you are going through a midlife crisis. Am I right?"

"I don't' think I'd call it that, I'm too young."

"Sean smiled, "Look, big brother, if I can help in any way I'm at your beck and call. That's what best friends are for."

"I know, Sean, and I truly appreciate that. I just have to try to muddle through this phase of my life by myself for a little while longer."

"By the way, Joe, what exactly are you doing in these proceedings?"

"I have been assigned as an assistant to one of the bishops. His name is Albino Luciani. He's only been a bishop for about three years. He's smart, very warm and friendly and actually listens to other people's opinions. He and I have been assigned to the Pontifical Commission on Population, Family and Birth-rate, more popularly known as the Birth Control Commission.

"The Commission is comprised of 72 members from five continents. Included in this group are 16 theologians, 13 physicians, 5 women, and an executive committee of 16 bishops and cardinals.

"In 1930, Pope Pius XI issued his encyclical, 'Casti Connubii', meaning Chaste Marriage, which prohibited Catholics from using artificial methods of birth control.

"The introduction of the oral contraceptive pill just a few years ago created an overwhelming demand from the laity, as well as many of my colleagues, to have this method approved by the Church. We believe that this is not an artificial method.

"The commission gives us the opportunity to do a complete study on the entire subject of birth control as well as human sexuality and make recommendations for change, if necessary.

Sean said, "You couldn't have asked for a more controversial and history-making commission than that."

"I agree. The whole world will be paying close attention to us.

"Good luck with that."

"Thanks, we are all going to need it."

Sarah questioned Joe, "Why has your church been so adamantly opposed to birth control, except by the rhythm method? Most of the other major religions don't feel the same way."

"That's an excellent question and one that we constantly hear from almost all of our married couples.

"The primary reason is based on the biblical story of Onan found in Genesis 38:3-10."

Sarah said, "I know that story. I read it in my study of the Torah when I was growing up. As I recall, Onan had an older brother named Er who was married to Tamar. Er died before they had any children.

"At that time in Jewish history, there was an interesting rule in effect, called the levirate marriage law. It required the brother of the deceased to marry the childless widow and try to father a son who could care for her.

"Onan's father, Judah, told him that he had a duty to marry Tamar, and he did so.

"However, any time that Onan had sex with Tamar, he disregarded his obligation by withdrawing before he climaxed and, as the bible said, 'spilled his seed on the ground'. This is an early example of birth control that we now call coitus interruptus or early withdrawal."

"You have a good memory, Sarah. Then what happened to Onan?"

"The bible says that God was offended by Onan and took his life."

"That's right. The early Church leaders believed that God was angry at Onan's contraceptive act and punished him for it. However, most of my theologian colleagues, and I, believe that this analysis was incorrect. We believe that God's anger was directed not at the sexual act, but at Onan's disobedience by refusing to obey the law and impregnate his brother's widow. Here's the rest of the story.

"Onan was, at that time, the middle of the three children of Judah, father of the tribe which eventually produced both King Solomon and King David. His older brother, Er, would eventually become the leader of the tribe upon Jonah's death. Since Er died without producing an heir, it was an obligation for the younger brother to take his deceased brother's wife and provide her with a son.

"Under the levirate law, Onan's biological son, produced in this manner, would not be considered his own. If Onan provided his older brother's widow with a son, that child would inherit the office of chief of the tribe upon Jonah's death.

"This meant that Onan would be inferior to his own biological child. It also meant that Onan would receive a much smaller inheritance because the laws of inheritance, in those days, required that the oldest brother receive a double portion. This meant that if Onan provided his brother with an heir, Judah's estate would be divided four ways, with two fourths going to this child while Onan and his younger sibling would only receive one fourth each.

"However, if Onan retained his status as oldest surviving son, the inheritance would be divided in just three ways, with Onan receiving two thirds and his sibling one third. He would also become the tribe's spiritual and moral leader.

"Onan showed himself to be unworthy of this office due to his selfishness, his disrespect for his brother, his wife, his father, and his disobedience to God's law.

"Jonah's tribe was of utmost importance in God's plan, as we learn from the gospel of Matthew 1:3. This passage gives a complete genealogy of Abraham, the founder of the Israelites. The list is quite long. It includes the names of Jonah and Tamar, who eventually did bear two sons. Her older son, Perez, continued the lineage which included the names of King David and King Solomon. The list ends with Jacob, the father of Joseph, who married Mary, the mother of Jesus Christ.

"I think you can understand why God didn't want Onan in this line of succession and punished him with death."

Sarah slapped her head. "Wow! I just realized something."

Sean asked, "What?"

"As I've told you before, my father says he is descended from the House of David. That means that I have some of the same genetic material that Jesus had. It blows my mind to think that I have some form of kinship with your Messiah."

Joe smiled. "That is quite a realization, Sarah. I almost feel honored to be in your presence."

Sean laughed, "Think how I now feel. I don't see how I can ever share the same bed with her."

Sarah started to smile, "OK, wise guys. You've had your fun. But I really do feel somewhat overwhelmed by the thought."

Joe said, "Seriously, I think you have a right to feel that way. You are very fortunate to know that you have such a unique link to your heritage."

Sean shook his head. "Joe, I wasn't aware of the whole story about Onan. Do you think you can convince the other members of your commission to share your opinion on Onan's actual transgression?"

"I think there is a very good chance. However, there are other arguments in favor of keeping the ban on artificial birth control based on natural law."

Sean said, "I remember that we studied natural law at Fordham. Refresh my memory on it."

"Basically, it is a system of law that is purportedly determined by nature, and thus universal. Classically, natural law refers to the use of reason to analyze human nature, both social and personal, and deduce binding rules of moral behavior from it.

"Thomas Aquinas was a champion of this concept and his interpretations form the basis of the Church's teachings in many areas. However, there are a host of other schools of thought with differing interpretations of the natural law and our committee will take a close look at them."

"I hope you're successful, Joe. I have a gut feeling that the recommendations of your commission will change the course of history for our Church."

"So do I, Sean. I hope the change is for the better. Time will tell."

Chapter 34

Joe had Sean and Sarah over to his place for a few drinks early in July of 1966. "Well, after about three years, we finally issued our report on birth control to the pope on June 28."

Sean inquired, "I know you couldn't discuss what was happening during your deliberations, but can you talk about it now?"

"Technically, I'm not supposed to, but I know you two will be discreet. Somebody associated with the commission has already started to leak information to the news media, so you deserve to get the straight scoop from me.

"Our commission took our job very, very seriously. We studied the history of Catholic teachings on contraception and found that many of the scientific and theological underpinnings of the prohibition on contraception were faulty or outdated. Lay members presented the findings of surveys they had conducted of devout Catholic couples about their experiences with the rhythm method; some of the women present testified about their own use of the method.

"What we heard challenged our thinking about the role of fertility and contraception within marriage. We learned that, contrary to the assertion of the hierarchy that natural family planning brought couples closer together, it often drove them apart.

"In the end, the vote was 65 to 7 to change the Church's stance on birth control. The official report of the Commission said the teaching on birth control was not infallible; that the traditional basis for the prohibition on contraception, the biblical story of Onan and his spilled seed, had been interpreted incorrectly in the past; that the regulation of fertility was necessary for responsible parenthood and could properly be accomplished by intervening with natural processes; that artificial birth control was not Intrinsically evil, and that the use of contraceptives should be regarded as an extension of the already accepted rhythm method.

"An obstetrician, who was a member of the commission, put it another way, saying, 'I cannot believe that salvation is based on contraception by temperature and damnation is based on contraception by rubber.'

"We said that Catholic couples should be allowed to decide for themselves about the methods to be employed in non-abortive methods of family planning that would work best for them."

Sean exclaimed, "Wow! I would never have guessed that you guys would have come up with such an earth shaking recommendation. The laity will be awestruck."

"Hold on, Sean. This is just our recommendation. The pope still has to make the final decision. It's not a sure thing."

"Joe, I don't see how he could possibly reject your proposal."

"Silly boy. You don't know the extent of the machinations of the ultraconservatives in the Vatican.

"I understand that the seven dissenters, comprised of 4 theologian priests, 1 cardinal and 2 bishops are in the process of submitting a minority report recommending that the Church's teaching remain unchanged.

"All we can do now is wait to see who the pope believes."

Two years later, on the evening of July 26, 1968, Joe knocked on Sean's apartment door. Sean greeted him warmly but then he noticed that Joe seemed to be down in the dumps. "What's wrong, Joe? I've never seen you look so unhappy. Sit down. Let's have an adult beverage to change your attitude. Tell me what happened."

Sarah was in the kitchen and heard the exchange. She proceeded to mix a pitcher of Margaritas. After they had a few sips, Joe asked, "Have you read the Vatican newspaper today, Sean?"

"No, not yet. What does it say?"

"It published Pope Paul VI's new encyclical, 'Humanae Vitae' that declares that the only methods of birth control acceptable to the Church were abstinence and the rhythm method. He summarily rejected our report. He chose to assert the power and authority of his office over the collegially discerned recommendations of the Commission, which had acted in the spirit of Vatican Council II. He chose to say that he knew better what was for the good of married couples than the 3,000 or so couples consulted by the Commission, and that he understood theology and the moral law more clearly than the collective intelligence of the bishops, cardinals, and theologians serving on the Commission."

Sean shook his head, sadly. "What's wrong with that guy? The report was leaked months ago. The people were overjoyed and fully expected him to approve it. He will rue the day that he overruled your recommendations."

"I totally agree. This will turn out to be an unmitigated disaster."

Sarah chimed in. "As somewhat of an outsider, even I cannot understand why he took such a controversial stand."

"The pope believed that if it should be declared that contraception is not evil in itself, then he would have to concede that for many years, the Holy Spirit failed to protect Pius XI, Pius XII, and a large part of the Catholic hierarchy from a very serious error.

"Furthermore, to admit error in the case of contraception would open a Pandora's Box to the possibility of changes in some other highly contentious areas such as a married clergy, divorce, the ordination of women, and even the question of papal infallibility."

Sarah asked Joe, "I never fully understood the notion of papal infallibility. Can you explain it to me"?

"The doctrine of Papal Infallibility does not mean the Pope is always right in all his personal teachings. Most Catholics are quite aware that, despite his great learning, the Pope is very much a human being and therefore liable to commit human error. The doctrine simply means that the Pope is divinely protected from error when, acting in his official capacity as chief shepherd of the Catholic fold, he promulgates a decision which is binding on the conscience of all Catholics throughout the world. In other words, his infallibility is limited to his specialty, the Faith of Jesus Christ.

"The Pope has no authority to originate new doctrine. He is not the author of revelation, only its guardian and expounder. He has no power to distort a single word of Scripture, or change one iota of divine tradition. His infallibility is limited strictly to the province of doctrinal interpretation. It is used in order to clarify or define some point of the ancient Christian tradition.

"Infallible teachings are very rarely issued. As a matter of fact, there is no official listing of infallible doctrines. This causes a good deal of confusion among the laity as well as the priesthood."

"Joe, does this mean that the ruling on birth control can't be changed?"

"The simple answer is no, it can be changed. The pope didn't go so far as to say that his teaching is infallible, therefore the possibility exists that it can be changed sometime down the road. There are precedents for changing the Church's stance on certain issues. For example, the Church, for centuries, accepted the legitimacy of slavery. It wasn't until 1891 that Pope Leo XIII condemned it. Another example was the question of usury, the lending of money at extremely high interest. The Church did not condemn this practice until the nineteenth century.

"Not too long ago, Catholics were forbidden to eat meat on Fridays, under pain of grave sin. The sinful act was not that of eating meat, but that of disobedience to the command of the pope and bishops. Once the bishops decided that they would no longer command under the pain of sin, which they have the power to do, the faithful were released from that level of obligation.

"The people accepted these changes without any uproar because they understood that these laws were the laws of man, not of God. As such, they were not deemed to be infallible and that the Church had the authority to make changes."

Over the ensuing years, the repercussions of the encyclical turned out to be monumental. Just as stunning as the indifference with which the Catholic faithful met the new encyclical was the response of the world's Catholic theologians and bishops. There was a torrent of dissent from inside the church, most of it asserting that Catholics were free to follow their consciences on the issue of birth control. Many of the world's most noted theologians, including Bernard Haring, Karl Rahner, Hans Kung, Edward

Schillebeeckx, and Richard McCormick, dissented from the encyclical.

The theological faculties of Fordham University, St. Peter's College, Marquette University, Boston College and the Pope John XXIII National Seminary issued public statements of dissent, as did 20 of the most prominent theologians in Europe.

Humanae Vitae forever altered the relationship between Catholics and the hierarchy. Catholics realized that they could disagree with the pope on nonfallible issues and still remain a good Catholic. This created a lot of tension regarding the credibility of the church.

Joe put it this way, "This is a perfect example of the law of unintended consequences. The very thing that Pope Paul had feared most, that changing the teaching on birth control would erode the hierarchy's authority on other matters, happened precisely because the teaching was not changed."

Chapter 35

During her years in Rome, Sarah had put a great deal of energy into her work. She traveled extensively, taught seminars, and published numerous papers. She used her maiden name for professional purposes. She became well renowned and respected in her field.

She postponed motherhood until she had accomplished certain goals. After ten years of marriage, she felt the time was right to have children. However, after a few years of failing to become pregnant, she started to worry. She thought that the stress of her grueling schedule was a major factor. Feeling that her biological clock was running out, she underwent a series of medical tests that revealed blockages in her fallopian tubes. She underwent an operation to correct this problem and, shortly thereafter, become pregnant.

She and Sean agreed that they had spent enough time in Europe. They wanted their baby to be born in the United States so that, as Sean laughingly said, "He or she could be eligible to become president of the United States." Sean requested a transfer to the New York office. His request was immediately accepted. He was promoted to a major vice president position.

Sean had been paid handsomely in salary, bonuses and stock options over the years and had made wise investments. Sarah had also contributed to the family coffers. They took great pride in the fact that they had done so well financially, strictly on their own merits. They bought a comfortable two- story house on Bleeker St. in Greenwich Village, not too far from their old apartment.

The Village had changed quite a bit since they had previously lived there. It had become gentrified. More artists were moving in, renting converted loft buildings for their endeavors. Boutique shops were opening up and there was an increase in small nightclubs and restaurants. It was an interesting and vibrant part of Manhattan.

Sarah decided not to go back to work during her pregnancy, especially after her obstetrician informed her that she was going to be the mother of identical twin boys.

The proud parents-to-be spent some time discussing names for the boys. They decided on Brian David and Liam Daniel. The middle names were chosen to honor both of their grandfathers.

Sarah's pregnancy was uneventful, and she continued with her daily activities into the ninth month. A few days before the expected delivery date, Sarah was lying in bed when she felt the first contractions in the middle of the night. "Sean, it's time to go to the hospital."

Sean was prepared for this moment. He immediately jumped out of bed. He and Sarah dressed quickly. Sean picked up the phone, placed a call to the doctor, and left a message to meet him at the hospital. An overnight bag had been prepared many days beforehand. Sean grabbed it as he walked Sarah to the car.

St. Vincent's Hospital was less than a mile away. When they arrived there, Sarah was taken immediately to the delivery room while Sean filled out the paperwork.

The delivery proved to be a very difficult one. The doctor decided that the prudent thing to do, in order to protect both the mother and the babies, was to perform a cesarean section. The baby boys emerged in good health and were administered to by the doctor and the nurses while Sarah was wheeled to her private room.

Sometime later, Sean visited Sarah. She was still a little bit groggy from the anesthesia, but she was smiling very happily. The babies were brought in and the proud parents got their first chance to hold and cuddle them. The babies started to cry because they were hungry. The nurses then suggested that Sarah feed them. The boys were each pressed to one of her breasts and seemed to enjoy their very first meal.

Sean stayed in the room for about another hour and then left because Sarah became exhausted. He came back early the following day to see how everyone was. The babies were in the bed with Sarah. Each of the boys wore a plastic bracelet imprinted with their names.

Sarah said, "Sean, these two little guys are as identical as two peas in a pod. I can't tell them apart. This will be so confusing when they grow up and we have to call them by name."

Sean smiled and told her, "I considered the problem and I made provisions to solve it."

"What do you mean you've solved it?"

Sean reached over the bed, uncovered the two boys, and removed their diapers. Sarah looked at her naked babies and then started to laugh. She saw that only one of the boys was circumcised, Brian, the firstborn.

"That was quite an ingenious solution to the problem, Sean, but now, for the rest of their lives, we'll have to have the boys drop their pants in order to positively identify who is who."

Sean started to giggle and said, "You're right. I guess we'll have to be extra cautious when we have company over and they want to know which one is Brian and which one is Liam."

Sarah's parents were ecstatic. Her grandparents were even more so. They had waited so long for this event and were beginning to despair that it wouldn't happen in their lifetime.

When Sarah was released from the hospital, the whole family gathered at her parents' New York apartment to celebrate. Saul Goldman and Isaac Silverman stood on either side of Sean with a twinkle in their eyes. Saul pulled an envelope out of his breast pocket, handed it to Sean, and said, "This is for you."

Sean arched his eyebrows, opened it, took out a yellowed piece of paper and read it aloud, "It says: Invoice for one diamond engagement ring and it's stamped PAID IN FULL."

Sean laughed and said, "I'm sorry that you two had to wait so long for your final payment. All I can say is that Sarah and I spent many a sleepless night trying to fulfill my obligation. You will notice, no doubt, that I provided you with double interest on your installment plan. Thank you."

Everyone laughed. Saul, beaming, said, "Isaac and I are the ones to be thankful. We have never seen such a happy couple. We are so proud of both of you for what you have accomplished in life, and now, you have given us these beautiful boys to continue our lineage."

When Sarah visited her doctor for the twins' first checkup, he told her, "When I performed your Caesarian, I noticed that both of your ovaries had developed small tumors. I was concerned that they might be cancerous so I took a biopsy. The results confirmed my suspicions. I don't think the cancer has spread but, to be on the safe side, I strongly recommend that you have a hysterectomy."

Sarah was momentarily stunned. Regaining her composure, she said, "I see. Well, I certainly realize how serious this could be so let's make an appointment for the procedure. This means that I can never have any more children."

"Yes, it does, Sarah. I'm sorry. I'll call you tomorrow and we can finalize the date for the procedure."

Sarah broke the news to Sean. "I saw the biopsy report and I have to agree with the doctor's diagnosis. I know that he has had a great deal of experience with this procedure and I think the odds are greatly in my favor. Obviously, the major negative factor is that I can no longer have more children."

She then broke down in tears.

Sean hugged her and whispered, "The most important thing to me is that you be well. God was nice enough to give us two healthy children, which is more than many other families can say."

Then, in an attempt to lighten up the moment, he smiled and said, "You have to realize that you have already fulfilled every Jewish mother's dream. When you walk the babies in their carriage, you can introduce them to other people by proudly saying, 'This is my son, the doctor and this is my son, the lawyer.' What more could you want?"

Despite her sadness, Sarah smiled. "That's funny. Thanks for trying to cheer me up. I was afraid you might be disappointed."

"Of course not. I could never be disappointed in you. The important thing is that you're going to be alright."

The operation was successful and Sarah recuperated quickly. Caring for the twins was the best therapy possible. They required her full attention and left no time for feeling sorry for herself.

She and Sean knew how valuable it was for an individual to be multilingual. They devised a regimen wherein they would talk to the twins in a different language on certain days of the week. The boys, therefore, were exposed to a similar set of circumstances that their father had experienced. After a few years of total immersion in this environment, the boys could carry on a conversation in many languages. Needless to say, the grandparents and great grandparents were overjoyed to hear the boys talking to them in Russian and Hebrew.

When the boys were three years old, Sarah hired a live-in nanny and did some part time research work at Columbia University, her old alma mater.

In 1971, both of Sarah's grandparents went on a trip to Israel. Their plane ran into engine trouble over the Atlantic and crashed. There were no survivors but their bodies were recovered.

A few weeks after the funeral, Sean and Sarah, along with David and Nancy Goldman, met in a lawyer's office for a reading of the grandparents' wills. Both grandparents made large contributions to their favorite charities. The remainder of their multimillion-dollar estates was bequeathed to a stunned Sarah and Sean.

Sean was the first to speak. "That can't be right. There must be some mistake."

David replied, "Why do you think there is a mistake?"

"Because you and Nancy were completely cut out of the wills. I'm not even a blood relative and I get a large amount of money? That's just not right."

David smiled and said, "Calm down Sean, let me explain something. Nancy and I owned a number of investments with our parents as joint tenants. When they died, we became sole owners of those assets, which, I might add, comes to a considerable sum.

"Nancy and I had discussions with our parents about their estate plans, some time ago. They knew that we had accumulated more than enough money on our own to last us many lifetimes. We didn't need nor want any more. We suggested that they give their estates to Sarah and you.

"Sean, you know how much they loved Sarah from the day she was born. When you entered our lives and also showed them how much you loved her, they were extremely pleased. When you provided them with the twins, their happiness knew no bounds. They wanted to show their appreciation for the joy you gave to Sarah and them, but they knew how independent you were and how you gently and repeatedly refused their many offers of financial gifts. Sarah went along with you in that. They admired you both for your attitudes. But, they reasoned that you couldn't refuse their final wishes to include you in an inheritance."

Sarah was choked with emotion. She walked over to her parents and hugged them warmly "Thanks mom and dad. I'm so lucky to have the best parents and grandparents in the world."

Her father replied, "And we feel that we have the best daughter and son-in-law in the world."

Sean, still somewhat dazed by the whole scenario, joined in a group hug.

A few days later, when the shock had worn off, Sean said to Sarah, "I just don't feel comfortable about all the money your grandparents left me. God has been very good to us. You and I really don't need it."

"I know. I feel that I'm merely the lucky winner of the gene pool lottery. I really haven't done anything to deserve the money either. What do you think we should do about it?"

"Well, your faith and mine place a good deal of emphasis on charity. They both teach that we are merely stewards of the gifts that God has provided and that we will eventually be judged on our stewardship. We should share our good fortune."

"I agree. How should we go about it?"

"Suppose we set up a charitable foundation and give most of the money to those causes that we feel passionate about. If God continues to smile on us, we can add more money to it as the years go by."

"That's a wonderful idea. What should we call it?"

Sean paused for a few moments. "How about the GSG Foundation?"

Sarah smiled. "Oh, I get it. The initials stand for the last names of all three families. My grandparents would have been so pleased and proud of the idea. I love it. Let's do it."

The following year, Sarah's father retired from JP Morgan due to their mandatory retirement at age. He was elected to their Board of Directors.

Chapter 36

A few years later, Sean and Sarah were having dinner at home. Sarah said, "Sean, you haven't been your usual self lately. Is something wrong? Do you feel alright?"

"Physically, I'm fine. It's just that I'm getting more and more frustrated with my job. With each new added responsibility, a new level of bureaucracy is created beneath me. I am getting further and further away from a real love of mine, helping small companies to start up and expand. Now I am dealing with top executives from the Fortune 500 companies. I don't get the same sense of satisfaction in working with them.

"With the startup companies, I was dealing with very smart, innovative people. They had a degree of passion that was contagious. I miss that. I don't find that kind of passion in my current clients.

"I'm so fed up that I'm seriously thinking of quitting."

"Well, dear, you certainly have the financial independence to explore that option. There's no reason for you to be frustrated and unhappy. If you're unhappy, the whole family will eventually become unhappy. What would you like to do?"

"I've been thinking of getting into the venture capital field. Our economy is starting to explode. There are a great many small startup companies that could use financing and business advice in order to grow. Entrepreneurs are very good at coming up with ideas and starting up on a shoestring. However, most of them don't have the administrative and business savvy to grow the company beyond a certain point. I think I know how to help them do that."

"What kind of businesses are you thinking about?"

"New technical fields such as computers, communications, and biotech. I have been exposed to some of these small startup firms but I can't convince my bosses to allow me to get more personally involved. They tell me not to waste my valuable time with the small fry. They want my junior staff members to handle them. They don't seem to realize that even their biggest boys once started out as small fry, working out of their garages. The little guys need more personal help than the big boys. I think there is a golden opportunity in these areas."

"Dear, I think you should follow your heart. Why don't you talk to my dad about it? I'm sure he would make a good sounding board."

"I will. I wouldn't dream of making such an important career move without discussing it with him."

Shortly after this conversation, Sean sat down with David and told him what he was thinking. David listened attentively.

"I can empathize with you, Sean. I have often thought that you were the kind of person that couldn't be comfortable by being a small part of a large corporation. You have that independent entrepreneurial streak in you and you need to be your own boss."

He smiled, and continued, "I'm reminded that my Harvard roommate was once given an assignment to come up with three characteristics of an individual that would almost guarantee his business success. His answer consisted of just one word and he received an A on the assignment. The word was DBLITY. You are the only person I have ever met who epitomizes the term."

Sean looked puzzled. "DBLITY? What does that mean?"

"It's an acronym for Dress British, Look Irish, Think Yiddish."

Sean let out a hearty laugh. "That's a good one. I'll have to tell Sarah that. However, I believe I have another characteristic that is equally important."

"What's that?"

"I have had the advantage of a disadvantaged background."

David furrowed his brows for a moment and then replied, "I see what you mean. You never felt you were entitled to anything. Nobody handed anything to you on a silver platter. You had to work hard for everything you got. Yes, I agree that is a great advantage, especially in this day and age.

"My advice is follow your heart, Sean. I know you will be successful. Do it"

Sean gave him a big bear hug, "Thanks so much for your confidence in me. I couldn't have asked for a better father-in-law."

David replied, "Ruth and I are so proud of both of you and we love you dearly. You have made our Sarah one of the happiest people in the world. The two of you have exceeded all of our fondest dreams.

"Why don't you flesh out your ideas on paper and then let's get together again."

A week later, Sean showed up with a brief business plan and went over it with David. Basically, venture capitalist firms raise a pool of money and invest it in a number of privately owned start-up companies in exchange for stock and loans. They also can act as mentors. If necessary, they will add additional personnel and equipment. Despite all of this help, some will fail. Some will do fairly well and will return the investment plus a modest return. The big payoff comes if a few do extremely well. These successful companies can then be brought public by issuing stock via an IPO. A successful stock offering can make the founders very wealthy as well as bring a healthy return to the investors.

Sean identified the types of companies he thought would offer the best opportunity for success. He outlined the amount of money needed and the approximate time and effort that may be required to start seeing results

David looked over Sean's proposal and said, "What you have here is quite interesting. Where do you think you'll get the pool of money needed for your venture?"

"Well, I thought I would put in some of my own money to seed it, and then try to raise the rest. I have worked with some state retirement funds and know that many set aside about five or ten percent of their portfolios to invest in higher risk/reward ventures. Large universities, unions, corporations, and foundations do the same thing."

"I agree. But it would be well to think of tapping wealthy individuals also. They would probably be easier to work with. For example, I would be extremely interested in investing in your enterprise, and I have a number of friends would be eager to do the same. With your reputation and extensive contacts, raising money should be the least of your problems.

"I think you should do it and I would love to help you raise whatever money you need. I have lots of time on my hands now and I think it would be a lot of fun."

Sean smiled and said, "I was going to ask you if you were interested in joining me. I was afraid it might seem awkward for you to be working for me."

"Not at all, Sean. As I once told you, many of us at the company felt that we would be working for you someday, one way or another. This is your show. You have the youth, enthusiasm and experience. I have gotten bored with retirement. I would look forward to getting back into some kind of action."

Sean shook his hand and said, "That's great! I would love to have you. I treasure your experience and advice above all others. We will work out the details as we go along."

Shortly thereafter, Sean resigned from J P Morgan and flew to San Francisco with Sarah. He was interested in seeing firsthand what was happening around the campus of Stanford University, an area that was seeing explosive growth due to venture capitalist investments.

During the 1940s and 1950s, Frederick Terman, Stanford's provost and dean of engineering, encouraged faculty and graduates to start their own companies. He was credited with nurturing Hewlett-Packard, Varian Associates, and other high-tech firms. As a result of these successes, the area around the Stanford campus become known as Silicon Valley and Terman became known as "the father of Silicon Valley".

Sean visited some of the local venture capitalists, most of which were housed on Sand Hill Road. He posed as a prospective investor. Many of these people knew of him and were quite eager to explain their operations.

When Sean felt that he had learned enough, he and Sarah flew down to San Diego. In 1960, her old friend and mentor, Francis Crick, had become a Non-resident Fellow at La Jolla's Salk Institute for Biological Studies. He, along with James Watson, received the expected Nobel Prize in Physiology in 1962.

In 1976, he left Cambridge University and came to work full time at the institute. Sarah wanted to spend a few days visiting with him and catching up on his current situation.

Crick greeted his old protégé with a warm embrace. They chatted amiably about their experiences since Cambridge. Crick spent a great deal of time showing the couple around the beautiful, architectural award winning buildings at Salk. He explained the research they were doing there in three fields: genetics, neurosciences, and plant biology. Sarah was extremely impressed, as was Sean.

Over lunch, Sean talked about his recent experience in the Stanford University area. Crick said, "The same thing could happen right here in San Diego. UCSD has outstanding programs in computer science, engineering, and medical sciences. We have some young outstanding talent right here at Salk. A venture capital firm, such as yours, could find some very fertile fields here. This is a virtually untapped area with a great deal of potential."

Sean said, "I like that idea. Do you know anyone at the university I could talk to?"

"Yes. I know the president personally. I can give him a call and get the names of the people that you might be interested in talking to."

"I would certainly appreciate that."

Crick turned to Sarah, "Sarah, if you and Sean should decide to move to California, La Jolla is the ideal place for you. I would love to have you join my staff. You have had a great deal of experience in Europe in the field of genetics. I have read all your papers. I could really use you here. You would be a great asset to me."

Sarah beamed and replied, "I would love to do that. Let me think it over and I'll get back to you."

Sean and Sarah decided to stay for a few weeks in La Jolla, at the La Valencia Hotel, for further investigation of the area. Sean talked with a few of the local bankers. Every one of them was enthused about the vision of San Diego becoming a world-class center of research and innovation. They said that San Diego had outgrown the image of a sleepy little navy town and was now ready for the big time.

Crick gave Sean the name of a professor of computer science at UCSD. His name was Elwin Law. He spent a number of hours with Sean, explaining the programs at UCSD.

He agreed with Sean's suggestion that the school could emulate Stanford in its approach to encourage graduate students to start their own companies. "As a matter of fact, I have a few former students that have done just that. I stay in touch with them and act as a kind of mentor. Some of them are doing excellent work. They would welcome help from venture capitalists."

At the conclusion of the meeting, Sean told him, "Thanks, for your time. I really appreciate it. You have given me a great deal of food for thought. Once I have digested it, I would like to meet with you again."

"Anytime. I would be delighted to hear what you have to say."

Sean decided that La Jolla would be his base of operations. Sarah wholeheartedly agreed. Now that the twins would be entering school, she was eager to get back into harness and continue her research career. Salk would be the ideal place.

They spent some time with a real estate agent and wound up buying a large lot on La Jolla Farms Road, atop the bluff overlooking the Pacific Ocean. It was only a stone's throw away from both the Salk Institute and UCSD. They also met with an architect and discussed their building plans.

They decided on a large, one story, U shaped, Spanish style house with a red tiled roof. One of the wings would serve as Sean's office. They also made provision for a separate guesthouse that featured two large master bedrooms with baths, along with a kitchen and living/dining room. This could provide private quarters for Sarah's parents, or other visiting guests.

They returned to New York to announce their decision and to prepare for the move. Sarah's mother was less than enthusiastic to learn that her only child, and grandchildren, were going to move three thousand miles away.

Sarah mollified her when she told her about the guest cottage. "We hope you will visit us often. Besides, we will be making frequent trips to New York. I'm sure dad will also have to make trips to La Jolla, to consult with Sean and vice versa. We will still be seeing a lot of each other."

Over the next few months, Sean was busy in New York setting up his company and attracting investors. He and David easily raised over one hundred million dollars. David's role was to be Sean's partner and representative on the east coast. Sean named the company Emerald Enterprises. Sarah flew to San Diego a few times to meet with their architect and contractor to review the status of their new home. The following year, Sean sold the house in the Village. The family packed up and moved to their new home in La Jolla.

The twins took to their new home immediately. They had a large lawn, which they didn't have in Manhattan. They could play outdoors all year round. What was not to enjoy for two active young boys?

There was a gated, paved path nearby, for the local homeowners that extended from the top of the bluff down to Black's Beach, one of the best surfing spots in San Diego. The boys eventually became excellent surfers.

Black's Beach was unique in that it was the only clothing optional beach in San Diego. It abutted the very popular, family-oriented La Jolla Shores Beach. However, it was almost impossible to go from there to Black's Beach due to a natural obstruction in the shoreline created by the bluff, which rose abruptly at that very junction.

Most people had to go to the glider port parking lot, next to Salk, and then climb down the cliff via a steep and dangerous dirt path to the beach. As a result, the beach was quite secluded and never crowded. Nudists liked the isolation. Surfers were never daunted by any difficult trek to outstanding surfing venues. At Black's they didn't have to fight off too many Hodads for the bodacious waves.

Sean took great delight in taking out-of-town visitors and houseguests down the gated private path to the beach, without telling them about the clothing optional feature. He found the expressions on their faces to be priceless when they first saw young men and women playing beach volleyball in the buff, with various body parts wiggling and jiggling. Other extracurricular activities were also evident. His guests' experiences became great conversation starters at cocktail parties.

They enrolled the boys in All Hallows Academy, the local parish grammar school. Sarah signed on at the Salk Institute as a researcher in genetics. Her schedule allowed her to be home when the boys got out of school.

She also became an adjunct professor at the University of California San Diego, giving occasional lectures on genetics.

Sean flew to Washington, D.C., to seek advice from his old mentor, John McCooe, who had retired from the CIA. They had stayed in close touch over the years. Sean had acted as his financial advisor and they had remained good friends.

McCooe greeted him warmly. "Sean, it's good to see you again. It's been a while. What have you been up to lately? Did you get your VC company off the ground?"

"Yes, I did. I have the organizational structure in place with the help of my father-in-law. Now, I just have to choose the right kind of companies in which to invest. Since you have had a unique global perspective on what is happening throughout the world, I thought I would pick your brain for some ideas."

"I'm flattered that you would ask me for advice. What would you like to know?"

"We have all seen how Stanford University has encouraged its faculty and graduates to start their own high-tech companies. That approach seems to be working quite well. I think that UCSD has the opportunity to do the same thing. It has excellent engineering and computer science programs as well as a fine medical school. I was wondering which of those areas you think might prove to have the best growth prospects for a start-up company."

"Sean, have you ever heard of DARPA, the Defense Advanced Research Project Agency?"

"I've heard of it, but I'm afraid I don't know much about it."

"It's an agency responsible for the development of new technology for use by the military. Many of these technologies have eventually been successfully transferred to the business world."

Sean said, "In other words, it's inclined to act like a kind of incubator for new ideas."

"Exactly. My best friend, Joe Garon, heads up the agency. Right now, he's very excited about computers. He is utterly

The Almega Project

convinced that they are going to be the biggest benefit to humanity since the invention of electricity.

"As you well know, computers can store huge amounts of data. Joe says that we need better ways to mine these data banks in order to retrieve and analyze specific information. He says he is data rich but information poor.

"Up to this point, computers have been quite large and relatively expensive, but Joe says that, in the near future, they will be cheap enough and small enough to fit on your desk. Almost everybody will be able to afford one.

"He also needs a better method of sharing information between computers. He has already developed a computer communication network, which he calls ARPANET. It is able to link computers together for the exchange of information over telephone lines for short distances. Right now, it's very cumbersome and very slow. He's looking for ways to improve the speed and volume of digital data transmissions.

"Joe plans to spend a major part of his future budgets in funding these areas for the military. Speedy access to stored, meaningful information will give us a tremendous advantage over our enemies."

Sean said, "I can see how that same technology would eventually be of enormous benefit to businesses as well as individuals. It would be like having the entire Library of Congress and other data banks at your fingertips. That would be incredible."

John said, "Exactly. It's an area just in its infancy. If you could get into it early, it could be a real blockbuster."

"That sounds like an area that's right down UCSD's alley. Can you arrange a meeting with your DARPA friend?"

"I sure can. How about dinner with him tomorrow evening?"

"That would be great."

The following evening, McCooe introduced Sean to Joe Garon, who said, "John has told me a great deal about you and your plans. I was impressed. If you come up with companies that have expertise in the computer data retrieval and transmission areas, I would like to see them. Keep in mind that much of the work we do is classified and our suppliers have to able to pass a background security check. I don't see that will be a problem for you."

"I don't either."

During dinner, Garon proceeded to answer detailed questions from Sean, who took a number of notes.

At the conclusion of the meal, he said to Sean, "It's been a pleasure meeting you. I hope you can come up with some companies that can help solve some of my problems. I'll warn you that it's sometimes hard to get hold of me since I'm frequently out of the office. Your best bet is to stay in close touch with John. I confide in him a lot and he has extensive knowledge of my plans. He always knows where I am and can relay any message you may have.

"I look forward to seeing you again."

The following morning, Sean met with McCooe. "I can't tell you how much I appreciate your arranging for me to meet with your friend, Joe. I now know what to focus on when I get back home."

"You're welcome, Sean, I was glad to do it. Is there anything more I can do for you?"

"As a matter of fact, there is."

"What?"

"I would like you to become the first outside member of my Board of Directors."

"Really? What would I have to do?"

"You would, of course, have to attend a few Board meetings a year. I know the CIA has been using secret advanced computers for years and your experience in this field would be invaluable. You obviously have an interesting Rolodex file and have direct access to a number of important people throughout the world.

"But, most of all, I consider you a true friend, I trust you implicitly, and value your insights."

"I'm pleased to hear you say that, Sean. I think you know how strongly I feel about you."

Sean continued, "You will be compensated by an annual Director's fee and a generous stock option plan.

"Are you interested?"

John raised his eyebrows and, after a short pause, replied, "I've never done anything like that before. I think it would be quite interesting. My answer is a wholehearted yes."

Sean smiled. "I am so glad you agreed. I'll go back home and see if I can find the companies with the technologies that Joe Garon is interested in. Then, I would like you to come out and visit them to determine if you think they are on the right track.

"If they are, you can set up an appointment with Joe for an official presentation.

"How does that sound?"

"It sounds like the right approach to me. I'm already starting to get excited. Go for it."

Upon returning to La Jolla, Sean met with Professor Law, and told him of his meetings with Joe Garon and what DARPA was looking for.

Law said, "That's great news. I think I have a couple of ideal candidates for you. They are former graduate students of mine. They are very bright and ambitious, and each one of them started up a company shortly after they graduated.

"One of them is doing some interesting work developing algebraic algorithms for artificial intelligence applications. Their programs are designed for analyzing and uncovering patterns in massive databases. They use a fairly new mathematical technique called fuzzy logic.

Sean raised his eyebrows. "What the heck is fuzzy logic?"

"It's a type of reasoning based on the recognition that logical statements are not only true or false but can also range in vagueness from 'almost certain' to 'very unlikely'. Our impression of the real world is pervaded by concepts which do not have strictly defined boundaries. For example, words such as many, tall, much larger than, young, etc. are true only to some degree, and they are false to some extent as well.

"For example, if someone says that today is sunny, it might be 100% true if there are no clouds, 80% true if there are a few clouds, 50% true if it's hazy and 0% true if it rains all day. These concepts can be called fuzzy or vague concepts – a human brain can work with them, while computers may not do so since they basically reason only with strings of 0 and 1.

"Software based on applications of fuzzy-logic, as compared with that based on formal logic, allows computers to mimic human reasoning more closely, so that decisions can be made with incomplete or uncertain data. This approach will yield much greater useful information when mining vast sources of data. It is the wave of the future."

Sean said, "That sounds fascinating. What's next?"

"The other company is developing software and hardware methods for speedy data communication between computers, over long distances, via telephone lines. They are also developing techniques that will compress video images that can be transmitted over regular telephone lines. They visualize companies being able to have face to face conferences with their remote offices or with their key customers. This will save a lot on travel expenses."

Sean nodded. "Those projects sound like exactly what DARPA is looking for. I would like to meet your two young men."

"That can be arranged."

Professor Law accompanied Sean to the two startup companies. The young entrepreneurs enthusiastically demonstrated their nascent work. They both expressed an interest in getting outside help to continue their research.

When the meetings were over, Sean asked the professor, "Are you convinced that these young men are working on truly viable programs?"

"Absolutely. They have already made major inroads in their fields. Their technologies are on the cutting edge. All they need is enough time and money to develop their technology further and test their products thoroughly I have the utmost confidence in their ability to succeed."

Sean said, "Based on your endorsement, I would be willing to invest in their companies, under two conditions."

"What are they?"

"The first is to have my friend come visit them and validate your opinion of their potential.

"If he does, the second condition is that you become a member of my Board of Directors and continue to be a mentor to these two young men. You would, of course, be paid an annual Directors fee as well as a generous stock option plan. Are you interested?"

The professor didn't hesitate too long before saying, "Yes, of course. I have the utmost confidence in these protégés of mine."

John McCooe come out to visit the two companies. He was quite impressed. "I love that fuzzy logic approach. It will be a great advance in artificial intelligence. I can see that we would be able to mine our databases for more meaningful results. It would give us a huge advantage over our enemies. I can also see that a huge potential is there in the commercial world."

McCooe arranged for Joe Garon to visit the firms. He was impressed enough to grant both of them a series of development contracts based upon reaching certain benchmarks.

Sean signed up the two firms and agreed to fund their operation and provide whatever other assistance would be necessary. Both companies were then able to buy new equipment and hire additional computer programmers.

After one year, both companies had exceeded the benchmarks that DARPA had given them. The military branches as well as the CIA, NSA, and various other arms of the Department of Defense and Department of Justice immediately bought into the programs. Improvements continued to be made over time. All of the clients were immensely satisfied with their newfound technology. It gave them a huge advantage over their enemies.

When the internet became viable in the civilian field, Sean's companies had mature, tested programs ready to take advantage of it. They went public just as the dot-com frenzy started. Their stocks became some of the hottest items in the market. The founders and employees of the two companies became instant multimillionaires. Sean, his board members, and investors also shared generously in the bonanza.

A good portion of Sean's newly acquired wealth went to the GSG Foundation which grew to be one of the largest in the country.

Sean couldn't believe that he had batted a thousand on his first try. He knew that it was just beginners luck. However, over the next twenty years, he had a healthy success ratio. In addition to UCSD, San Diego State University, the Scripps Research Institute, the Salk Institute, and the Burnham Institute, there were various other enterprises that spawned a number of young men who started their own computer, communication, and biotech companies. Sean had a fertile field from which to choose.

During this time, the twins grew to be tall, handsome young men. When they graduated from the University of San Diego High School, they enrolled at Fordham. They were frequent visitors to their grandparents' nearby home on Long Island. The Goldmans loved it, and so did the boys.

They graduated from college with honors. They had no difficulty in being accepted into Harvard for post-graduate degrees.

Brian received a joint MBA and law degree with a concentration in intellectual property. He joined a law firm in San Diego that specialized in that field. Not surprisingly, the firm's largest client soon became Emerald Enterprises.

Liam received his medical degree and joined the staff of the UCSD hospital where he did cancer research.

Chapter 37

In late 1996, Sean and Sarah took a vacation and flew to Rome to visit their good friend, Joe. They hadn't seen each other for quite a while. Sarah always looked forward to their conversations because they were usually quite spirited, and she always learned something new.

During one of their meetings, Sarah playfully tweaked Joe by saying, "I was surprised to read about some remarks that Pope John Paul II has recently issued. First, he admitted that the Church made a mistake in condemning Galileo, centuries ago. Then he also admitted that evolution was more than a hypothesis, more than a hundred years after science had proven its reality. Such rapid changes of thought are making my head spin. I'm feeling so dizzy."

Joe smiled. "I don't blame you for being sarcastic, Sarah, but we are starting to make some progress. I think change in the Church is going to come faster, not with this pope, but, hopefully, with succeeding popes."

"Joe, why did it take the pope so long to admit that evolution was no longer a theory?

"The Catholic Church had a serious problem with evolution because it ran counter to the traditional interpretation of creation found in the Bible, as well as the concept of original sin.

"In the Book of Genesis, specifically chapters one to three, early theologians thought they found an explanation of the creation of the world in seven days, the creation of Adam and Eve, and the story of how they sinned by disobeying God's command not to eat the forbidden fruit from the tree of knowledge.

"The bible tells us that God punished them by taking away their preternatural gifts and expelling them from the Garden of

Eden. They, and their progeny, were doomed to suffer the pains of evil and death as a result of their original sin.

"Modern day science has, of course, determined the world was not created in seven days. We now know that the actual age of the universe is close to fourteen billion years and our planet is about four and a half billion years old.

"Darwin's theory of evolution opened up a very messy can of worms for the Church. It said, in essence, that there never was an Adam and Eve. But, if there never was an Adam and Eve, how could we explain the existence of evil and death in our world?"

Sarah said, "That's what I would like to know."

"Well, Pierre Teilhard de Chardin started to change the Church's thinking about evolution. He argued that the scientific evidence for human evolution was compelling, and, though subject to occasional revisions in its workings, is a generally accurate account of the way life developed on earth."

Sarah added, "I think the strongest evidence for evolution was the discovery, by twentieth century molecular biologists, that the DNA of the most primitive bacterial genes contains the same molecular structure as the genes of plants, animals, and humans. It showed that the genetic code is universal, and that all living things have a common evolutionary ancestor."

Joe continued, "That's right. As a result of all these discoveries, modern day biblical scholars concluded that Genesis had been misread in too literal a fashion. The creation account of Adam and Eve in Genesis does not relate to actual historical facts. They think it may be an Old Testament parable based on some earlier traditions. We now characterize this story as rationalized myth about the mystery and reality of evil in the world.

"What did the biblical writers really attempt to tell us? Essentially, that Adam is Man, Eve is Woman, and God is the potter who formed them from the 'clay of the ground' as it says in Genesis. He created them in His own divine image. Since God is a pure spirit that means He infused their mortal, material bodies, somewhere along the line, with an immortal, spiritual element that we call a soul. He gave them a singular likeness to divinity in their free will and intelligence."

Sean interjected, saying, "I understand what you are saying, Joe, but the church still talks about the existence of original sin.

How do you theologians now explain the concept of original sin since there never was an Adam and Eve?"

Joe responded, "I'm getting there. Let me refer to Chardin, once again.

"Chardin expanded on Darwin's theory. He added a Christian perspective to evolution. Whereas Darwin's theory concerned only the physical evolution of man, Chardin added the element of a spiritual evolution.

"He believed that, from the moment of creation, 'a certain mass of elementary consciousness was originally imprisoned in the matter of the earth', a cosmic natural order of things. As you know, Teilhard explained this cosmic law as the trend toward 'complexity/consciousness', which stated that increasing complexity is accompanied by an increased consciousness.

"In other words, as the first primitive life forms ascend each step up the evolutionary ladder, from plant to animal to humans, there is a corresponding higher degree of consciousness.

"With Chardin's theory in mind, this is what some of us theologians have done. We examined the concept of original sin from a contemporary point of view. We looked to the study of animal behavior as expressed in the works of people such as Jane Goodall and Frans de Waal."

"Isn't Jane Goodall the gorilla lady?" asked Sean.

"Yes, she is. And Frans de Waal wrote an interesting book called 'Chimpanzee Politics: Power and Sex among the Apes'. These two, as well as other scientists, have taught us how animals, especially our closest primate relatives, react in the wild and among themselves. The picture is not altogether pretty. From ants to apes, the animal world is awash in intraspecies aggression, theft, exploitation, infanticide, deceit, and cannibalism.

"Our closest cousins, the great apes and chimpanzees, have been shown to be adept at political intrigue, and quite capable of serial murder and lethal warfare. The inescapable fact is that there is virtually no known human behavior that we call 'sin' that is not also found among nonhuman animals."

Sarah asked, "Joe, you're not trying to tell us that animals can sin, are you?"

"Of course not. They do not have the same level of consciousness as we do. They are simply doing things that would be sinful, if done by morally reflective human beings.

"They also do many things we can applaud, such as peacemaking and reconciliation. Humans and other animals display these patterns of behavior because they inherited them from a common ancestor, who also possessed them. This common ancestor existed long before the first humans and cannot be identified with the biblical Adam.

"These behavior patterns exist because they promote the survival and reproduction of those creatures that perform them. They persisted because they are favored by natural selection for survival in the organism's natural environment. Since these behaviors are directed to self-perpetuation, and succeed in the world of finite resources only at the expense of others, it is accurate to call them selfish.

"Natural selection enforces selfish behavior as the price of survival and self-perpetuation in all living things. Where cooperative or seemingly altruistic behavior has evolved, it seems always, at least in nonhuman creatures, to be explainable in terms of selfishness and individual advantage."

Sarah chimed in, "My evolutionary biologist friends call this reciprocal altruism."

"Exactly. Humans sin because we all inherited, from the very first living things on earth, a powerful tendency to act selfishly, no matter the cost for others. Free will, embedded in our higher consciousness, enables us to override this tendency. However, we don't always do so because it takes a lot of effort. It's easier to act in our own interest. This tendency in all of us is what my colleagues and I now call the stain of original sin. It is not the result of a 'fall' in our pre-history since we were never more selfless than we are now. It is present even in infants who are undeniably the most self-centered of all, but are obviously guiltless of actual sin."

Sean interjected, "What you are saying is that we incur guilt only when we freely choose to act on this tendency to the detriment of others. In other words, not all self-centered acts are sinful but all sins are instances of selfishness."

"Yes. We learn to sin from the sinful society into which we are born. Even the very first humans learned to sin from the selfish pre-human society into which they were born. But, even without that legacy of learned behavior, we would still be urged to sin by the genetically programmed selfishness dating from the dawn of life that underlies it and gave rise to it.

"Life itself could not spread and evolve on a finite planet if death did not recycle space, energy, and materials, and cull undesirable genes for the benefit of the living.

"As single cells evolved into multicellular organisms, it became necessary for some cells to self-destruct according to a precise and genetically programmed timetable in order for the organism to grow and function properly. For example, deciduous trees annually inundate us with dead leaves, and a woman's uterus sheds its lining every month. This programmed suicide of cells, what Sarah and her colleagues call 'apoptosis', even generates some of our skin, hair, fingernails and the lenses of our eyes. However, it also leads to senescence, or aging.

"Programmed cell death and senescence first appeared, perhaps a billion years after the origin of life, when single celled organisms began to have sex and eventually evolved into multicellular ones. Sex increased genetic variety, speeding up evolution and, together with multi-cellularity, it made possible the large complex kinds of creatures that we are today."

Sarah agreed and added, "But the cost of this complexity was increased wear and tear on our DNA, the 'instruction manuals' in each of the body's cells.

"That's exactly right," said Joe. "This stark fact of biology, which came into clear focus only in the last couple of decades, can be stated more generally and simply, perhaps, by the science of physics. We now know that all matter is made up of atoms, quarks, and other entities, all in constant motion. Experience teaches us that anything with moving parts eventually breaks down. Nothing in the known universe has more complex moving parts than living organisms, especially us. It is physically impossible for any living matter to be immune from the material breakdown and dissolution that we experience as suffering and death.

"God's decision to create a material world was, inescapably, a decision to create breakable, mortal beings. In a nutshell, what we now call Darwinian natural selection enforces selfish behavior on the part of all living things as the price of survival and evolutionary progress, even though this selfishness can eventually entail sin on the part of moral creatures. Life cannot evolve any other way.

"This explains why evil exists. God did not create a static world in which things remained unchanged. He created a dynamic, living, material world. Once He did that, the world necessarily became a place where bad things could and did happen."

Sarah questioned him, "Why would a perfect, divine being, who is all good, want to create an environment which allows the existence of what I would call non-goodness, or evil?"

"Sarah, some years ago, you asked a somewhat similar question. You wanted to know why God created us in the first place because He certainly didn't need us."

Sarah nodded. "I remember some of that conversation. I think you talked about Aristotle and his comments on love between God and man."

"That's right. Aristotle believed that the only true love that existed was that between beings that were similar. He reasoned that since God was a self-created and perfect being and man was an imperfect being, God could not love man.

"I told you that I belonged to a school of thought that believes that God gave man a free will which enabled him to evolve into an entity that could overcome selfishness and develop a great love of God. In other words, he could use his free will to become more god-like and, therefore, be more worthy of God's love."

Sarah said, "What you're saying, essentially, is that God is testing us to see if we are worthy."

"I think so. In our Christian view, God knew that we would eventually need an incarnate example of perfect, divine altruism to show us how to transcend our original selfishness, and the limited self-centered sort of altruism that evolution can create. So, He sent us Christ, His only begotten son, to be our role model.

"Christ came to earth to preach the message of love and divine altruism. If we faithfully followed His directions, He promised us a resurrection into an everlasting life."

Sarah exhaled loudly and said, "I've never had such a clear explanation of what the bible was trying to say. As a scientist, I can relate to everything you said about the physical side of human beings. However, scientists generally don't speculate on the spiritual aspect. You made the marriage between the two very understandable. You have given me a whole new perspective on religion and on my work. Thanks."

"You are very welcome, Sarah. As you know from past experience, Sean and I enjoy talking about philosophy and theology. It's part of our Jesuit training. You, with your unique background, have added an interesting element to our verbal jousting. I really enjoy your participation."

"That's very kind of you to say that. The next time we meet, you will have to visit us in La Jolla. You are always welcome to stay as long as you like."

"I really appreciate your invitation, Sarah, and I will definitely take you up on it. I look forward to seeing you two guys there."

Chapter 38

The following year, Sarah was working in her laboratory at the Salk Institute, on a Monday afternoon, when her secretary entered the room and said, "Excuse me, but Dr. Crick is on the phone. He has just finished meeting with a group of visiting Israeli dignitaries. You're scheduled to meet them next. They're waiting for you in the small conference room downstairs."

"Good. Tell him that I will join them shortly, I just have to clean up my desk."

A few minutes later, Sarah entered the conference room, and introduced herself to the visitors. They were an eclectic mix of Israeli government functionaries, scientists, business people, and a rabbi. After an exchange of pleasantries, Herman Lieberman, who had introduced himself as a representative of the Israeli Prime Minister, acted as spokesman for the group and said, "Dr. Gallagher, we were looking forward to meeting you. We have an important request to make."

"How may I help you?"

"Doctor, I believe that you, as a Jew, share our pain over the loss of six million of our fellow Jews in the Holocaust."

"Yes, of course."

"As a geneticist, you, above all, are very well aware of the fact that the Jewish gene pool suffered a devastating loss. We were deprived of so many potentially talented people. This has put our race and nation at a great disadvantage.

"Israel still finds itself surrounded on all sides by bitter enemies bent on its destruction. Now, more than ever, we need to develop more men and women with proven genius and ability in various fields of endeavor if we are to survive this new century.

"We are in the forefront of computers, communications, and biotech research, as well as a producer of high-end products, and some of the most advanced engineering and scientific projects in the world. The gap between Israel and our neighbors has never been greater. Arab wealth is a product of what is hidden in the ground, Jewish success is a result of what is hidden in our people's minds."

"I agree with you," said Sarah, "but how can I be of help?"

"We need your expertise. You are a recognized leader in the field of genetics. In 1996, Scottish scientists succeeded in cloning the first animal, a sheep named Dolly.

"The whole world is well aware of the fact that a religious cult, called the Raëlians, formed a company earlier this year, named Clonaids, to perform research in human cloning. They have raised millions of dollars in donations and are openly advertising on the Internet for volunteers. They claim their scientists will have successfully cloned a human being by next year."

Sarah interjected, "I'm very aware of the Raëlians and their claims. They are a religious group that believes that life on earth was created by aliens. I think they are crazy and I don't believe they can do what they claim."

Lieberman continued, "I understand that current human cloning experiments are being conducted with DNA from living people. Our question to you is whether or not it is possible to clone humans from DNA extracted from the dead?

"If we provided the DNA material of a prominent Jew of the past, such as Albert Einstein, could someone such as you clone him?

"The reason we ask this question is that we strongly believe that such a human cloning program could provide at least a partial restitution of past iniquities to the Jewish race. It would give us the opportunity to make up for the Holocaust."

Taken by surprise, Sarah quipped, "It looks like you folks are planning a sequel to 'The Boys from Brazil.' What are you going to call it? 'The Boys from Tel Aviv?'"

"Dr. Gallagher, we are deadly serious about this."

"I'm sorry, gentlemen. I apologize for my flippant remark. It's just that I have never encountered this question before.

"Let me try to answer it this way. All blood and human tissue contains DNA and could potentially be a source for cloning. Unfortunately, DNA begins to slowly decompose a few weeks after death, destroying segments of the genetic code. For example, only a few short fragments of dinosaur DNA have survived after 60 million years, so the chances for realizing a Jurassic Park are slim. However, the prospects are good for recovering a complete DNA sequence from human samples because much less time has elapsed.

"Think of the genetic code as a very large book of blueprints for making a car, and from which paragraphs or pages are randomly erased over time. If we only have one copy of the damaged book, the complete set of blueprints cannot be recovered. Luckily, we have more than one copy. In bone, blood or tissue samples, there will be many thousands of cells, each with its own copy of the DNA code. This is like having thousands of copies of the same book. If, for instance, page ten has been erased in one book, that page may still be intact in another one, so that it is possible to recover a perfect copy of the original genetic code by combining information from many 'pages' or cells.

"Another positive, mitigating, factor is the fact that only a small percentage of the three billion symbols in the human genetic code is responsible for individual differences. For example, the genetic codes for chimpanzees and humans are actually about 99% identical. This means that only about 1% of the code, the part that determines human individual differences, needs to be recovered. The rest could be spliced in from any living human cell. Scientists are still working on the technology for this process.

"In short, the answer to your question is yes, it is possible, in theory, to do what you ask. However, a great deal more research work is needed and that would require a great deal of time and money."

"Dr. Gallagher," said Mr. Lieberman, "the state of Israel and a group of our business leaders are ready, willing, and able to fund such a research project, if you agree to be in charge. We consider this a project of vital national importance to the state of Israel. It may even guarantee its survival."

Sarah was stunned. It took her a few moments to compose herself. She finally spoke to them, "Gentlemen, I'm at a loss for words. This is such a revolutionary concept. I couldn't possibly answer your question right now. I need time to give it some very serious thought."

"We understand," said Mr. Lieberman. "We'll be staying in La Jolla, at the La Valencia hotel, for the next five days and then we must return to Israel. Would you be able to give us your decision by then? "

"Yes, of course. You'll have my answer before you leave town."

Shortly after the meeting, Sarah went home to ponder over what had just transpired. It was too important a decision to make on her own. She wanted Sean's opinion. She didn't want to do anything that would be contrary to his religious or ethical beliefs.

She looked at the clock. Sean should be home shortly. She got out the blender and mixed a batch of Margaritas while murmuring, "I think we will both need a few of these tonight".

While she was finishing, Sean arrived home. She met him at the door, drink in hand. He was surprised at this unusual reception and said, "You must have had a really hard day at the office if you are this anxious to have an early adult beverage. What happened?"

As they sat down in the living room, Sarah told him what had transpired that day.

He was amazed as the story unfolded but kept his silence until Sarah had finished.

"There it is, Sean. It's a fascinating challenge but I wouldn't dream of saying yes if you strongly disapprove. What do you think I should do?"

Sean shook his head and shrugged his shoulders. "I'm so flabbergasted that I can't think rationally right now. My gut instinct is to say don't do it. You know full well the moral, ethical and legal questions involved. A great number of people have been studying these for years and there is still no universal consensus on what's right. However, these Israelis have added a new wrinkle which I have never thought of. They make a very interesting and plausible new argument in favor of such a project

"I find the idea of restocking the Jewish gene pool mind boggling. Just think of the possibility of Einstein along with other Jewish Nobel Prize winners, and historical figures that might be assembled at one time. They would form the most fantastic brain trust the world has ever seen at one time. What a boon that would be, not only to your people, but also to all of humanity!

"By the way, did the Israelis have a list of people they had in mind?"

"If they did, they didn't tell me. Einstein was the only one they mentioned by name."

"Let me do some serious thinking and then I will give you my recommendation. You have until Friday, right?"

"Yes."

Sean spent much of the next two days browsing through some of his old college books on religion and philosophy. He also did some research on the internet. On Wednesday, he decided to have lunch downtown at his favorite place, The Cottage. He left there after devouring one of their famous tuna melt sandwiches and decided to walk over to Warwick's Book Store.

He and Bob Warwick were old friends. Bob was easy to spot. He was a tall handsome man with white hair. As usual, he was roaming the store, chatting with customers and helping his staff as needed. When he saw Sean, he came over and greeted him. They exchanged a few pleasantries and Bob asked him, "Is there anything in particular we can do for you today?"

"Not really. I am just browsing but I am interested in looking at whatever you have in your Religion or Philosophy sections."

Bob said, "We have a somewhat limited selection on those subjects but we can order whatever books you want. Why don't you go over there and talk to Mary, our specialist in that area?"

As Sean approached that section, he saw that Mary was having trouble trying to place a book in an upper shelf.

"Hello, Mary."

Mary turned, "Why, hello Sean. I haven't seen you or your lovely wife for a while. Is there anything I can help you with?"

"Maybe, but right now, I think I can help you put that book in its proper place."

"Thanks. I wish I were tall, like you. This job would be so much easier. Would you please put this book on the top shelf?"

Sean looked at the cover of the book which was titled, "The Resurrection of the Shroud", by Mark Antonacci. The subtitle was "New Scientific, Medical and Archeological Evidence."

Intrigued by the title, Sean started to thumb through it. There were a number of illustrations of the Shroud of Turin. They brought back memories of his visit to Turin many years ago.

"On second thought, Mary, I think I'll buy this for myself."

Sean drove home and spent the next few hours reading the book. When he finished it, he had a broad grin on his face.

That evening, he sat down with Sarah to discuss her situation. "After much soul searching, I think you should accept the project.'

"Really? I'm quite surprised. I thought that your religion would frown on such a thing. What made you decide?"

"It's true that the Catholic Church frowns on such a thing, but you're not Catholic and, if the Jewish government and a rabbi have sanctioned the project, then I would expect that they had examined the ethical aspects of this venture and decided that it did not contravene their moral precepts. I would not want to stand in the way of your helping in the survival of your people. Lord knows, they need all the help they can get. Besides, the project gave me another idea, which I don't want to discuss with you at this time. I'll tell you about it if you successfully complete this project."

Sarah was so overwhelmed with emotion that she started to cry. She threw her arms around Sean, kissed him, and said, "I was hoping you would say yes. I love you so much. You are such a sensitive and thoughtful soul."

Chapter 39

Herman Lieberman called on Friday. "Dr. Gallagher, have you reached a decision?"

"Yes, Mr. Lieberman. My husband and I have discussed your proposal at great length and have come to a decision. We would like to talk to you in person. Can you come to my home this evening?"

"Of course, I'll be there at six."

When Lieberman arrived, Sarah introduced him to Sean.

"I'm pleased to meet you, Mr. Gallagher. I almost feel that I know you since I have read so much about you in the news media. I am very impressed with what you have accomplished in your life.

"I am also thankful for the many generous contributions that you and your wife have given to Jewish causes through your charitable foundation."

Sean replied, "Thank you for your kind words but, please call me Sean. I hate being formal."

"Very well, Sean. I would like it very much if you and your wife would call me Herman. Sarah, I'm anxious to hear your decision."

"Herman, I have decided to accept your offer. I didn't want to pursue this venture unless I had the full-fledged cooperation of my husband. Initially, he was not in favor of such a project, but after a good deal of soul searching, he changed his mind. He now wants to support me in any way he can."

"I'm so relieved to hear you say that. Frankly, I don't know what I would have done if you turned me down. How soon can you start?"

"Well, I know that you feel that time is of the essence, but there are certain steps that we must put in place first. As you know, our government frowns on human cloning and continues to pass restrictions on such activities. We would have to establish a lab outside this country. Then, of course, I must find reliable people to staff that lab, people who can be sworn to secrecy."

"Sarah, I can be of help there. We have a number of trained scientists in Israel who are more than willing to come here and help."

Sean spoke up, "That would certainly solve the security problem. However, my suggestion is to establish Sarah's lab in Mexico, where the laws are more, shall we say, elastic? Tijuana is only a few miles from here. I go there fairly often because I have investments in a few U. S. biotech firms that also have facilities there. I am a familiar face to the government and the scientific community in TJ. I can easily set up a dummy firm and use it as a cover. That should arouse no suspicion.

"Sarah has suggested that she cut back on her work here and, therefore, be able to spend more time supervising the operation down south. Maintaining her connections with the Salk Institute and the University on a part time basis will help her research."

Lieberman looked pleased. "Sarah, you and Sean have obviously thought things through. With the background and resources that you both possess, I have every expectation that this project will be successful."

"Let's hope," said Sarah "that your confidence turns out to be well founded."

"I'm sure it will. I'm going to give you my phone numbers and e-mail address. Our Intelligence Service will set up secure lines. Word of this project must not leak out. Our enemies have many ears. They would stop at nothing to sabotage us."

"Believe me, Herman," said Sean, "I have access to some of the most sophisticated computer security software in the world. I'll work with your people to make sure that our electronic communications will be secure."

"Good. I must leave for Israel tomorrow. Send me a list of what you require in the way of money and other resources. We will get whatever you need. Again, you have my thanks and the thanks of my entire country."

When Lieberman departed, Sarah and Sean spent the next few days outlining the essential details of the project. They went over the list of equipment and supplies that they would need.

Sarah said, "Our first major problem concerns computers. In order to do the massive research for our project, we really need access to a supercomputer. I can only get a limited amount of time on the one at the University. That means that it will take many months, perhaps years, to get the information we need. A new supercomputer would be nice to have all to ourselves, but I know that they are prohibitively expensive."

"You're right", said Sean. "A supercomputer, like a Cray, can cost about thirty million dollars or more. But a more serious obstacle is that, even if you order a new one today, it won't be delivered for over a year or so. Maybe there's another way. Why don't you tell me a little bit about the kind of problems you need to solve on that type of computer."

"Alright. Let's start with the basic development of an adult organism. In humans, this process starts with a single cell, the fertilized egg, or zygote. The zygote undergoes about 50 cell divisions to create about 1 quadrillion cells that form the newborn infant. At the same time, the single cell type of the zygote differentiates to form the roughly 260 cell types of nerve cells, red blood cells, muscle cells, and so forth.

"The genetic instructions controlling development lie in the DNA within the nucleus of each cell. This genetic system harbors about 100,000 different genes, each encoding a different protein. Remarkably, the set of genes in all cell types is virtually identical. Cells differ because different subsets of genes are active within them, producing various enzymes and other proteins. Red blood cells have hemoglobin, muscle cells abound in the actin and myosin that form muscle fibers, and so forth.

"Genes and their RNA and protein products form a complex network, switching one another on and off in a wondrously precise manner. The network within each cell is the result of at least 1 billion years of evolution. "

"You make it sound as if this genomic system is like a chemical computer."

"Actually, you're right. However, this computer differs from the familiar serial-processing computer, which carries out one action at a time. In the genomic computer system, many genes and their products are active at the same time so the system is more like a parallel-processing chemical computer of some kind."

Sean's eyes lit up. He smiled and said, "You just gave me an idea on how to solve your problem."

"I did?"

"Yes. One of my computer software companies is a pioneer in a new technology called grid computing. The idea is to tackle a large problem, such as yours, by slicing it into thousands of tiny pieces that can be solved independently. These tiny pieces can be transmitted over the internet to hundreds, or even thousands, of smaller, cheaper, desktop computers and servers. These computers attack the problem when they aren't busy handling other tasks. When they finish their part of the problem, the information is transmitted back to the main frame computer office where it is spliced together.

"For example, you could break out each of your 100,000 genes and assign them to a host of small computers. There are thousands of computers in the corporations I control, and I can have all of them tied into such a grid. They can grind away on your problems all during the night, on weekends, and at various times during the day when they aren't busy. This approach won't be very expensive. All we need to get is a good mainframe computer with the necessary capacity to handle and organize the program. It will probably even do the job faster than one giant super computer."

"Sean, that sounds fantastic."

"That's the easy part. The harder, and more important part, is the writing of the software to tell the computers what to do. But that's a manageable problem. It will just take a bit of time to get the right head programmer and assemble a crew."

"I have a question for you, Sean. The project has to have a name. What should we call it?"

Sean pondered for a while, and then a puckish smile formed on his lips as he said, "Let's call it the 'Lazarus Project' as a part of 'Lazarus Industries, Inc.'"

Sarah frowned for a moment and said, "Lazarus? What an odd choice. Oh, wait a minute, now I get it. Wasn't he the guy in the New Testament that rose from the dead?"

"That's right"

"Sean, you have a weird sense of humor but you know what? I like it. I think that would make a great name. I hope that Mr. Lieberman has the same sense of irony."

The following week, Sean drove to Tijuana and started the search for a building. He soon found one to his liking. It was in an industrial park that contained a number of other American firms that were in the biomedical field. Delivery trucks with chemicals and lab equipment for Lazarus Industries, Inc. would arouse no suspicions in that area.

He completed the necessary paper work to establish the corporation. It was set up through a dizzying array of interconnected corporations so that it was almost impossible to determine who owned it. Financial transactions would be handled by the Thornton bank in the Cayman Islands. It would be virtually impossible to trace the flow of money through the complicated maze he created. Drug lords would have envied his sophisticated scheme.

He established secure, encrypted communication system with the Israelis. He gave them a list of the required equipment and cash needs. The money was transferred to the Thornton bank in the Cayman Islands and then, in a circuitous route, to a Mexican bank account the following day. Any specialized equipment available from Israeli manufacturers was shipped by air to the Tijuana plant. Sean was careful to purchase the rest of it from various firms throughout the world. Sean did not buy too much specialized equipment from one source. Other companies had a sixth sense about what you were doing by analyzing your purchases.

The project was launched.

Chapter 40

Within a few weeks, the Israeli scientists, technicians, and security personnel arrived in Tijuana, headed by one of Sarah's friends, Dr. Richard Blumenthal. Sean leased an entire wing of a nearby hotel and housed them there.

The hotel was called King's Inn. It was owned by a Pakistani named Ibraheen Malik. In Arabic, Malik means "king", one of the names of Allah, the king of all. For business purposes, he decided to use the Anglicized version of his family name for the hotel. Although he was born a Muslim, he did not practice his religion. He left Pakistan years ago because of his dissatisfaction with the religious extremists there.

The hotel was a family enterprise. His wife, children, and various relatives staffed the main positions. All of them were fluent in Spanish and English. One of his sons, Mansoor, was a medical student in Saudi Arabia. He came home during summer vacations.

One day, during the following summer of 1998, Mansoor was checking the rooms in the hotel to see if everything was cleaned properly. He entered a room occupied by one of the Israeli scientists and noticed a laptop computer on the desk. This was unusual because these secretive guests invariably took their laptops and documents with them when they left their rooms. The screen was blank, but he decided to hit the Enter key. To his surprise, the screen lit up, apparently the computer was in the sleep mode. The owner forgot to turn it off. Mansoor decided to look at the documents files to see if there was anything interesting. He found many scientific documents that seemed to concentrate on genetic research. This was a field of study that he was interested in at his medical school. He wanted to study the files in more detail but didn't want to spend more time in the room, in case the occupant returned. He went to his room and got out his own laptop.

He took the lipstick sized flash drive from its USB port and carried it back to the other room. He inserted it into the laptop and copied all the files. He returned the laptop to the sleep mode and left.

Over the next few days, Mansoor read all of the documents he had copied. He found numerous references to a Lazarus project and to various Israeli historic figures. He didn't fully understand all of the technical details but he knew someone who would, his teacher in Saudi Arabia. When his summer vacation ended, he took his flash drive with him.

When Mansoor arrived at King Saud University's College of Medicine in Riyadh, he met with his faculty advisor, Professor Badar Jamil, and showed him the contents of his flash drive. Jamil made a copy for himself so that he could study it at his leisure.

Jamil was a radical Sunni Muslim. For many years, he had studied under Wahabbi clerics, who were strict fundamentalists. Anyone, including other Muslims, who did not follow the Wahabbi belief, was considered to be an infidel, to be despised, even killed. Jews were especially reviled.

In addition to his teaching duties, the professor also did research in the field of genetics and was internationally known. While reading Mansoor's purloined documents, he came across the name of Sarah Goldman many times. It appeared she was in charge of the project. He, of course, knew of her. As a matter of fact, he had briefly met her at an international genetics symposium in Switzerland some years ago. He was very impressed with her and with the published works that she issued from the Salk Institute.

He also found the names of some Israeli scientists, some of whom he recognized and some of whom he didn't. It struck him as odd that so many Jewish geneticists were working together at an obscure building in Mexico. He could only surmise that they were working on a top secret project that had been named Lazarus. What could it be?

The technical documents gave very little clues. They seemed to be about normal research in the cloning of cells. He had conducted similar experiments in his own lab. There had to be something more, something so important that they had to work in Mexico, below the radar screen.

He also found references to many other people, all of whom appeared to be Jewish. He, of course, recognized Albert Einstein and Niels Bohr, the atomic physicist, but he didn't recognize most of the rest, so he made a list and had an assistant research them. After a few days, the assistant gave him the report. Many of the names on the list were Nobel Laureates in various fields, and most of them had been dead for a few years. Was Sarah Goldman conducting research on the DNA of these scientists to uncover the genetic basis of their genius? That surely would be an extremely important study, if it were successful and they could replicate those genes. That must be it. However, he wanted to make sure, if at all possible.

Jamil pondered the situation for many days and decided to discuss it with the Imam and other high members of his mosque. They mulled it over for many weeks and decided that it might be worthwhile to contact some of their followers in the United States, Mexico, and Israel and see if they could uncover any more information on this Lazarus Project.

Many months went by with little progress. The wall of security around the project made it almost impossible for them to gather any pertinent information. They did manage to uncover lists of chemical supplies and scientific instruments that were being delivered to the Lazarus Industries lab. They tried to intercept telephone and internet messages but they couldn't break the encryption codes.

In his university office, Jamil went over everything that he had collected on the Israeli program. It had something to do with genetic research, but why the extreme secrecy? Other labs throughout the world were conducting similar studies and publishing their results in order to be perceived as leaders in their field. It was curious that Sarah Goldman had stopped publishing any papers about the time that the Lazarus project started. She had previously been a fairly prolific writer on the subject of cloning. Come to think of it, the name Lazarus struck him as being somewhat odd. Why was it chosen? Since it was her project, she probably picked out the name. Was there something significant behind it? He knew that Americans often had an ironic sense of humor in concocting code names. For example, naming the first two atom bombs "Little Boy" and "Fat Man", or naming an extremely destructive ICBM the "Peacemaker."

He looked up the name Lazarus on the internet and saw a reference to the New Testament, the gospel of John, chapter 11. There, he refreshed his memory of the story about the raising of Lazarus from the dead. Was the name and story significant to Sarah's project? Then, it struck him! Was Sarah trying to clone all those Novel Laureates, essentially raising them from the dead? It would seem too preposterous to even be considered, but Sarah Goldman was an acknowledged leader in the field of cloning. If anyone could do it, she could.

Jamil pondered the implications of this possibility for many hours. If the Lazarus project became successful, it would have a major impact on the future of Israel, as well as the Muslim world. As a devout Sunni, he couldn't allow this to happen. Furthermore, he was the leader of a radical fundamentalist group known as "The Disciples of Muhammad." Their purpose was to eradicate Israel from the face of the earth and to spread their Muslim beliefs to the rest of the world, by force, if necessary.

He summoned Mansoor to his office.

"Mansoor, I have an important assignment for you. You have been a good Sunni Muslim and you know the importance of a jihad in defense of Islam."

"Of course, it is the will of Allah.'

"The computer documents that you gave me have been a great cause of alarm to me. The Israelis are apparently embarked on a secret experiment that could do our faith great harm. I need more information on what they are doing."

"How can I be of help, sir?"

"I want you to take time off from your studies and return to your family. I want you to implant listening devices in the bedrooms of the Israelis staying in your family's hotel. You will record all conversations and send them to me. You will also examine all their trash to see if anything of importance is there.

"If you find any more computers in the rooms, try to download them as you did before."

"I will gladly do as you ask, sir, but I do not have any expertise in installing listening devices."

"I know. I will send some specialists to you to take care of the technical matters. They will assist you on how to monitor the devices, and help you in other ways. Be ready to leave in a few days. May Allah be with you."

Mansoor returned to Mexico. He had written ahead to inform his father that he had been told to take a long vacation for health reasons, but that it was nothing serious.

Once he settled in, he met with three of Jamil's agents, headed by Omar Rajib. They set up the bugging devices in the Israelis' rooms and they tapped their telephones. Omar was very skilled in his job. They could barely be detected with the naked eye.

After a few weeks of monitoring the rooms, it became apparent that the scientists were very careful in what they said to each other. They obviously had been warned not to discuss their work outside the confines of the lab. They did not leave their laptops unguarded and they did not discard any written material pertinent to their work.

Mansoor could only hope that, eventually, someone might get careless again. He dutifully sent the telephone recordings and any observations that he thought might be of value to professor Jamil.

Jamil read through them. The Israelis were very circumspect in their conversations. There were no startling revelations, but there were enough clues to make him think than his original guess about the cloning of Nobel Laureates was probably accurate. What should he do about it?

Time was probably not a critical factor. Research of this complexity would take quite a while. He didn't want to create an international incident by trying to bomb the lab or kill the scientists. The Israeli and U. S. intelligence agencies had an uncanny way of ferreting out the perpetrators of these incidents, and the Saudi royal family would not be happy.

It was apparent that Sarah Goldman was the key person behind this plan. He thought, "If I eliminate her, the project will fail, and the world will have one less Jew."

He contacted his agents in Mexico and gave them orders to assassinate Sarah. He wanted her death to be a spectacular event that would gain extensive media attention. He came up with the idea of the hang glider attack on Sarah's La Jolla home.

After the attack, he would send a message from the Disciples of Muhammad to the Al Jazeera TV network explaining the reason behind the killing, and taking credit for it.

Part 2

The Present

Trust no future, howe'er pleasant!
Let the dead Past bury its dead!
Act-act in the living Present!
Heart within, and God o'erhead!

Longfellow: A Psalm of Life

Tom Galligan

Chapter 41

As the SUV sped along Interstate 5 toward the Mexican border, the Israeli guards kept checking the rear view mirrors but could not see anyone following them.

Sean continued in his dreamlike state until he was aroused from his reverie when the SUV stopped at the immigration inspection site. The inspector asked them a few questions and then waved them through.

He looked over at Sarah who grabbed his hand. "I'm glad that you're awake. That was a close call. I'm still shaking. What are we going to do now?"

"Well, it's obvious some extremist group has found out what you are trying to do or, at least suspects that you are doing something important for the Israelis. You will have to keep a low profile until we find out if we have a leak in our organization."

After arriving in Tijuana, Sean met with the project's Mossad security chief, Capt. Cohen, and explained what had happened.

Cohen was completely surprised. "I don't understand how anyone could have discovered what we are doing here. We have the tightest security possible. Either we have a mole in our operation, or someone got careless. I'll get on it immediately."

When the captain left, Sarah turned to Sean. "What happens now?"

"Until we know more, we will increase our personal security. If necessary, we can always move the operation to Israel."

"Oh, I hope we don't have to do that, Sean. It would really upset the whole project. We have made a great deal more progress than I had ever envisioned. We're getting so close"

Sean said, "I hope we don't have to go to that extreme, either. Let's wait until we hear from Cohen."

Capt. Cohen conducted a thorough examination of facility's security system. He swept the premises for bugs but found nothing.

He extensively questioned the staff and reviewed their background checks. They had all proven to be long term loyal citizens. Cohen pondered his approach to determine if he had overlooked anything. He finally realized that he had not examined the place where the employees were living.

He assembled his men, went to each room in the King Hotel, and covertly swept them for bugs. He was astounded to discover that each room had one or more cleverly concealed listening devices, and that all the phones were tapped. He was able to determine that the signals were being transmitted to Mansoor's room.

Cohen called his headquarters in Tel Aviv and asked them to run a background check on Mansoor. The following day, he received a reply. He was told that Mansoor was a medical student at the King Saud University. His faculty advisor was Professor Badar Jamil, a radical Muslim and the leader of The Disciples of Muhammad, a known terrorist group.

"That's it," shouted Cohen. "Mansoor is a spy. I bet he's an agent of his teacher's terrorist group."

He called a special meeting with Sean and of all the personnel in the project and explained to them what had happened. He told them that he was going to leave the devices in the rooms. He told them to continue their normal routine but to be extra careful what they said and what they left in their rooms.

He put a twenty-four hour surveillance team on Mansoor to determine his daily pattern of activity. Every Monday morning, Mansoor went to the local post office with a package to mail to Saudi Arabia to the attention of Professor Jamil. Cohen's agents were able to bribe the local postmaster who allowed them to open the packages and copy their contents. They were also allowed to intercept all incoming mail and copy it as well. A tap was put on Mansoor's phone.

The surveillance team saw Mansoor frequently visiting a house in town that was rented by three men, who were obviously Arabs. Cohen's team was able to place bugs in the house and

The Almega Project

intercept their mail as well. He learned that they were trained members of The Disciples of Muhammad, the same people who had planned the aerial suicide assault against Sean and Sarah.

From the intercepted correspondence, it was evident that Jamil was aware of something called the Lazarus Project, but was unsure what it was all about. He guessed it had something to do with cloning and that the names of Albert Einstein and some other Jewish notables had been mentioned on more than one occasion. Jamil was upset about the failure of the attempt on Sarah's life. He urged Mansoor and the three-man team to learn more about the project in any way possible.

The Arab agents spent a good deal of time tailing various Israeli employees, in their off-hours, to see if they could catch them in any compromising situations for the purpose of blackmail. They hung around the restaurants and bars where the Israelis congregated and listened in on their conversations.

Cohen was relieved to learn that Jamil had not penetrated into the true secret of the Lazarus Project. The attempt on Sarah's life was apparently an attempt to force the Israelis to take some kind of drastic action. That would indicate that the project was of immense importance to them.

Cohen reasoned that the Muslims might even resort to force to uncover the secret of the experiment or, failing that, perhaps destroy everyone and everything connected with it. They had already proved that they were capable and willing to commit violence.

Cohen met with Sean, who asked, "What do you think we should do?"

"Obviously, we are not going to be intimidated by this nut group. We know that Mansoor and three other Muslims are behind the attempt to breach our security and the threat on Sarah's life as well as yours. It would be quite easy to arrange some kind of accident and kill them all at one time."

Sean frowned. "No, that's not a good idea at this point. Jamil would never believe that it was an accident. He would be absolutely convinced that we had discovered his plot and that our project was so important, and so close to a successful completion, that we had no qualms about killing his operatives.

"Yeah, on second thought, I think you're right, Sean."

Sean continued, "However, if Jamil was convinced that the experiment was a failure, he might lose all interest in us. Why don't you map out a plan to supply him with misinformation, over the next few weeks, to the effect that we had encountered some insurmountable problems and that we were discontinuing the project? We would ostensibly close the lab and send our scientists back home. In actuality, we would merely move to another location. I own some other companies down here that could easily accommodate our people and equipment. Our project would only be set back a week or so. I'll get working on that part right away."

The captain grinned, "That's a much better plan than mine. I'll set up the scenario tomorrow and get it started. It should be fun."

Cohen coached the Israeli personnel as to what they would do over the following weeks. He had small groups congregate in each other's rooms in the evenings for a few after dinner drinks. Some of the drinkers would apparently get drunk and start talking "out of school." They would complain about their bosses, about the fact that they were not allowed to go home for leave time, and the onerous security restrictions.

They voiced despair over the lack of progress they were making. They expressed fear over the rumors that Sarah Goldman was on the verge of aborting the whole thing. Empty liquor bottles were left in trash baskets. Torn up copies of internal memos started to appear there. They groused about everything. Laptop computers would occasionally be left unattended in a room. The documents found on these computers had been crafted to lead a reader to conclude that the project had hit a brick wall and was a complete failure.

They started a pool as to what day the project would be aborted. The winner would get five hundred dollars. They felt their days were numbered and they no longer cared about security.

Mansoor dutifully sent each week's recordings, torn up memos, flash drives with downloaded files from the laptop computers, and personal observations to Jamil.

After Cohen's scenario ran for a few weeks, Sarah issued a surprise announcement to the Israelis that the project was, indeed, a failure. She was shutting down the lab. A discarded memo of the announcement was found in a few of the rooms. It said that all the employees would be put on a plane to return to Israel within a few days.

On the evening before their departure, the employees held a going away party in one of the local cantinas. They got drunk and boisterous. They appeared to be a very disgruntled group as they loudly lamented about the project's failure, the incompetence of their bosses, and a host of other things. It was a typical bitch fest that could be expected in any corporate downsizing or plant closure.

The Muslim operatives were present in the cantina and noted everything.

The Israelis made a great show of packing their belongings, checking out of the hotel and driving to the airport. There they boarded a chartered El Al plane. Its final destination was listed as Tel Aviv. Mansoor and the Muslim operatives watched them take off.

Lab and office equipment was packed and moved out of the building. A For Rent sign appeared on the front entrance.

Jamil was, of course, informed about all of this. He expressed his gratitude to Mansoor for his efforts to uncover a potential threat to the Islamic world. He was glad that the threat no longer existed. Mansoor was free to return to Saudi Arabia and continue his studies.

The three Muslim operatives were given orders to return to Saudi Arabia. In the middle of the night before their departure, the gas line to the heater in their house mysteriously sprung a leak. All three men were asphyxiated and died in their sleep.

Captain Cohen smiled and wondered how many virgins awaited them in heaven.

The Mexican police investigated the incident and ruled the deaths an unfortunate accident. They saw many such happenings each year in their town.

Chapter 42

The chartered plane landed in Phoenix and disgorged its passengers to awaiting buses. The plane then continued on to Tel Aviv. The Israelis were driven to a nearby motel for the night. The next afternoon, the Israelis boarded another plane and flew back to Lindbergh Field. They were then bused to a new location in Tijuana.

Sean had made arrangements to have the Israelis move into the Tijuana headquarters of Gamma Pharmaceuticals, a company which he controlled. Gamma was a large research and development company that had long term contracts from major drug companies throughout the world. They had over three hundred employees in a four building complex.

The new arrivals were given one of the buildings which had recently been vacated. The nice thing about it was that it was just a few miles away from their original lab. It only took a week to get their equipment back and set up. Extra security measures were put into effect and strictly enforced.

The many previous months of research on reconstituting the DNA of dead animals for cloning purposes had finally produced positive results. Previous cloning processes historically had a high rate of failure but Sarah developed a method that virtually guaranteed success in every case.

Over the following months, these procedures were tested and modified for humans. Eventually, they proved successful as well. Sarah was now ready for Albert Einstein.

An egg cell was taken from a donor, had its cytoplasm removed and placed in a Petri dish, together with Einstein's genetic material. Using an electric current, the two were fused.

Sarah would always remember how she had held her breath while peering into her electron microscope as she witnessed this historic union. Over the next six days, the cells reached the blastocyst stage, the critical step in the cloning process.

The embryo was then planted into the womb of a volunteer Israeli surrogate mother. After nine months, a baby was born. She named it Albert Melamed, the Yiddish word for teacher.

Once Sarah was satisfied that the baby was healthy, she had her scientists spend the following months working on the DNA of the other individuals supplied by the Israelis. All of them were successfully cloned. Israel would eventually have an assembly of some of the greatest minds in their history.

The Lazarus project was more successful than anyone had expected. The Israeli government sent Sarah a letter of appreciation. They apologized for not giving her public recognition because of obvious security reasons. Sarah understood. She told them she didn't do it for vainglory. The feeling of possibly helping the survival of her people was reward enough.

Once the Israeli scientists packed up and left, Sean said to Sarah, "Now that you have made history in the field of genetics, I have another project for you that may prove to be even more historical."

"That certainly sounds intriguing. What do you have in mind?"

"The cloning of the most famous Jew of all time."

"And who might that be?"

"Jesus Christ."

Sarah's eyes grew in astonishment and she said, "But Sean, that's impossible. I know that you, as a Catholic, believe that Jesus rose from the dead on Easter Sunday and ascended into heaven. Therefore, there couldn't be any physical remains."

"I used to think so, too. Then I remembered the work you did for STURP."

STURP was the acronym for the Shroud of Turin Research Project. In October of 1978, a group of esteemed physicists, chemists, pathologists, engineers, and photographers came from some of the most renowned institutions in the world: NASA, Sandia Laboratory, Jet Propulsion Laboratory, the U. S. Air Force, and Los Alamos Scientific Laboratory. They met in Turin, Italy, to examine the same shroud that Sean and Sarah had seen with Father Joe in 1954.

The group came with three million dollars' worth of scientific equipment that weighed more than eight tons. They spent more than one hundred and twenty hours examining and taking samples from the cloth.

Their purpose was to determine if it was the actual burial cloth of Jesus Christ, as many Christians believed. The Catholic Church had still not issued an opinion on its authenticity, but it was interested in having it examined to determine if the possibility existed.

The initial STURP reports appeared during the 1980s in scientific journals. The conflicting conclusions of the scientists cast a great deal of doubt on the shroud's date and, therefore, its authenticity. However, over the next twenty years, things changed dramatically. New scientific instruments came into being, and different scientists re-examined the data. Sarah, herself, was asked to review certain findings.

Sean asked Sarah, "Didn't the STURP people give you, and a few other scientists, a sample of some dried blood? Weren't you able to verify that it was type AB, and contained X and Y chromosomes, proving that it came from a male?"

"Yes."

"And didn't they also find some dried bodily fluids on the cloth and maybe even hair follicles?"

"Yes."

"Well, then, wouldn't these samples contain a good deal of DNA?"

"Yes."

"I thought so. I am now fully convinced that the Shroud was the authentic burial cloth of Christ and that, consequently, most of the DNA found on it belongs to Him."

"What convinced you?"

"A number of things. First, some recent research showed me that reevaluations of the initial findings seem to be mounting up in favor of the Shroud's authenticity. Some time ago, I went downtown to browse through Warwick's Book Store. I came across a fascinating book, just recently published, called 'The Resurrection of the Shroud', by Mark Antonacci. The author summarizes the original findings, presents some new scientific data, and makes a very convincing argument in favor of its authenticity.

"What initially impressed me the most was the conclusion of one of the original STURP examiners mentioned in the book, who happens to be a Jew."

"Who is he? Do I know him?" asked Sarah.

"I don't think so. His name is Barrie M. Schwortz. He's in Los Angeles. He was the Documenting Photographer for the STURP project. I want you to take a look at the web site he established and continues to update."

Sean booted up the computer on his desk and typed in www.shroud.com. "Read what Barrie has to say about his STURP experience."

Sarah peered at the screen and read the following:

"In the earliest stages of my involvement, I wondered whether someone raised as an Orthodox Jew should be a part of such a 'Christian' project. Even then I clearly understood that this was probably the most important relic of Christianity. In my heart I asked myself, 'Should I be a part of this?' But my good friend and fellow team member, the late Don Lynn, of NASA's Jet Propulsion Lab, was quick to remind me that the man in question was also a Jew. He urged me to 'go to Turin and do the best job possible' and worry about 'why and for what purpose' when I got back.' He suggested that, one day, I would know. I have never regretted taking his advice.

Now, over twenty years later, my 'purpose' has become very clear. As the Documenting Photographer for the project, I felt a responsibility to complete what I began, and make available some of the 2700 photographs and other materials I collected during the four years of the project. And finally tell the story of what took place in my own words and from my perspective. Frankly, I am still Jewish, yet I believe the Shroud of Turin is the cloth that wrapped the man Jesus after he was crucified. That is not meant as a religious statement, but one based on my privileged position of direct involvement with many of the serious Shroud researchers in the world, and a thorough knowledge of the scientific data, unclouded by media exaggeration and hype. The only reason I am still involved with the Shroud of Turin is because knowing the unbiased facts continues to convince me of its authenticity."

Sarah said, "That's quite interesting. I hadn't seen that before."

"There was another Jew mentioned in the book who also impressed me with his findings. His name is Dr. Avinoam Danin, a world-renowned professor of Botany at Hebrew University in Jerusalem. From his analysis of the cloth, the images of flowers that had lain on the Shroud, and various pollens lifted from the Shroud, he came to certain conclusions. He determined that the cloth was woven in the land of Israel. He was also able to determine that the period of its use as a shroud was either March or April, the Easter season, and that one of the flowers laid on the shroud was only found in and around Israel and was picked around 3 or 4:00 o'clock in the afternoon. These findings are totally consistent with the writings from the Bible. He, however, could not evaluate the age of the cloth."

"Sean, as I recall, the Vatican allowed some scientists to take a small swatch from the shroud in 1988 to do some carbon dating. University labs in Arizona, Oxford and Zurich tested pieces of that swatch and concluded that the age of the shroud was somewhere between 1260 and 1390 A. D. I thought that pretty well ended the authenticity controversy."

"Not quite. Something very interesting happened in 1995 in Columbus, Ohio. Sue Benford, a registered nurse, as well as an Executive Director of a non-profit biomedical organization, along with her husband, Joe Marino, a former Benedictine priest, teamed up to examine photographs of the shroud taken by the STURP scientists. When they minutely reviewed the section from which the swatch was taken for carbon dating, they noticed something peculiar. The herringbone weave used throughout the shroud was misaligned in that area.

"They suspected that the 1988 sample was from a damaged section of the linen shroud that was repaired in the 16th century, after being damaged in a fire. They concluded that a process known as French reweaving had repaired this section of the shroud. In this intricate process, new cotton threads were combined with the original linen threads to form an almost invisible repair. They sent pictures of this area to a few textile experts, without identifying where the fabric came from. Each of them confirmed that this area had been rewoven.

"The couple maintained that the combination of sixteenth century cotton threads, and first century linen threads, would have drastically skewed the carbon dating tests, yielding the faulty results announced by the labs. They just published their findings earlier this year.

"Raymond Rogers, a Los Alamos chemist on the original STURP team, said he was so irritated by the claim of these two non-scientists that he was determined to prove them wrong. He thought he could do it in five minutes.

"He still had some threads from 1978. Under a powerful microscope, he re-examined those linen threads, luckily from the same section as the 1988 sample, and found that they were, indeed, combined with cotton. He said the cotton fibers were heavily coated with dye in order to match the linen coloring during a repair. The repair had gone undetected because it was so expertly done, and there was no record of it. No one on the STURP team was a textile expert, and the area had not previously been a focus of any major Shroud researchers' attention because it was outside the body image area.

"He confirmed that Sue and Joe were right! Now can you see why I believe in the authenticity of the shroud?"

"Yes. But, even if you are right, how could you have the chutzpah to try to do such a thing? How could you, a practicing Catholic, justify what would seem to be a sacrilegious act?"

"That's a valid question. I wrestled with my conscience for many days over that. I found an answer in the teachings of Teilhard de Chardin."

Sarah cut in. "I remember that you and Joe have talked about him quite often over the years."

"Yes. Some of what I'm going to explain to you will be simplistic and redundant due to your scientific background. But, bear with me because I want to explain to you how I tried, step by step, to integrate the theories of Chardin, together with those of Charles Darwin and George Lemaître in order to come up with my idea."

"OK, I'll try to keep quiet until you finish."

"Good. I'll start with Chardin. He believed that the concept of evolution held as much weight as scripture. However, his theory ran completely counter to Darwin's, in that the success of humanity's evolution would not be determined by a random 'survival of the fittest,' but by an evolution mapped out by a divine intelligence.

"He believed that, from the moment of creation, 'a certain mass of elementary consciousness was originally imprisoned in the matter of the earth'. In other words, there was an inherent compulsion in matter to arrange itself in more complex groupings, exhibiting higher levels of consciousness. In essence, he said that evolution is an ongoing ascent towards higher and higher complexity and consciousness.

"I thought his theory nicely complemented those of Darwin and of Georges Lemaître. Lemaître was a Belgian Catholic priest as well as a mathematician and a physicist. He first proposed the Big Bang theory of an expanding universe in 1927. According to this theory, in the very beginning, there appeared a glowing ball of energy, so compact and heavy that it defies our comprehension. This cosmic egg, small enough to be held in one's hand, had within itself, all the enfolded information that would forever fuel the unfolding cosmos. This object was heated to an estimated 100 billion degrees centigrade, a temperature at which no stable particles could take shape, and, therefore, none of our current laws of physics applied.

"This primordial ball exploded and unfolded everywhere. Every particle rushed away from every other particle. The explosion filled all space, a space that curves back upon itself like the surface of a sphere. Eventually, the frenzied particles calmed, dissolving into a great scattering, and the cosmos began to transfigure itself. As this initial plasmic wave cooled, the microscopic stuff of stars, planets and DNA molecules began to weave themselves out of the initial chaos. It fashioned the galaxies. These gigantic self-organizing systems pinwheeled and clustered across the outer mantle of the universe.

"By feeding on helium and hydrogen, brilliant stars and planets were born. The early planets bubbled forth as gaseous soups that cooled into planetary crusts. Chemical creativity began to churn away.

"Darwin's theory of evolution tells us that on one of these planets, the Earth, the first living cell appeared. Our earliest single-celled ancestors reproduced by asexual cell division, as modern bacteria do. When single-celled organisms began to have sex they evolved into multi-cellular ones

"Multicelled organisms began as corals, became worms, and insects, and fish. They wiggled and flashed about in the sea and on the land. They multiplied into many life forms. Experimenting, they discarded some forms and built up others. As organisms became more complex, they developed a greater sense of consciousness. About two hundred million years ago, mammals entered into the life of the Earth and man became the highest mammal with the highest form of consciousness.

"An animal is only conscious of what it knows through the five senses of its material body. Man, on the other hand, is conscious of being conscious. He is aware of being aware, he can reflect back on himself. In short, he has a cognitive faculty, or intellect, that the animal does not possess.

"Man is capable of forming abstract ideas such as charity, or oneness, or justice, which are not found in any specific material object. Abstract ideas are immaterial and, by definition, immaterial means spiritual. Since the material cannot produce the immaterial, man must have a component in his being that is immaterial. The major religions call this component man's soul.

"They believe that God, who is the only being that can truly create something out of nothing, infuses each human being with a spiritual soul, that part of man made in His image and likeness. The exact moment of this infusion has been the subject of great debate among scholars and theologians down through the centuries."

Sarah said, "That's one of the big issues in the current abortion controversy."

"That's right. According to Teilhard's theory, human beings, in today's societies, have become more and more specialized in areas of expertise. The incredible rate at which scientific discoveries and technologies advance, today, ensures that the need to specialize will only increase. As humans become even more specialized in narrow fields of expertise, the need for cooperation becomes even greater.

"People throughout the world are becoming increasingly interdependent. Of necessity, they are forming more and more complex economic and political arrangements. People are becoming increasingly aware of how much they have in common with each other, more conscious of their unity, or oneness. After all, each person is basically made of the same stardust, the hydrogen and helium atoms that were forged at the beginning of the universe into all the other elements from which life emerged. Man is in the universe and the universe is in man.

"Teilhard theorized that society can thus be viewed as a multicellular organism, with individuals in the role of the cells. These organisms are now aggregating to form an organism of organisms: a 'superorganism'. This more complex superorganism, in turn, gives rise to a higher form of consciousness, a 'superconsciousness', which he called the noosphere. He regarded the noosphere as a 'thinking layer' surrounding the earth. Others have called it a 'global brain'.

"When socialization has reached its highest peak, he believed that our social development would then lead us into one unified society. As people realize they share a oneness with each other, they should find it more and more difficult to hate one another. To do so would be to hate themselves. The unifying factor is love. Christ's teaching 'to love one another as yourself' would seem, then, to have come to fruition.

"Teilhard believed that both the biological and social evolutions are not ends in themselves but strive to reach the highest evolution possible, what he called the Omega Point, the final unity of all men with Christ, the Son of God. He saw the role of Christ, in His Second Coming, as initiating this ultimate convergence."

Sarah frowned. "That was quite an explanation. Do you really think that civilization has reached this evolutionary level of superconsciousness? Do you actually believe that this so called noosphere, or global brain, really exists today?"

"Sarah, I want to point out to you that Teilhard wrote his book in 1947, but it wasn't published until after his death in1955. His prophetic vision was deemed by many, at that time, to be just so much science fiction. After all, in 1947, the computer was then little more than a glorified abacus, and Sputnik would not be launched until 1957.

"If you walk out onto our patio right now and look through a telescope at the night sky, you can actually see a physical manifestation of Teilhard's 'thinking layer'. In the heavens, you can see hundreds of satellites used by the internet, circling the globe, with hundreds more to come. They enable millions of worldwide computers to share the collective knowledge of mankind, almost instantaneously. They have formed what is essentially a giant neural network, a web of wisdom, Teilhard's global super-consciousness. We now have another word for it, cyberspace.

"Teilhard is now regarded by many as the patron saint of the internet and cyberspace."

"Sean, I'm still a little confused. Where are you heading with this?"

"Here's what I think could happen. Remember when you watched some football games with me and you often saw some people in the end zone stands holding up a sign that read 'John, 3:16'? That bible passage says 'God so loved the world that He sent His only Son, so that everyone who believes in Him might not perish but might have eternal life.'

"Christians believe that Jesus is the Son of God and that He came to earth once, to preach the gospel of love to all mankind, and to serve as the ideal role model. He also promised to return sometime after His death. I think this might be close to that time. Maybe you and I were destined to be the instruments for this historic second coming. Maybe we were meant to be the modern day Joseph and Mary by cloning their Son."

"Sean, that's incredible. You can't be serious."

"Why not?"

"Because I don't think the world has evolved to the state of 'oneness' that seems to be essential to your theory. There is still so much hostility and hatred especially in the underdeveloped parts of our world. Right now, for instance, I can't foresee the Jews and the Muslims ever getting together."

"Perhaps. But let's assume that our cloning experiment proved to be successful within the next few years. According to the bible, the original Jesus didn't start his public ministry until He was about thirty years old. Much could occur in the next thirty, or so, years. Look what happened to the fall of Russian Communism. Hardly anyone anticipated that it would collapse in the twentieth century. Chinese communism looks like it's on its last legs. Even the Muslim countries are starting to change. Technology is accelerating change more and more each year because our ability to communicate and share information gets better with each passing day. It's as if we are running our lives on fast forward.

"When Jesus came to earth the first time, He preached mainly to the poor and oppressed. He probably only talked to a total of a few thousand people during the course of His thirty-three years on earth. Many accepted His teachings, and His followers increased a million fold over the centuries. He changed the course of human history.

"I can envision the future Jesus clone reaching out to the entire world through cyberspace, Teilhard's global brain. He could preach His doctrine of love and salvation to the poor and oppressed as well as to the rest of the world at the same time. Just think of it, Sarah, everyone on earth could log on to the Son of God at www.Jesus.com, or tune in to Him on CNN or on their cell phone!

"Isn't it possible that this is how the promised second coming would come to pass?"

"Sean, are you trying to tell me that this new Bethlehem of yours would be located in a Petri dish and we would be substitutes for Mary and Joseph?"

"That's an interesting way to put it, but why not? We all know that God works in mysterious ways."

"I'll grant you that, but this idea of yours is mind boggling. What would the rest of the world say if they found out about such a project?"

"That, I think, could create the greatest controversy the world has ever seen. The current pope would obviously condemn it, but he's not going to live much longer. Perhaps succeeding popes would look at things with a different viewpoint. I know that most of today's Catholic theologians, like Joe, look at things much differently than the current pope. In the past, the Catholic Church has evolved very slowly. Everything else in life now seems to be on fast forward, perhaps the Church will eventually be swept up in that trend."

Sarah said, "Interesting. How would the other Christian religions react? What would the Orthodox, Conservative and Reformed rabbis say? What could be expected from the rapidly growing Muslim world? When would this Jesus clone realize that He was the new Messiah? What new message would He bring? Would His second coming be the harbinger of the end of the world as your bible indicates?"

Sean shrugged his shoulders. "I obviously don't have all the answers to your questions, but maybe, over time, you and I can find some of them. Are you willing to try this?"

Sarah looked at Sean intently and said, "I know how much this means to you. Of course I'll do it. You supported me, now it's my turn to support you. I could never imagine a more interesting challenge in my life. I'm getting goose bumps just thinking about it.

"You have to realize that this project would be more complicated, but I believe that the Lazarus project has given me the methodology to be successful. We have the experience, and we have newer and better hardware and computer software now. What we lack is genetic material. Can you get it?"

"I hope so. Remember, Joe is coming next month to stay with us for a few days. He is still intimately involved with the preservation of the Shroud. I'll try to find a way to persuade him to help us, but I know it won't be easy."

Chapter 43

The first day of May, 2002, was warm and sunny when Sean met Joe at Lindbergh Field. They greeted each other like long lost brothers. They then proceeded to La Jolla, where Sarah embraced her old friend.

That evening, Sean prepared their favorite meal, Osso Buco Morelli, which he paired with some fine bottles of California wine. When they had finished, Joe remarked, "I haven't seen you two for quite a while, tell me what you have been up to lately?"

Sarah, arching her eyebrows, looked at Sean and said, "Shall we tell him?"

Sean nodded his head. "Go ahead, you tell him."

"All right. Joe, you have to promise that you will listen to me all the way through my story without interrupting."

"Boy that sounds mighty mysterious. You have my undivided attention."

Sarah proceeded to tell Joe about the Israeli offer for her to clone dead Jewish historical figures.

Joe shook his head in awe. "That's the most incredible thing I have ever heard. What was your answer?"

"I agreed to do it."

Joe looked at Sean and asked, "What was your reaction?"

"As a matter of fact, I encouraged her to do it."

"Why would you do such a thing, Sean? You know the Church's stand against cloning."

"Of course I do. But Sarah's not Catholic. She feels strongly about the survival of her race. She believes that she is more qualified in her field than almost anyone else. If she can be the first to succeed, she will have given her people a great gift, an advantage that could change the odds in her people's favor. She is just following her conscience.

"I preferred to see her succeed in this field rather than some Islamist extremist or some other whacko. As a matter of fact, she was recently successful in cloning Albert Einstein as well as some other Jewish notables. It is a fantastic historical achievement. You are now one of the very few people to know about it."

While Joe sat there with a stunned expression on his face, Sarah interjected, "Remember, Joe, we once had a discussion about the first book of Genesis. Didn't God command Adam and Eve to be fruitful and multiply? He didn't specify how. If He didn't want humans to be able to be cloned, He could have changed the way DNA functions."

Sean added, "Maybe it was God's will that, when man had evolved to the proper stage, he could have available the ability to be more in control of life and, therefore, have more options to heed the command to multiply and fill the earth."

Sarah continued, "We Jews are God's chosen people. Jesus was a Jew. I feel as if I am helping God to choose the best and the brightest of our race in order for us to survive another perilous time in our history. In the Old Testament, God always provided such heroes as Moses, David, Solomon, and many others, when the Jews faced dire circumstances. Why can't I, a woman, be His instrument and co-creator to provide the future leaders and heroes to fulfill His commandments?"

Joe took a few moments before replying, "That's an interesting interpretation, but I'm not sure that I can agree with you."

Sarah pressed forward, "Perhaps your Church should reconsider its stance on this subject. Would they ever even consider it, Joe?"

"No, and I doubt that they ever will, at least not in our lifetimes. There are so many other problems that have been lingering for centuries that they haven't yet addressed. As I have previously told you two, I have become extremely frustrated with what is happening, or, perhaps I should say, what is not happening in the Church.

"As a matter of fact, the reason I'm here for a vacation is that I need time off to examine my life. I'm going through a serious crisis of faith. My initial idealism and enthusiasm have been eroded against the grindstone of reality. I'm not sure what I should do."

Sean furrowed his brow. "Really? I know you have been upset with the Church for a number of years over various things but I never dreamed that you would come to this point."

"The aftermath of Vatican II, and especially Humanae Vitae, has caused forty years of heady change and controversy for the Church. It was as if the Church was reborn and went through another stage of awkward adolescence. These new hormones made its body grow so rapidly that its limbs became gangly and uncoordinated. It seemed that the Church was constantly tripping over its feet, which had become disproportionately large. It started to develop what I call ecclesiastical acne and its voice started to change."

Sean interjected, "Too bad that its gonads didn't drop."

Joe chuckled, "I agree with you. As you two well know, I was in the forefront of the liberal and progressive wing that tried to push the Church forward to new insights and change. However, the conservatives in the Vatican, including the current pope, still controlled the power and were frightened by what was happening. Over the years, they have been methodically dismantling many of the changes we fought so hard for.

"Our present pope, John Paul II, has changed nothing. As a matter of fact, he has exacerbated the problems in the Church. He seems to fear and resist the modern world. I finally realized that he bears the scars of having been forged in a doubly persecuted church, first by the Nazis, then by the Communists. People in persecuted churches cling to every traditional symbol or practice of the church out of a fierce defiance to those who would crush it.

"That no doubt was why one of the pope's first acts in office was to order priests back into their Roman collars, and nuns back into their habits. It was a brave act to wear a Roman collar in Poland during his earlier days. But to treat the entire world as if it is plotting against you is to encourage a paranoid style of rule. The pope distrusts his own bishops and his own laity. He has emasculated the authority of the United States Conference of Catholic Bishops. He showers favor on those who share his paranoid concerns, who think of themselves as a besieged church within the church. It's like living in the Kremlin.

"The Church has become smaller, more insular, more dismissive of its members, more authoritarian, and more entrenched than ever. That it has become so after the spirit of the openness and the promise of collegiality of the Second Vatican Council is a betrayal of epic proportions.

"The net result has been a huge decline in the number of penitents and a loss of authority for confessors, particularly in sexual matters. As the educated laity questioned more and more precepts and became increasingly autonomous morally, the church became more and more irrelevant in their minds. This was a great tipping point in church history.

"The Catholic Church, at least here in the United States, has become virtually a voluntary association with Catholics increasingly finding authority in their individual consciences."

Sean spoke, "I agree with what you are saying. I have the impression that the pope and cardinals are acting like the ship's stewards who are rearranging the deck chairs while the Titanic is sinking."

"That's not a bad analogy, Sean. The question is whether the Church can redefine itself in terms of simple truth, or whether it will continue as an empty shell, acting in direct contradiction to its own sacred precepts, and in disdain for those it intends to protect and teach.

"The educated laity has become very restless and critical of the status quo. There is very little consultation with their local bishop. The people want their opinions to be heard and evaluated.

"Women are still treated like second class citizens and are refusing to accept it any longer. As a result, church attendance is substantially down in the industrialized nations. Our growth is now coming from people in the poor third world countries.

"After all, who is the Church? Why all of us, of course, both the laity and the priesthood. The laity far outnumbers the priesthood. They rightfully want their voices to be heard, and they are being ignored. It's an untenable situation.

"Priestly celibacy is being increasingly questioned by the priesthood as well as the laity. The bible tells us that St. Peter, the first pope, and the rock on whom the church was founded, was married. St. Paul, in his First Letter to the Corinthians, Chapter 9, acknowledges that other apostles were married.

"In his First Letter to Timothy, Chapter 3, St. Paul refers to married bishops and their children. It's quite clear that the precedent of a married clergy was established from the very beginning of Christianity.

"Celibacy only became mandatory in the 10th century. Maybe there was a need for it then because of the rampant corruption and abuses within the church at the time, but is it really necessary in this day and age?

"We are losing a tremendous amount of talent because so many men won't enter the priesthood because they can't marry. We have more and more parishes that no longer have a priest. We have the greatest message to give the world but we are running out of messengers. I'm beginning to feel that the future is pretty bleak."

Sean said, "Those are strong words, Joe, but I can't say that I am completely surprised at the depth of your feelings. I fully agree with you. One thing that has always bugged me is the fact that married Anglican priests who convert to Catholicism, and become Catholic priests, are allowed to remain married.

"And what about the priests in the Eastern rites? They are allowed to be married. Why does the Vatican talk out of both sides of its mouth about celibacy? It is the most hypocritical thing I have ever seen."

"Sean, I agree. It's very frustrating for me and many of my colleagues."

"So, Joe, what would you do if you were running things?"

"Well, first of all, I strongly believe that we have to make the church more participative. This, after all was one of the goals of Vatican II. Vatican administrators should not be allowed to become cardinals and, thereby, be able to vote for a new pope. Like all bureaucrats, they are too entrenched and isolated from the real world, and fiercely resistant to change. I mentioned this to you some time ago. This one change would create a monumental power shift away from the mainly ultraconservative Italian faction and open the door to the fresh air of new ideas as envisioned by John XXIII.

"I would also allow women to play a more important role in the church by initially becoming Deacons. There is a biblical precedent for this.

"In St. Paul's First Letter to Timothy, Chapter Three, he refers to women Deacons. There is documented proof that female Deacons existed in the Church until the fifth century.

Sean asked him, "Does your use of the word 'initially' mean that you would favor women becoming priests?"

"I haven't quite made a firm decision on that issue. There is a need to reexamine the role of women in society during Jesus' time versus today. Women are no longer chattel. Why should we waste the tremendous talents of over fifty percent of our congregations?

"Let's face it, women were also made in the same image and likeness of God. God is sexless. Souls are sexless. Women have the same intelligence and free will as men. We need all the help we can get."

Sarah smiled. "I say amen to that, Joe. Today's women have proven their capabilities in all walks of life when given the opportunity."

Joe nodded. "Sarah, you're a perfect example of that."

"Thank you."

"I also believe that laypeople should be able to help select pastors and bishops. Prior to the 1800s, priests played a major role in the selection of bishops. The current situation in which the pope has the sole authority to appoint bishops and cardinals is no longer tenable. We don't need more sycophants. Vatican II promised us a new era of collegiality. It hasn't happened.

"My most radical idea is to propose the establishment of a College of the Laity as a much needed counterbalance and co-equal to the College of Cardinals. It would share and supplement the functions of the College of Cardinals. Its membership would be composed of men and women from a variety of countries, occupations, and walks of life. I firmly believe that Church leadership should not be limited only to elderly male priests.

"I want to point out the fact that the office of Cardinal is honorary, it has no sacramental or intrinsic connection to Holy Orders. Its members function as papal advisors and diplomatic envoys. There are ecclesial jobs that a layperson can handle very well, probably even more effectively than an ordained priest.

"This new College of the Laity would add a badly needed perspective on the impact of the teachings and practices of the Church. The combined Colleges would more accurately represent the true face of the Church and would provide more realistic advice and proposals to the pope.

"Furthermore, I think that the members of the College of the Laity should also be allowed to vote for new popes. It's a little known fact that any male Catholic can be elected pope. He doesn't even have to be a priest."

Sarah questioned Joe, "Do you mean that even Sean could be elected pope?"

"That's right. If that happened, he would have to be quickly ordained a priest, then a bishop and a cardinal. It has happened once before, in 1032, with the election of Pope Benedict IX at age eighteen, the youngest pope ever. The tradition has already been established, and we all know how strongly the Vatican loves tradition."

Sarah smiled. "I would love to see Sean become pope. Just think, he would be the first married pope with a Jewish wife. With all those beautiful robes, I would be the envy of all my friends."

Joe had a hearty laugh. "I also would love to see that."

Sean added, "So would I. But, seriously, I love the idea of a College of the Laity. I've cringed at the secretive, irrational, and incomprehensible way the Vatican is handling the clergy sexual abuse problem versus the straightforward way a corporation handles similar problems of sexual abuse within its ranks. A corporate offender would not simply be transferred to another division. He, or she, would be fired, or be forced to resign. In most cases, the police would be informed.

"I don't think the Vatican's egregious mishandling of the problem would have happened if a College of the Laity was in existence to give hardnosed practical advice to the pope. The average person hates the hypocrisy and deceit that has been foisted on us.

"Furthermore, the Vatican could really use the business acumen and expertise of such an advisory assembly. It has an urgent need to learn about the benefits of a more efficient management of human, financial, and physical resources.

"Look at the scandals that have revolved around the Vatican Bank over the years in its mishandling of funds and its alleged ties to the Mafia. It wasn't that way years ago when I worked with Msgr. Fellini.

"You have told me in the past that administrators and members of the Curia are not promoted on the basis of expertise or merit. That's felony stupid considering the enormous responsibility attached to many of the jobs.

"I would make it mandatory that seminaries include certain basic business courses in their curriculum, such as finance and management. Promotions to higher offices and the Curia should favor those priests who continue to take some advanced business courses. Lord knows, we have a lot of Catholic universities that offer excellent programs. Many of them provide courses over the internet.

"I have personally seen that members of the Curia are deeply influenced by Italianate work habits. Its members usually leave work in the early afternoon, so they have plenty of time to study."

Joe said, "I hadn't thought of that. It sounds interesting. Do you have any other suggestions?

"Yes, I do. Members of the Vatican are human beings with the same strengths and weaknesses of character that we laymen have. There have been strong rumors of greed, corruption, nepotism, cronyism, and sexual misconduct among them. They have proven that they are unwilling or unable to police themselves and have been resorting to subterfuge and cover-ups of massive proportions. An outside force, such as the College of the Laity, could form an oversight committee on accountability to investigate and put a stop to this hypocrisy and thereby regain the people's trust and respect."

"Sean, you're making some very good points. We desperately need to bring the church into the twenty-first century. I fear the office of the pope is being compromised by the Curia and other staff members and is losing its moral authority with the people.

"As long as I am talking about the pope, why is it that he holds the office for life? Priests and bishops are required to retire at age seventy-five. The pope is just as human and subject to the same vicissitudes of old age. Too often have we seen popes who have become physically unable to perform many of their duties in their later years. I have to assume that some of them have also been afflicted with diminished mental capacity. However, they are so well insulated from us, inside the Vatican, that we never know the truth. Without a healthy and vigorous pope, the Curia takes over, much to our detriment."

Sean asked, "If I remember correctly, weren't there some popes that resigned?

"Yes. There have been a few. The last one was Pope Gregory XII in 1415. The historical precedent has already been established."

Sean shook his head. "Boy, you really have quite a number of radical ideas there, Joe. Do you think any of them will ever be implemented?"

"Some of them might. I do know that radical changes have to be made fairly soon, otherwise the Church will continue to lose members in larger and larger numbers.

"Exegetists in our Church, as well as those in other denominations, are constantly examining new discoveries by archeologists, biologists, linguists, and other scientists, which give us new insights into the interpretation of the scriptures and the times in which they were written.

"Saint Thomas Aquinas and Saint Augustine are the two past theologians who have had the major influence on Church teachings. Their philosophy and theology was based on their belief that the universe was static. We now know that is not the case. As we discussed before, many of my theologian colleagues agree with Teilhard de Chardin that, since the entire universe is constantly evolving, our theology must also evolve when we discover new evidence. The hierarchy, however, is still mired in the distant past and refuses to open its mind and heart to new ideas."

Sean commented, "It has always seemed to me that Theology is like a matryoshka doll."

Joe had a puzzled look. "What is that?'

"That's a set of Russian nesting dolls, which consists of a wooden figure that separates, top from bottom, to reveal a smaller figure inside that has, in turn, another figure inside of it, and so on. The smallest, innermost doll, is typically a baby lathed from a single small piece of wood and is non-opening."

"That's an interesting analogy, Sean. You're saying that the job of us theologians is to open and examine the various teachings of the Church until we come to find the baby, the Christ child, whose basic message is a simple four letter word, LOVE."

"That's exactly what I mean."

Joe shook his head. "I like that analogy. Unfortunately, I feel that the current hierarchy of the Church doesn't want us to keep opening those dolls. They are quite content with the status quo."

Sean, with a sly grin, said, "Joe, I've been thinking that, if some dramatic changes won't be made in our Church, I would form my own alternative religion."

Joe decided to play along with him. "I would like to hear more about that. I might be interested in joining it. What would you call it?"

"I'm torn between the 'Church of the Holy Tabernacle Door Half Open', or, 'The Church of Our Lady of Questionable Taste.' Instead of the Ten Commandments, we would have the 'Seven Suggestions and Three Do the Best You Can.'"

Joe had a good laugh at that. "You probably would have a huge congregation, especially here in California."

Sean, still smiling, said, "I'm sure I would. But let me get back to the more serious part of our conversation. As I understand it, then, you think the Church is being torn apart because the pope and cardinals seem to be getting more and more remote from the concerns of the priesthood and laity, there is less and less transparency in the operation of the inner workings of the Church and that the line of communication with the laity, as well as the bishops, is strictly one way."

"Yes. Let's face it, thanks to your companies and many others, we are immediately able to access whatever information we want over the internet. Today's Catholics, especially here in America, are extremely well educated and are quite able to think for themselves. They aren't reluctant to question and challenge authority when things don't seem to make sense, or even when they do.

"The lack of communication between the laity, the priesthood, and the hierarchy is one of our most serious problems. In 1969, as Archbishop of Cracow, Pope John Paul II, encouraged both the faithful and theologians to public discourse and dissent when he said, 'Conformity means death for any community. A loyal opposition is a necessity in any community.'

"A decade later, as pope, he declared, 'The Church needs her theologians, particularly in this time and age. We desire to listen to you and we are eager to receive the valued assistance of your responsible scholarship.' Unfortunately, the pope doesn't practice what he preaches. He has, since then, arbitrarily muzzled a goodly number of theologians because he doesn't like what they say and he hasn't allowed them any discussion or recourse. I find this kind of censorship to be stifling. We have very little dialogue, it's mostly a monologue.

"The role of theologians requires us to explore the perceived difficulties with current authoritative teaching. We must challenge what we perceive to be faulty theological arguments in contemporary teachings that appear to be at variance with our intuitions and experiences, as well as those of the faithful.

"Why should the Pope and the magisterium be afraid of honest inquiry? If their authoritative teaching on a subject is in fact authentic, its validity can only be enhanced. If it is not authentic, the inquiry could lead to the development of a substantive change in its teaching. This logical approach could possibly change people's minds about leaving what they think is a moribund Church."

Sean interrupted, "If I remember correctly, didn't St. Paul strongly disagree with St. Peter's position on regulations for Christian converts, and didn't St. Peter, who is regarded as the first pope, change his mind?"

"Yes, that's true. A loyal opposition was in place from the very beginning of Christianity. As a theologian, I feel strongly about my role as a member of the loyal opposition. Right now, I am deeply discouraged. I believe that what the Church desperately needs now is a catharsis, a revitalization of faith, a revolution of sorts, something that would bring mankind closer to the ideal of Jesus Christ."

Sean smiled at his friend. "You just brought up the topic of revolution. I was waiting to talk to you about that."

Chapter 44

Joe asked Sean, "You want to talk about revolution? What is that all about?"

"Actually, I want to discuss two revolutionaries, namely, Jesus Christ and Chardin."

"That's an interesting pairing. What are you getting at, Sean?"

"Let me explain. When Sarah agreed to the Israeli's request, it started me thinking. Who was the greatest Jew of all time?"

Joe replied, "Jesus Christ, of course."

"Of course. So, it got me pondering about a hypothetical question. Since Sarah was successful in her cloning of Jewish notables, why not try to clone the most notable of all Jews, Jesus?"

"Sean, that's ridiculous. I know that you believe Christ rose from the dead and ascended bodily into heaven. That would be impossible, there are no remains."

"That's not quite true, Joe. Remember when you showed us the Shroud of Turin way back in 1954? We saw blood stains on that linen fabric. I don't have to remind you that you were there when scientists from the 1978 STURP project took some blood and tissue samples found on the Shroud. They were able to determine that the blood was type AB and contained human DNA with XY chromosomes. This confirmed that the samples came from a human male.

"For many years, the scientists disagreed on the age of the shroud. However, as you well know, recent findings have pretty much proved that the shroud came from the first century. I believe that the shroud is authentic as I think you do."

"Yes, I do."

"Sarah thinks that her science has since progressed to the point that she could use the genetic material on the shroud to reconstruct Christ's DNA for cloning purposes."

"Sean, that's the most incredible idea I have ever heard of. Why would you even think of attempting such a sacrilege?"

Sarah smiled. "Let me answer that one, Sean. Joe, I recently saw a cartoon in one of my medical journals which shows a woman talking to a man at a cocktail party. The caption reads: 'All I'm saying is that if God created man in his own image, he was a bit of a cloner Himself.' "

Joe laughed. "That was a good one. Touché."

"On a more serious note, Joe, let me explain my viewpoint. Having listened to you and Sean discuss religion and philosophy for all these years has made me reflect more deeply on my own Jewish heritage and religion.

"Jews do not accept Jesus as the Messiah for two reasons. First, Jesus did not fulfill what we believe were the messianic requirements to restore the national sovereignty of the Jewish people in the land of Israel, and to gather in all the exiles.

"Secondly, Jesus did not fulfill the messianic criteria to bring about God's universal kingdom of justice and peace on earth.

"Christians say that's true, He didn't do those things at that time, but He will when He returns once more. Jews say that, if He didn't do that when He was here, then He wasn't The One. And, if He does come back and perform what a Messiah must do, we'll all be happy to call Him the real Messiah.

"Here's how I address the first argument. I think that, today, we Jews have the strongest military might in the Middle East. We have a really good chance of gaining sovereignty in the land of Israel in the not too distant future. I believe my successful efforts to clone our Jewish heroes will help to accelerate this process.

"Furthermore, as you know, we have already gathered almost all the exiles who wish to return to Israel.

"As a result of these two things, I believe that the way is close to being prepared for the second coming of Jesus which your bible has predicted. If He comes a second time, there might well be more fertile ground for Him to bring about a kingdom of justice and peace. I would like to be instrumental in helping that prophecy to be fulfilled."

Joe looked at Sarah and shook his head. "That certainly is a unique way of looking at things."

Sean said, "Joe, here's what I think. You have often told us that Chardin revolutionized Catholic Theology with his teaching on human evolution, and his belief in an evolving universe. I thought that this cloning idea was something that he would have encouraged, if he had been alive today. You, yourself, strongly maintain the position that theology should be an evolving field."

Joe replied, "What makes you believe that he would have condoned such a bizarre scheme such as this?"

"Two words: Omega Point."

"Omega Point? What do you mean by that?"

Sean answered, "I know you share his primary thesis that the cosmic natural order of evolution is an ongoing ascent toward higher and higher complexity and consciousness as well as an increased ascent to greater unity."

"Of course I do."

"You also know that Chardin viewed human societies as multicellular organisms, with individuals in the role of the cells. I believe that, today, these organisms are aggregating to form an organism of organisms, a 'superorganism'. This more complex superorganism, in turn, gives rise to a higher form of consciousness, a 'superconsciousness', what Teilhard called the 'noosphere', a 'thinking layer surrounding the earth. Others have called it a 'global brain'. Today, a more popular term is cyberspace."

Joe said, "Tell me something I don't know."

"Well, I believe that, today, man is entering the stage of super complexity and, therefore, a stage of superconsciousness."

"What makes you think that?"

Sean continued, "As I once explained to Sarah, if you look at the sky at night, you can actually see a physical manifestation of Teilhard's noosphere or cyberspace. In the heavens, you can see hundreds of satellites used by the internet, circling the globe, with hundreds more to come. They enable millions of worldwide computers to share the collective knowledge of mankind, almost instantly, by contacting a specifically chosen search engine on the web. This is rather slow and awkward when compared to the speed and flexibility with which our own brain thinks.

"Right now, some of my technology companies are in the beta stage of testing 'wearable computers'. You can have these miniaturized powerful processors with you continuously, perhaps attached to a belt. They will have access to the World Wide Web through the almost ubiquitous WI-FI networks, cell phone towers, or satellites.

"They come with special glasses that allow you to see information from the computer, superimposed on a normal view of your surroundings. Thus, the computer can constantly provide you with information about the things you see, and warn you when an important message arrives.

"These computers use multimedia interfaces, allowing them to harness the full bandwidth of three-dimensional audio, visual, and tactile perceptions in order to communicate information to your brain.

"The complementary technologies of speech, or gesture recognition, make the input of information by the user much easier. For example, the wearable computers are connected to a small microphone, into which you can speak, and a glove, or sophisticated trackball kept in your pocket, with which you can steer the cursor or manipulate virtual objects.

"We are also doing advanced research on the next phase of information technology, what is called BCI, for Brain Computer Interface. This is based on neural network interfaces, providing a direct connection between nerves and computer.

"For example, you would be able to steer a cursor on your wearable computer screen simply by thinking about it. Your brain waves, associated with particular thoughts such as up, down, left or right, are registered by sensors attached to your head and interpreted by neural network and artificial intelligence software. These interpretations are passed on to the computer interface in the form of a command, which is then executed. Eventually, we may even be able to attain telepathic communication with each other.

"Once these technologies have become more sophisticated, we could imagine the following scenario: at any moment, a thought might form in your brain, and then be translated, automatically, via a neural interface to the external 'global brain', accessing various data banks, and come back to your own brain in a much enriched form. With a good enough interface, there should not really be a border between 'internal' and 'external' thought processes: the one would flow naturally and immediately into the other. We will be able to access the entire knowledge of the human race instantaneously.

"At this point, we will have reached the complexity level of a superorganism with its corresponding superconsciousness. This may well be the final level of our evolution."

Joe nodded his head and said, "That's a fascinating scenario you have painted. What do you see happening after that?"

"The bible tells us that Christ will come again. If Christ were to reappear on earth at that point, He could be the catalyst that accelerates the process leading to the ultimate evolutionary level, the Omega Point.

"He could easily tap into the World Wide Web and spread His gospel of love, harmony, and unity throughout the world. He first came to earth to show us and teach us what the ideal human being should be. Why not repeat it? He would certainly have more fertile ground the next time.

"I look at it this way. Our souls are that part of us made in the image and likeness of God. I picture them as little mirrors that both absorb and reflect the blinding love and glory of the creator. Suppose all these soul 'mirrors' came into harmony with one another by becoming properly aligned like mirrors that form a huge parabolic dish. They would reflect and concentrate their light of love on one focus point, God, who is both the originator and receptor of that light. This interaction would be the ultimate unity of man and his creator. This could well be the Omega Point predicted by Chardin."

Joe looked at Sean for a few moments, mulling over what he had just heard. "I see what you're getting at. You're referring to the fact that Chardin described the Omega Point as 'a time when light would blaze across the planet, not physical light but the light of consciousness.' Am I right?"

"Yes. Each of the mirrors, polished to give a perfect reflection, and united with all those other apparently separate rays of consciousness, would know themselves to be part of the same eternal light of consciousness. Man would experience a feeling of oneness with humanity and with God. At this Omega Point, our evolution's ever-accelerating trend would at last come to an end. Man would have become more Christ-like and be united with Him by fulfilling God's greatest commandments: to love God and one's neighbor.

"Joe, I remember a previous conversation that we had concerning the question of why God created man. My theory fleshes out your thesis. You might think of this evolutionary stage as the creation, by humanity itself, of an entity that would be more Christ-like, an entity that God could love and be united with."

Joe merely replied, "That's a fascinating theory, Sean. You make it sound so simple and logical."

Sean replied, "I applied the principle of Occam's razor to come to this conclusion."

Sarah frowned. "I've heard the term Occam's razor but have forgotten what it is."

Joe said, "Let me answer that question. The term Occam's razor is attributed to a 14th century English Franciscan friar, logician and theologian by the name of William of Occam. The principle states that, other things being equal, a simpler explanation is better than a more complex one. The term razor refers to distinguishing between two theories either by shaving away unnecessary assumptions or cutting apart two similar theories.

"Sean, I think you have successfully applied a razor to your presentation. I applaud your creativity. You really did cut through some very complex and competing philosophical theories and came up with a simple and elegant solution to your problem.

"Sometimes I think I am too close to the trees to see the forest. You have just given me a refreshing new perspective on the subject. I think you missed your calling."

"I'm very flattered, Joe. I think our Jesuit training and our conversational jousting over many years has led me to come to this conclusion."

Sarah looked at the two men and said, "This is pretty deep stuff for me, but I think I understand what Sean is saying. Joe, what do you think might happen if we ever reach this Omega Point?"

"I really don't know, Sarah. We theologians have been debating that question for many years and haven't come to a common conclusion.

"Perhaps, at that point, we will witness the final judgment and resurrection, forecast in the bible, when God will separate the good from the bad. Since we consist of a material body and an immaterial soul, it would be reasonable to assume that our resurrected and reunited bodies would participate in whatever reward or punishment we merit.

"It would probably be the end of the world as we know it now, but it wouldn't necessarily mean the destruction of the real world. With superconsciousness, we might find ourselves in a totally different kind of reality."

Sarah cut in, saying, "That's a very interesting point. Ever since Einstein came up with his theories of relativity, mathematicians and physicists have tried to come up with a single, elegant 'Theory of Everything' that would be used as the basic unifying principle for nature. Some of them now think they may have discovered it.

"They call it the M-Theory. It postulates the existence of as many as eleven dimensions, and the existence of parallel universes, each with a different law of physics. Do you think it possible that we might find our new existence in one of those parallel universes?"

"Sarah, that's a great insight. It's interesting to speculate that, in one of these parallel universes, our resurrected bodies could live on with different attributes, similar to those preternatural gifts found in the parable of Adam and Eve in the Garden of Eden. After all, Christ's incarnation demonstrated that our physical death is ultimately to be connected with a resurrection into a new and changed eternal life. But, I'm afraid that we will have to await the answer to this question when, and if, the Omega Point occurs."

Sean replied, "That leads me to ask you why can't we hasten this inevitable conclusion to our destinies? If we could clone Jesus, it might take Him about thirty years to fulfill His mission, the same amount of time as His first historical appearance. Our world has changed dramatically in the past thirty years and it will change even more dramatically in the next thirty, or so, years. It's as if the whole world is now on fast forward. The world may be ready for the new Messiah in thirty years.

"What do you think of this scenario? Could you approve of it?"

Joe pursed his lips. A smile appeared as he answered Sean, "My gut reaction is, of course, no, but I would like to think about it overnight."

On the following morning, the three of them had breakfast. Sean asked Joe, "Well, how do you feel about our previous conversation?"

"I've been up all night thinking about it. As I mentioned earlier, my initial reaction was to reject your idea outright. Then I reviewed your explanation of Chardin's theory of superconsciousness and the Omega Point, and that struck a deep chord within me. It put things in an entirely different light. It made me think that, if man could be a co-creator of the Son of God, man would have achieved the absolute pinnacle of his existence. What a wondrous thought! The idea overwhelmed me."

"Joe, would you like to help make that scenario come true?"

"How?"

"Sarah would need to have access to the Shroud of Turin in order to collect whatever genetic material that may still be there. I know that you are still the key person entrusted with its preservation. Could you get her that access?"

Joe slapped his head and exclaimed, "Oh, my god! This couldn't be just a coincidence."

"What are you talking about, Joe?"

"It just so happens that many months ago I scheduled the Shroud to undergo a major restoration a few weeks from now, between June 20 and July 22. I chose the team that is going to do the work and I will be overseeing the operation.

"In 1534, a linen backing fabric, called holland cloth, was sewn to the back of the Shroud to provide stability and help to preserve it."

Sarah said, "I remember seeing that."

"This backing cloth will be removed for the first time since then, and a new cloth will take its place. Even the STURP people didn't have full access to the back of the Shroud.

"I'm getting this eerie feeling that the timing of your request and the timing of the restoration have been preordained by a higher power, and not by chance."

Sean and Sarah stared at each other in utter amazement. Sean finally spoke, "Joe, I think you're right. This is a message that can't be ignored. It was meant to be. Will you help Sarah?"

Joe shrugged his shoulders and raised his hands in surrender. "It pains me to say this, but I don't believe I have a choice to do otherwise. Besides, I'm rapidly approaching mandatory retirement age and this may be my last shot at making a meaningful change in my moribund Church. Yes, count me in."

Chapter 45

Joe spent the next few weeks relaxing with his friends, thinking, and planning the upcoming restoration of the Shroud. When he felt fully reenergized, the trio flew to Rome.

Sarah told Sean, "It's so exciting to realize that I'll be one of the first people to examine the back of the shroud in almost five hundred years. The STURP people didn't have that advantage and I think that's why there has been so much controversy about their results. We have a much better chance of gathering enough DNA to give us a fairly decent shot at achieving our goal. I can hardly wait."

The restoration of the shroud was carried out in the sacristy of the Turin Cathedral. It was being done by a team headed by Swiss expert Mechtild Flury-Lemberg, former director of the Abegg Museum in Berne.

Joe introduced Sarah to the restoration team as his personal representative and advisor. Most of them were aware of her reputation and greeted her cordially.

During 40 days of work, starting on June 20, experts removed patches that Clarisse nuns sewed on the cloth after it was damaged in a fire in the French Cathedral of Chambery in 1532. After the holland cloth was removed, both sides of the shroud were scanned digitally for the first time, measurements and other observations were painstakingly recorded and photographs were taken at each step of the work.

The nuns replaced its backing of holland cloth, also dating to the 16th century, and vacuumed up particles of pollen, burnt cloth and other impurities that had accumulated on the cloth over the centuries. All the material removed was catalogued and placed in safekeeping. When the restoration team left the room each evening, Sarah stayed to collect her genetic samples. She had the advantage of studying the prior STURP notes and photographs so she knew where to concentrate her efforts in extracting samples of the blood and bodily fluids she needed.

When the work was finally completed, Sarah packed up her instruments and the trio left Tours to return to Joe's apartment in Rome.

Joe asked her, "Do you think you got enough samples for your project?"

"Yes, I do. Sean and I certainly want to thank you for your cooperation. We know how difficult it was for you to make this decision."

"Yes, it was the most difficult decision in my life. It required a great leap of faith, but I was reminded of an old saying that you can't leap across a wide chasm in two short jumps. I think the three of us just jumped the world's widest chasm. I pray to God that we are right."

The following day, Sean and Sarah flew back to La Jolla. Once back in the privacy of their home, Sarah discussed the Almega project with Sean.

"The methodology we developed for cloning the Israelis has given us excellent results. Trying to clone Jesus from His DNA will be a little more difficult but I believe it's doable. The shroud has been contaminated by many people over the centuries but I think that I can identify and isolate the remnants of His particular DNA and reconstruct it. It really boils down to just a matter of time for our newer hardware and software to analyze and solve this complicated jigsaw puzzle. I think we will have the answer in the near future."

A few months later, Sarah told Sean that she had replicated the DNA that she believed belonged to Jesus. She took Sean into her lab to view the experiment. "I have a surprise for you, Sean. The ovum I'm using is my own. Prior to having my hysterectomy many years ago, I had the doctor remove a number of my eggs and had them frozen, just in case you were unhappy with having only two children. Since I am a descendant of the House of David, and since Joe once made me aware of my distant kinship with Jesus, I thought it would be appropriate to make use of one of my eggs at this time."

Sean gave her a warm hug. "Dear, you never cease to amaze me."

They both watched the successful uniting of the egg and the DNA through a powerful microscope. Sean was so overcome with emotion that he started to shiver violently for a few moments.

Sarah had asked a young Israeli volunteer, named Ruth, to remain behind when the Lazarus project ended. Sarah told Ruth that she had a special surrogate project for her.

Ruth was a healthy, vivacious twenty-one year old virgin who had been born and raised in Jerusalem. She was told only that the baby she would be carrying was the clone of one of the most important Jews that had ever lived. The Torah had foretold that he would be a great leader. His reincarnation would be a major factor in establishing the rightful destiny of Israel. She was thrilled with the honor.

She was also warned that the baby might have some powerful enemies. If they even suspected who the baby was, they would try to kill him and her. That was the reason why Ruth could not be told the baby's identity, and why she had to be isolated from the others.

Sarah had her live in the guest house in La Jolla after she was impregnated. Sarah closely monitored her progress. She gave Ruth a special medal to wear. It was made of gold, and contained the Star of David on the front. The back contained a strange inscription, which Ruth didn't understand. It said ALMEGA.

When Ruth entered her ninth month, Sarah chartered a private plane to fly Ruth to a special obstetric clinic in Mexico City, where she would be completely anonymous. Sarah and Sean planned to join her later for the birth.

As they watched the plane depart, Sarah said to Sean, "I have never been so excited in my life. I can't wait until the baby is born. What if we were wrong in attempting this? Will god punish us for our hubris?"

Sean replied, "We will soon find out. If we are successful, the world will never be the same. If we are wrong, I hope that God grades on a curve."

Chapter 46

The plane encountered a severe thunderstorm in the area around Puebla, Mexico. A bolt of lightning struck the plane and disabled the engines and electrical systems. The plane crash-landed in a lake and began to sink rapidly. The pilot was killed instantly.

Ruth was seriously injured but managed to escape through the broken windshield of the cockpit, severely cutting herself. She was barely able to swim the fifty yards to the shoreline. She managed to crawl out of the water onto the shore where she lapsed into unconsciousness.

When she awoke, it was dark. She was bleeding profusely from her wounds and was in a state of shock. She looked around for help and saw a faint glow of light in the distance.

One leg was broken so she could not walk. However, she managed to crawl slowly and painfully through the drenching rain towards the light. She eventually reached its source, and found that it was coming from a window that appeared to be a barn, adjacent to a farm house. With a superhuman effort, she was able to crawl to the door and pound furiously on it.

The barn was part of a farm owned by José Benveniste and his wife, Maria. Jose's ancestors were Sephardic Jews who had been exiled from Spain by the Catholic Monarchs, Ferdinand, and Isabella, in 1492. Their descendants wandered through Europe for centuries. Some of them eventually sailed to the New World and settled in Mexico. Since they spoke Ladino, a Spanish dialect spoken by Ferdinand, Isabella, Columbus, and Cervantes, they easily adapted to their new country.

José had inherited the farm from his father, Juan, who had been a rabbi in the small Jewish community of Puebla. José was very proud of his father and, when he was very young, he dreamed of following in his footsteps. He studied hard in school and was a good student. At home, his father taught him the Hebrew language and had him study the Torah. When he came of age, he made his Bar Mitzvah.

While attending school, he found that he had a natural talent for art. His beautiful drawings impressed both his classmates and teachers. When he finished high school, he decided that he no longer wanted to be a rabbi, he wanted to study art. His father, needless to say, was disappointed, but José was an only child and the father didn't want to stifle his ambitions. He reluctantly agreed to send José to the university in Mexico City to pursue his dream. The university was only a couple of hours away, so the parents would be able to see their son on a regular basis.

José took the usual art courses but he became particularly interested in creating sculptures. He learned to work in clay, metal, and stone, but he found his true love in wood. He could take a piece of wood, look into its soul, and sense the kind of figures that would best take advantage of the wood's grain and color. He discovered that his artistic talents also allowed him to design and make elegant custom pieces of furniture.

After graduation, he stayed in Mexico City and worked under some master craftsmen, in order to hone his skills. After a few years, his name became well known in the art world. He started to receive commissions to create statues and furniture for some of the wealthy families in the city.

He had met a sweet young Jewish student, named Maria Sanchez, while attending the university. She worked part time as a model in the art classes in order to pay her tuition. José fell in love with her. José's father married them when they graduated. They set up house in Mexico City.

When his parents were badly injured in a car accident, José moved back home to Puebla to supervise their care. Both parents died within a few weeks of his arrival. He decided to remain in Puebla because he never really liked the hustle and bustle of Mexico City. Furthermore, the city was becoming more and more dangerous. He feared for Maria's safety. He reasoned that he could work in peace and quiet in Puebla and drive to the big city whenever it became necessary.

The Almega Project

The family farm was in an ideal location. It was far enough away from the town so that few visitors wandered by to interrupt his work. The farm sat on top of a small hill. He could see for miles in every direction. There was a large lake nearby. In his youth, José had spent many hours fishing and swimming in it.

The farm contained a small barn, which housed the few cows, pigs, sheep and chickens that his mother had tended. Maria had also been raised on a farm. She loved animals and persuaded José to keep them. José agreed, he felt that Maria wouldn't be quite so lonely while he was pursuing his career.

Since he needed a lot of room to work, he decided to enlarge the barn by adding a new, walled-off, section, which would serve as his workshop/studio. He put in many windows to give him the natural light, which he favored. It proved to be the ideal environment to inspire his creative juices.

The young couple wanted to have children and they were delighted when Maria became pregnant.

A month before the baby was due, José had to visit some clients in Mexico City. Maria went with him. While they were there, Maria started to hemorrhage. José rushed her to the hospital where the doctors had to perform an emergency Caesarean. The baby was stillborn. The doctors also had to perform a hysterectomy in order to stop the hemorrhaging. That ended her hopes of ever becoming a mother. The couple was heartbroken. When Maria was released from the hospital, they drove back to Puebla.

José was at work in the studio section of the building, carving intricate designs on an elaborate desk that had been commissioned by a wealthy banker. Maria was keeping him company. She found that helping him kept her mind off her recent tragedy. Jose was working under a few kerosene lanterns. A strong thunderstorm had been in the area all day and had knocked out the electricity and phone lines. The roads had become impassable.

Maria heard a noise and said, "José, I think someone is knocking on the barn door."

"I doubt it. No one would be out on a night such as this. It was probably one of the animals making that noise."

"No, I'm sure it was somebody knocking. I'm going to see."

"Wait, I'll come with you. We'll need a lantern to see what's out there."

They walked out of the studio into the stable area and opened the barn door. They found a woman lying in the mud. She was semi-conscious, and her wet clothing was heavily stained with blood.

"Oh, my God," cried Maria. "That poor woman. José, carry her into the barn. I'll put some clean straw on the floor. Let's see what wrong with her."

José lifted the woman and carried her inside. He gently placed her on the straw pallet that Maria had hastily put together.

Maria said, "She's as white as a ghost. She must have lost a lot of blood. She feels so cold, she must be freezing to death. We have to get her out of those wet clothes. I'll do that while you get some of the horse blankets to warm her up until we find something better."

José nodded and quickly grabbed two blankets as Maria undressed the woman. Maria shouted, "Oh this poor woman is pregnant. From the looks of her, she must be in her ninth month. Maria put her ear to the woman's stomach. "The baby is still alive. It's really kicking up a storm. I think it's ready to be born."

"Speaking of a storm," said José, "We can't get any medical help out here, and we can't get her to a hospital until this storm ends and the roads are passable. She has a serious wound in her chest and it looks like she's going in shock due to all the blood she has lost. Her pulse is very weak. I'm not sure that she is going to survive much longer. You get her as warm as possible. I'll get the First Aid kit from the studio and see if we can stop the bleeding."

José came back with his kit and applied pressure bandages to the woman's wounds. Her eyes fluttered open, and she tried to speak.

"There, there," whispered Maria as she soothed the woman's forehead. "Take it easy. We're going to take care of you."

In a weak voice, the woman said, in Hebrew, "I know I'm dying. Promise that you won't let my baby son die too."

Maria answered her, in Hebrew. "I promise. Can you tell us your name and what happened to you?"

"No. You would be in danger if I told you my name. I can't even tell you how I got here. Evil men may try to kill my son.

This baby boy that I'm carrying is a special gift from God. He must live at all costs. The prophets in the Torah have predicted that he will be a great man. If I die, bury me in an unmarked grave. Tell no one about me. If my son survives, don't tell anyone. Raise him as your own. You will be proud of him and God will reward you. This is my dying wish. Will you promise me?"

With tears in her eyes, Maria replied, "I promise you."

The woman smiled as her eyelids closed. A deep sigh escaped from her mouth as her spirit left her body.

Maria put a finger on the woman's throat in order to feel a pulse. There was none. "Oh, my God, José, She's dead. What about the baby? "

José put his hand on the woman's stomach. "He's kicking. He's still alive, but he won't last much longer."

"Do something, José, do something. I promised her."

José paused for a moment and then ran into his studio. He soon returned, carrying a case of his wood carving tools. He told Maria, "Look, I'm going to try to perform a Caesarean section. I took a lot of anatomy courses in art school. The woman is dead, so I don't have to worry about her. Let's try to save the baby."

José could still feel the baby feebly kicking in the womb. He took one of his cutting tools and made a transverse slice across the woman's lower abdomen. Then he carefully started to cut through the muscles and flesh. He eventually reached the womb, and carefully opened it. He grasped the baby boy by the feet, pulled him out, hung him upside down, and slapped his bottom. The baby screamed to let him know that he didn't appreciate this introduction into the real world.

José placed the babe in Maria's hand, and then tied off and cut the umbilical cord. Maria wrapped the baby in her shawl and nuzzled the wrinkled tyke to her bosom.

"What do we do now?" asked Maria.

"We'll do what the lady wanted. I don't understand why she said the things she said, but I think it would be prudent to believe her until we find out differently."

Maria agreed. José wrapped the woman's body in a blanket and laid it in one of the stalls until such time as he could dig a grave. Maria held the baby close to her body as they went back to the house. José set a roaring fire and the three of them warmed themselves before the hearth.

The baby in Maria's arms started to cry. "I think he's hungry, José."

Maria unbuttoned her blouse and exposed her right breast, which was still swollen with milk, and offered it to the child. The baby eagerly accepted the gift and started to nurse greedily. Maria felt a sense of euphoria. The body, which had prepared itself for her own child, was now being used to sustain life for another helpless human being.

The storm abated by the next morning. José and Maria went to the barn to prepare the dead woman's body for burial. Maria washed the blood from the nude woman and started to close the large gaping wounds from the Caesarian section. José had made one of the incisions all the way down through her groin. Maria was startled at what she saw there.

"José, come over here, I want to show you something."

"What is it?"

"Look, this woman's hymen is still intact. She was a virgin. How could this be?"

He shook his head, slowly "I have no idea. It just adds to the mystery that this woman has brought into our lives. I think the best thing to do is to honor her request to remain anonymous and take care of her child."

José buried the body under a tree on the hill overlooking the lake. He covered the grave and said a silent prayer. He left no marker. No one, but he, would ever know the location of this burial site.

Earlier that morning he had searched through her tattered clothing but found no identification, not even a label. He had, however, found a small gold chain around her neck. On it, hung a small medal with the Star of David on the front. On the back was inscribed the word "ALMEGA." He puzzled over the meaning of the word but could not come up with an explanation. He removed the chain and put it in his pocket. He would hold it for her son in case he ever decided to tell the boy the truth about his real mother.

He and Maria discussed what they should do next. No one in the Mexico City hospital knew them. Maria's case was an emergency procedure, and José had never completely filled out the paperwork for the hospital. He had paid the bill in cash when they checked out. There was not much of a paper trail if anyone was even remotely interested in tracking them down. They had returned to Puebla without meeting anyone. No one knew what had happened to her child.

José said, "Everybody in this town knows that you were pregnant and due soon. Why not just pass this baby off as our own?"

Maria said, "But that would be a lie."

"Yes, it would. But think of the consequences to the baby if what the woman said is true. If we reveal the truth as to how we came to have this child, its life could be in serious danger, maybe ours as well. Besides, we promised her that we would raise it as our own. What if she had knocked on the door of any other house in the area? She obviously was Jewish, and we are the only Jewish family for miles around here.

"I have this eerie feeling that we were meant to have this child. It's as if God had this all planned for us. There's something strange going on here that I can't explain."

"I have the same feeling, José. Every time I look at the baby sucking on my breast, his little eyes keep staring at me. I know that babies this young aren't supposed to see, but I swear that this one can. I get the feeling that he is able to see straight into my soul, and then I get this feeling of total peace. There's something very unusual about him. I just can't explain it. It's a mystical experience."

"Mystical is a good word, Maria. Remember what the woman said? Something about the prophets in the Torah saying that this child would be born and would be a great man. How could she say such a thing? How could she know such a thing?"

They had no answer to this puzzle, so they agreed that they would present the newborn as their own son. They waited at home for eight days and made arrangements for the boy to be circumcised.

On the eighth day, they put the baby into a portable bassinet that José had fashioned for it, and drove into town.

When they arrived at the temple in Puebla, Rabbi Jacobs greeted them warmly. He had been a family friend for many years and had replaced José's father as the head rabbi. Since he was getting along in years, he had turned many of the ceremonies over to younger men.

During the circumcision ceremony, the mohel performed the cutting of the foreskin. The rabbi then uttered the traditional prayer, "May the lad grow in vigor, of mind and body, to a love of the Torah, to the marriage canopy, and to a life of good works."

After the ceremony, José was talking to rabbi Jacobs, at the door to the temple, while Maria took the bassinet outside, and laid it nearby on the lawn.

The baby was happy, cooing, and waving his arms and legs in his comfortable bed, while looking up at the sky. A beautiful white dove grabbed his attention, as it flew in lazy circles overhead. Suddenly, a hawk streaked down from high in the sky and headed straight for the dove. Its talons hit the bird with such force that it broke the dove's neck. The hawk's momentum carried him close to the child but, as he broke out of his dive and started to ascend, he lost his grip on the dove, and the bird fell. It landed in the bassinet. Maria and the baby were startled by this sudden intrusion.

Maria reached into the bassinet and was relieved to see that the baby was not hurt. The bird had not landed directly on him. She took the lifeless creature in one hand to examine it. The baby made a loud gurgling sound, reached up and grabbed her hand.

"You don't want to touch this poor lifeless creature, now do you, baby? It's not a pretty sight for you to see."

She tried to pull her hand away, but the baby tightened his grip and wouldn't let go. She finally relented and lowered her hand so that he could see the bird. She noticed that his eyes examined the bird carefully. She could almost swear that she saw a tear of sadness in his eyes. However, she dismissed this notion as impossible for a child that young to feel such emotion.

The baby pulled her hand down lower, released his grip and took the bird in his own two small hands. He pulled it towards his face to examine it closer. Then, he breathed on it. The bird's eyes fluttered open, and it started to stir in his hands. The baby smiled and threw up his hands, releasing the bird into the air. The dove circled over him, and then flew away.

Maria was stunned. "I must be dreaming", she said to herself. "This couldn't have happened. I can't tell anybody what I just saw. They would tell me I was crazy. I don't understand it."

She turned her head to see if José had witnessed this event, but he had not. He was in the process of saying goodbye to Rabbi Jacobs.

As José turned to leave, she heard the rabbi say, "José, my hearing has gone bad in my old age, and I didn't hear much of the ceremony conducted by the mohel and the other rabbi. So I have a question, what name have you given to this boy?"

José had given much thought to this question. He had finally decided to give the boy the same name as his grandfather, a name that was commonplace in Mexico.

"Jesús."

AUTHOR

Tom Galligan hails from New York City. He is a graduate of Fordham University and holds an MBA degree from NYU.

After serving two years as an officer in the United States Air Force, he became a merchandise executive for a large national retail chain. After leaving that firm he co-founded a successful women's clothing manufacturing company in Los Angeles.

Upon retirement, he moved to La Jolla with his wife, Sara, a former school teacher. They have four children and six grandchildren, all of whom live in the southern California area.

In his spare time Tom enjoys playing tennis, scuba diving and reading.

His email address is: tomgall@san.rr.com

Made in the USA
San Bernardino, CA
22 June 2014